CHILDREN OF MONSTERS

An Inquiry into the Sons and Daughters of Dictators

Jay Nordlinger

ENCOUNTER BOOKS

New York • London

First American edition published in 2015 by Encounter Books,
an activity of Encounter for Culture and Education, Inc.,
a nonprofit, tax exempt corporation.
Encounter Books website address: www.encounterbooks.com

Manufactured in the United States and printed on
acid-free paper. The paper used in this publication meets
the minimum requirements of ANSI/NISO Z39.48–1992
(R 1997) (*Permanence of Paper*).

First paperback edition published in 2017.
Paperback edition ISBN: 978-1-59403-899-0

THE LIBRARY OF CONGRESS HAS CATALOGUED
THE HARDCOVER EDITION AS FOLLOWS:
Nordlinger, Jay, 1963–
Children of monsters : an inquiry into the sons and daughters of dictators / Jay Nordlinger.
pages cm
Includes bibliographical references and index.
ISBN 978-1-59403-815-0 (hardback)—ISBN 978-1-59403-816-7 (ebook)
1. Children of criminals. 2. Dictators—Family relationships. 3. Parent and child.
4. Totalitarianism—Social aspects. I. Title.
HV6251.N67 2015
321.9092′2—dc23
2015005297

To David Pryce-Jones, an exemplary thinker, writer, and friend

From the Same Author

Peace, They Say: A History of the Nobel Peace Prize, the Most Famous and Controversial Prize in the World (Encounter Books)

Here, There & Everywhere: Collected Writings of Jay Nordlinger (National Review Books)

CONTENTS

FOREWORD

This peculiar book came about in a peculiar way: In 2002, I was visiting Albania for the first time, speaking under State Department auspices. The country was ten years beyond the collapse of Communism. Many of the old structures were in place, however; democracy was not quite flourishing (nor is it today). For some 40 years, Albania had been ruled by a dictator outstanding in his cruelty: Enver Hoxha. Hoxha achieved an almost perfect tyranny. No one could breathe. One of his few rivals was Kim Il-sung, in North Korea. Hoxha was known as "Sole Force." In Albania, that was pretty much true.

Toward the end of my visit, a young intellectual from a government ministry was assigned to show me around. In the course of our tour, I thought about Hoxha and his complete domination of the country. He was gone now—dead. But I had a question for my guide: "Did Hoxha have children?" Yes, he did: three of them, two sons and a daughter. "Are they still in Albania?" Oh, yes. "And what are they doing?" Well, the daughter was an architect, and she had helped design the shrine to her father. As for the sons, they were dabbling in politics or business—it was a little unclear.

I wondered what it must be like to be the son or daughter of Hoxha. To bear a name synonymous with oppression, murder, terror, and evil. I thought it might make a good subject for a magazine article: the Hoxha children. I also thought a broader study of sons and daughters of dictators might make a good book. I tucked the idea away, mentally. Eventually, there came a time to act on it.

This book will present 20 dictators and their offspring. Twenty is a nice round number, and you might think I aimed for it—or added or subtracted a couple of brutes to arrive at it. In point of fact, I drew up a list of dictators I thought I should survey, and it came to 20. They are all modern dictators, by which I mean, they ruled in the 20th century. (One of them, Fidel Castro, ruled into the 21st. The son of one of them rules Syria right now. The grandson of another one rules North Korea—having taken over from his father, the son of the original dictator.)

I could have gone back to antiquity—Caligula had a child, just one. Her name was Julia Drusilla, and she was a chip off the old block. Suetonius, in his *Lives of the Twelve Caesars*, writes that Caligula knew she was his own, "for no better reason than her savage temper, which was such that, even in her infancy, she would attack with her nails the face and eyes of the children at play with her."

The little girl's parents were murdered on January 24 in 41 AD. She was just a year and a half. She was murdered the same day, her head bashed against a wall.

I could have gone to 16th-century Russia too, when Ivan the Terrible was on the throne. He beat his pregnant daughter-in-law, causing her to miscarry. When his son, the czarevitch, complained, he beat him too, bashing him with his scepter and killing him. The czar and father was immediately horrified by what he had done.

Ivan does not play a part in this book, but Bokassa the First does. He was the self-proclaimed, self-crowned emperor of the Central African Republic, or, as he styled it, the Central African Empire. He beat people to death with a kind of scepter—it was a ceremonial cane or walking stick, made of ebony. I must report, however, that he did not beat a son or daughter, at least not to death.

The book is called "Children of Monsters"—but the dictators are not equal in their monstrousness. Indeed, a few of them are hardly monsters at all. Mobutu of Zaire, for example, was an angel compared with his friend and neighbor Bokassa. Honestly, I feel a little sheepish about including Franco in this book. He was a dictator, and you and I, being good democrats, would not have wanted to live under him. But in the dictator business, we sometimes grade on a curve. Franco was a lamb compared with our genocidal monsters: Stalin, Mao, Pol Pot, et al. Yet I have included him because a) he is famous and b) he had a daughter, who is interesting. And c) he *was* a dictator.

If you yourself had drawn up a list of dictators, it may well have differed from mine. You may fault my book for omissions. From Soviet

Europe, I chose two dictators, Hoxha and his Romanian counterpart, Ceaușescu. One could have done East Germany's Honecker—who joined his family in Chile after his downfall. In the Caribbean, I might have included Trujillo, the dictator of the Dominican Republic. (He renamed the capital city after himself, a very dictatorial thing to do.)

As a rule, I went for the worst of the lot. You have to be very bad indeed—drenched in blood—to qualify for my book. Sorry to be ghoulish about it, but body count mattered. So, when it comes to Iran, you have Khomeini but not the shah. You and I would not have wanted to live under the shah. But we most likely would have been screaming for him to come back, after experiencing Khomeini and his gang.

This book has an organizational plan, of course, but it may take some explaining. I begin with dictators associated with World War II, plus Franco. I end this section, or grouping, with Tojo—then stay in the Far East, for Mao and Kim. Then I go to Eastern Europe, or Soviet Europe, as I have called it. Then the Caribbean. Then the Arab world. Then Iran. Then Africa. In each group, I tend to start with the dictator who took power first, then proceed chronologically—i.e., in the order of power-taking. This is just a tendency, though, not a hard-and-fast rule.

At the end of the book, I have a coda, if you will: on Pol Pot and his late-in-life daughter.

These sons and daughters of dictators will not get equal time. Some will get page after page, practically a mini-biography. Others will get a sentence or two. This has to do with how interesting or important they are, but it may also have to do with how much we know about them. Svetlana Stalin, for example, is interesting, important, and well-known, all three. She wrote about her life extensively. Other people have written about her, too. Mengistu, the "Stalin of Africa," had three children. ("Has," I should say—he is still alive, though not ruling.) About one of the kids, we have three or four scraps. About another, we have two or three scraps. About the third—a son, Tilahun—we have next to nothing. I can give you his name, and not much else.

Let me apologize in advance for some words that will appear in this book, over and over: "apparently," "evidently," "reportedly," "seemingly." I will write, "The story goes that..." and "He is believed to have..." No historian or journalist wants to write this way. We want hard facts, not "apparently." But when it comes to writing about dictators and their families, there is some guesswork, no matter how painstaking one's investigation is. Writing about Mengistu's family (to stay with him) is not like writing about Jimmy Carter's family. Writing about closed societies is not like writing about open societies. Sometimes it's hard to get the most basic information out of a dictatorship: How many children does the leader have? How many wives has he had? What are their names?

Not until midway through his reign did Mengistu permit an official biography to be printed about himself. About *himself*, let me emphasize, never mind his family. In Cuba, Fidel Castro forbids his media to mention his family. In 2000, a subhead in the *Miami Herald* read, "Fidel's private life with his wife and sons is so secret that even the CIA is left to wonder." (It is not altogether clear, by the way, that Castro has a wife.) The Kims' Korea is known as the "Hermit Kingdom." In truth, we are dealing with many hermit kingdoms.

But there are cracks, leaks, fissures. We have information from defectors, analysts, witnesses, friends, former friends—the principals themselves. In short, we have plenty of information. My job has been to sort it and adjudicate it, and to unearth more of it.

Bear in mind, this is a book about the sons and daughters of dictators, not the dictators themselves. There are biographies—usually many of them—to be had about *them*. I will do some sketching of them, of course. But this is the children's hour. In most cases, the children are bit players on the stage of history, not main players. They are footnotes, asides. But they are noteworthy footnotes and asides, and they are human beings—human beings born into a very strange position.

My book is, in part, a psychological study, I suppose. Obviously, there are themes, patterns, and connections among the children. These individuals share that "very strange position." But they are also that: individuals. And they have coped with their situation in various ways. While I was writing the book, I had lunch with my friend Tom Griesa, a judge in New York, and told him what my subject was. He had just one comment—simple yet oddly profound: "People are interesting." Yes, they are. Sometimes more interesting than they want to be.

Anyway, this is enough of a prelude. On with the show. We will begin with the most infamous dictator of all. Who really doesn't belong in this book, a book about children of dictators. Does he?

1

HITLER

Hitler had no children. He did not have a wife either, unless you count Eva Braun—the mistress whom he married just before his suicide (and hers). It must have been one of the strangest weddings in history, occurring in the bunker just after midnight. The reception consisted of some champagne, sandwiches, and awkward small talk. Two afternoons later, the newlyweds finished themselves off.

It was Hitler's conceit that he was really married to his cause, Germany (as he would have thought of it). He had relationships with women, and they were twisted relationships, unsurprisingly. These women had the habit of committing suicide, or attempting to do so. One of his women, in a sense, was his niece, Geli Raubal—daughter of his sister, or half-sister, Angela. Geli came to live with "Uncle Alf" in 1929, when she was 21, and the nature of their relationship has been the subject of much speculation. He enjoyed squiring her around, and he grew possessive of her, attached to her. In September 1931, she was found dead in his apartment, while he was away. Dead by his gun. Was it a straightforward suicide? Why did she do it? These questions, too, have been the subject of much speculation.

But Hitler had no children, and we need not spend any more time on him—except that a man claimed to be Hitler's son. Actually, it was his mother who claimed that he was Hitler's son, and he came to believe it, strongly. So have others. His name is—was—Jean-Marie Loret. (He died in 1985.) His mother's name was Charlotte Lobjoie. The story goes like this:

In the summer of 1917, she was a French girl cutting hay with her friends. Hitler was a soldier, fighting the world war in France. Charlotte and her friends noticed him across the way as he sketched in his artist's pad. She was appointed to go over and talk to him. They struck up a romance of sorts. She was 16, he 28. They would take long walks in the countryside, which didn't work out very well: He would give haranguing speeches on the histories of Prussia, Austria, and Bavaria. This was Charlotte's impression, anyway—she spoke no German, and he no French. One "tipsy evening," a son was conceived. Jean-Marie was born in March 1918.

He did not have an easy time of it growing up, taunted as a "fils de boche." (This was a rude way of describing the son of a German soldier.) In 1948, when he was 30, his mother told him that the late German chancellor had fathered him. She died in 1951. For about 20 years, he denied, in himself, what his mother had told him. But then he became obsessed with the question and devoted himself to investigating it. In 1981, he came out with a book, *Ton père s'appelait Hitler*. The title came from the words his mother had spoken to him: "Your father's name was Hitler."

The proffered evidence for Loret's sonship has to do with blood, handwriting, and other things. Charlotte is said to have kept paintings signed by Hitler. He is said to have painted a woman who looked just like her, after he was back in Germany. Envelopes of cash are said to have been ferried to Charlotte by German officers during World War II. There are other morsels and claims as well.

In 2012, a diary came to light—the diary of a British soldier, Leonard Wilkes, who had been with the Royal Engineers. On September 30, 1944, he wrote the following: "An interesting day today. Visited the house where Hitler stayed as a corporal in the last war, saw the woman who had a baby by him and she told us that the baby, a son, was now fighting in the French army against the Germans." This story caused some

Jean-Marie Loret

excitement around the world. Could Adolf Hitler, probably the most reviled man in history, have fathered a child?

Forgetting the handwriting, paintings, etc., it is a curious fact that Jean-Marie Loret looked like Hitler—a lot like him. So does his son Philippe (about whom more in a moment). Any number of mothers could have told their son that Hitler was his father. Why did Charlotte Lobjoie's have to look so much like him?

The consensus of historians is that Loret was not the son of Hitler, or that it is extremely unlikely that he was. That was the judgment of Ian Kershaw, in a footnote to Volume 1 of his acclaimed Hitler biography, published in 1998. In 2014, he confirmed to me that nothing has happened in the intervening years to alter his judgment. It may be a little odd to say, but, for purposes of my own book, the truth about Loret's parentage is almost irrelevant. What matters is that he *thought* himself Hitler's son. What effect did that have on him?

It was Loret's choice to grow a mustache—to have a Hitler mustache, specifically. This does not suggest distancing from the alleged father, to put it mildly. The man could easily have gone clean-shaven. Philippe Loret, too, has a mustache, or had one when London's *Daily Mail* came to call on him in April 2012. It was not a Hitler mustache, however; it was a longer one. Philippe's home was adorned with two portraits of Hitler. That does not suggest distancing, either. "Hitler is my family," he explained. "It's not my fault that I ended up as his grandson or that all the things happened during the war. What he did has nothing to do with me. He will always be family for me."

After his father died, Philippe Loret traveled to Munich, where he met a daughter of Himmler—who told him that insider Nazis always believed that Hitler had a secret son in France.

Philippe further told the *Daily Mail*, "I don't think evil passes on. Of course, qualities from your parents pass on to you, but you build your own life, and you make it what it is." About his father, he said, unequivocally, "He was proud of being Hitler's son."

That statement is hard to take, as is the mustache that Jean-Marie wore, as are the portraits that Philippe hung on the wall, as is the rendezvous with the Himmler child. But we might consider this: What if *your* mother, one fine day, told you that the father you had always wondered about was actually Adolf Hitler—a genocidal dictator whose name is a synonym for evil? That is a card dealt to virtually no one.

2

MUSSOLINI

Mussolini had five children, officially. How many unofficial children he had, no one can know: Mussolini was not the conjugal or monogamous type. He had a great many lovers or mistresses, including the one he died with, Claretta Petacci. They were shot, then hung upside down at the gas station in Milan.

There was definitely one unofficial child—a son named after him, Benito Albino Mussolini. His mother was Ida Dalser, with whom Mussolini began an affair in 1909 or so. Both were in their twenties. At some point, they may have married, but this is unclear. What is clear is that Benito was born in 1915. About a month later, Mussolini married someone else, Rachele Guidi.

The two women met once, stormily. It was in 1917, when Mussolini was in the hospital, recovering from a war injury. Many years later, Rachele told a son of hers, Romano, what happened: "She [Ida] threw herself at me in your father's room, insulting me and screaming, 'I am Mussolini's wife! Only I have the right to be at his side!' The soldiers there started to laugh. Wild with anger, I lunged at her and grabbed her by the neck. From his bed, looking like a mummy with bandages restraining his movement, Benito attempted to intervene. He got up from his bed to stop us while a doctor and two nurses also tried their best to separate us. Dalser fell back, and I burst into tears."

For a while, Mussolini accepted Benito Jr. as his son and made payments for his support. But when he rose to power in 1922, Ida and Benito became a nuisance to him. Ida kept showing up, demanding her rights, and especially those of her son. Mussolini had her confined to an insane asylum; he had Benito confined to a separate asylum. They were not crazy when they went in, but they were certainly tormented as "patients," or victims. Both died horribly: mother in 1937, when she was in her late fifties, and son in 1942, when he was in his mid-twenties.

These events came to light in the decade of the 2000s, when there were books and films. Mussolini did many cruel things in his life; almost never was he crueler than in his treatment of Ida Dalser and their son, Benito.

It was the presence of Ida that spurred Rachele to marry Mussolini. Ida, with her newborn, was calling herself "Signora Mussolini"; Rachele thought there could be only one of those, and it wasn't Ida. So, Rachele married Mussolini in a civil ceremony in December 1915. The groom himself was not present. He was laid up in bed—as he would be later, when Ida and Rachele met and fought. He sent a proxy. Also in attendance was a little girl, Edda. She was the five-year-old daughter of Mussolini and Rachele.

Edda had come along in September 1910. For many years, there was some question of her maternity—not paternity, but maternity, the questioning of which is rare. It was whispered that Edda was really the daughter of Angelica Balabanoff, a "Russian Jewess" with whom Mussolini had an affair. They were comrades in revolutionary circles. But the ultimate answer to this rumor is that Rachele Guidi Mussolini would never have accepted or raised Edda if she had not been her own. The Mussolinis' eldest son, Vittorio, put it this way in a memoir: "It is enough to have met my mother once to realize that some other woman's daughter would never have come into *her* house." Edda says much the same, in a memoir of her own.

Rachele and Mussolini were not the marrying kind, given their political and social beliefs. They were "good Socialist revolutionaries," as Edda writes, believing only in what was called a "free union." According to Vittorio, Rachele would say, "You don't hold a man with a stamped certificate." Besides, she wanted to be free to leave Mussolini quickly and easily, if he displeased her. But Ida Dalser, in a way, forced her into marriage. Ten years after the civil ceremony, in 1925, Rachele and Mussolini had a religious ceremony, for appearances' sake.

Mussolini, to say it once more, had a great many affairs. Vittorio relates that, when he learned of them as a boy, "it shook me terribly." It also "doubled my affection for my mother, whom I felt I must defend at all costs." But he came to accept his father's ways, and writes that he was "a good husband." (He also says, "I know only men will understand me.") It is sometimes said that Rachele accepted her husband's affairs nonchalantly or stoically, the good Italian wife, or dictator's wife. This is not necessarily true: When she learned of Claretta Petacci, she swallowed bleach. A maid found her, forced her to vomit, and sent for help. Romano writes that the maid saved his mother's life.

The couple had their five children: Edda, Vittorio, Bruno, Romano, and Anna Maria, born over a span of 19 years—1910 to 1929. In Fascist propaganda, Mussolini had a happy, full family life (unlike his weird partner in the Axis, Hitler). Biographers describe him as a distant father, rarely seeing his children, or wife, for that matter. But his children adored him. Perhaps they treasured their moments with him all the more, for the relative fewness of them. What everyone agrees on—certainly the children—is that Rachele was "the real dictator in the family." She had a rural simplicity, firmness, and savvy.

We will take a look at the children, one by one, starting with the eldest and proceeding to the youngest. We will also look at some of *their* children, i.e., Mussolini and Rachele's grandchildren. The first of the Mussolinis' children, Edda, had the most complicated and interesting relationship with her father. This must be expected, in view of the fact that he executed, or allowed the execution of, or failed to stop the execution of, her husband.

Mussolini absolutely adored Edda. Is there anything like a father's love for his daughter, especially a firstborn daughter? Edda was the apple of her daddy's eye, as everyone said. Romano put it nicely in his memoirs: "My father had a weakness for her, which he made no attempt to conceal." Mussolini insisted on being present at Edda's birth, and fainted. He would be daunted by her on later occasions as well. They were a lot alike. As Romano writes, "She had his temperament (energetic

Edda Mussolini Ciano

to the point of recklessness)" and other things. "She resembled him physically too, with that withering look she inherited from him."

Mussolini's adoration was returned, most of the time. Edda would write, "The degree of osmosis between my father and me was such that to please him and obey him I learned how to do everything: I was the first Italian woman to drive a car and to wear trousers," etc. She was maybe the only person who could talk back to him. Mussolini once remarked, "I have managed to bend Italy, but I doubt I will ever be able to bend Edda's will." Romano writes, "Even Hitler himself held her in high regard." (Those words "even Hitler himself" are characteristic of the Mussolini family. They held him in high regard, to borrow Romano's language.)

Fascinating, willful, and, let's face it, the daughter of the absolute ruler, Edda had more than her share of boyfriends and suitors. When she was 19, however, she was introduced to the man she would marry, Galeazzo Ciano, son of Costanzo Ciano. This elder Ciano was an admiral, war hero, and count. He was also a Fascist minister and close ally of

Mussolini. Indeed, he was Mussolini's designated successor. Galeazzo, like his father, was called "Count Ciano," and Edda would be known for the rest of her life as "the countess."

When the pair met, Ciano was working in the diplomatic corps. He was a bon vivant, a swell, a playboy. Donna Rachele, the matriarch, had little use for him, as she had little use for anyone whom she thought had airs. Yet Ciano was more than a spoiled, pleasure-seeking child: He was bright and capable, as his famous diary proves. The marriage between this prince and princess of Fascism, Galeazzo and Edda, took place on April 24, 1930. It was one of the great social occasions of the age. So reluctant was Mussolini to let Edda go, he followed her in his car as the newlyweds drove to their honeymoon on the Isle of Capri. About 15 miles outside of Rome, Edda had had enough. She confronted her father, demanding that he turn back. He pleaded, "I just wanted to accompany you some of the way." But turn back he did, with tears in his eyes.

The Cianos' marriage is sometimes described as an "open" one, or perhaps we could say a "free union," to use the earlier term. It is assumed that the count had a lot of women and the countess a lot of men. Amid this, they had three children together. Ciano was an aviator, and led a bomber squadron in the Ethiopian war (1935–36). When he returned home, he was named foreign minister by his father-in-law. He was young for the position, age 33. Before long, people thought of him as the heir to the throne. As the elder Count Ciano was once the designated successor, now the younger count was in waiting, or so it was assumed. Galeazzo certainly wanted the job. His wife would confirm it matter-of-factly in her memoirs: "Who does not dream of succeeding in life?"

People also noticed that Ciano looked and sounded a lot like Mussolini. As *Time* magazine put it, the foreign minister was "aping the postures, speech, and manners of his father-in-law." Here again, Edda is matter-of-fact: "My husband seemed to mimic my father simply because he met with him several times a day for years and so unconsciously adopted certain of his characteristics. There are families, the Agnellis, for example, in which all the brothers and their friends speak in exactly the same way." (The Agnellis are the industrialists who have forged and led Fiat, the automaker.)

That *Time* article appeared in the issue of July 24, 1939. Edda was on the cover, which advised, "She wears the diplomatic trousers." The story inside was titled "Lady of the Axis." It began, "Most noteworthy Italian exponent of the Fascist dictum that a woman's place is in the home is none other than Donna Rachele Mussolini." But "Italy's outstanding exception" to this dictum was the Mussolinis' eldest child. The article was entertaining, scalding, and sensational, depicting Ciano as a lightweight and mediocrity, and his wife as a conniving floozy—of dubious maternity.

Making a visit to Berlin, Edda "liked the heavy masculine atmosphere," said *Time*. "Handsome young Nordic men were always at hand to keep her in a proper Germanic frame of mind." In Budapest, "the Countess was said to have made eyes at one of the sons of old Regent Horthy. This could easily have been excused, but when the Count and Countess showed up for a hunting expedition arranged by the Regent four hours late with only the excuse they had overslept, there were strained feelings." Edda was also depicted as a raging, hard-line Fascist, which was quite true.

Whether she ever knew the contents of the article is unclear. In her memoirs, she writes, "*Time* even devoted its cover to me one week. What a boon to the ego!"

There were actually towns named for Edda, or at least one of them. After Mussolini invaded Albania in April 1939, he renamed Saranda, or "Santi Quaranta," as the Italians had called it, "Porto Edda." The name stuck until Italian fortunes were reversed later in the war.

Edda Mussolini Ciano loved Fascism, loved Nazism, and loved Hitler. In her memoirs—penned well after the war, in the mid-1970s—she is entirely open about this. In May 1940, she argued with her husband, expressing her disgust, indeed "shame," that Italy had yet to enter the war on Germany's side. Her father no doubt knew how she felt as well. And she did not have to endure her "shame" for much longer. "A month later," she writes, "Italy entered the war, but I must emphasize that, though I was delighted by my father's decision, I had absolutely nothing to do with it."

She nonetheless had a role to play in Axis relations. I will let her explain: "Given my Germanophile sympathies, I was, without being aware of it, the link between the Führer and my father. I found it normal that two dictators should be allies. And this all the more so since, as soon as he took power in 1933, I had begun to consider Hitler a veritable hero."

Edda writes fondly and tenderly about Hitler, recalling the time she joined him and the family of Joseph Goebbels, his propaganda minister, on the shores of Lake Wannsee. Hitler played with the Goebbels children, "giving all signs of pleasure at doing so and at hearing them call him 'uncle.'" She met with Hitler on several occasions, and "was always struck by his extraordinary kindness and affection toward me as well as by his patience." She had standing to argue with him—because "he knew that he could have confidence in my honesty, in my fidelity and in my friendly feelings toward his regime."

The countess gives us a clue about Hitler and women, a theme with which we started this book: "During the receptions at the Chancellery, I was often struck by the number of very beautiful women surrounding Hitler." At a particular reception, "a Nazi dignitary pointed out one of these women to me. She was a marvelously beautiful blonde with the body of a goddess, and he whispered in my ear that for the moment she had captured the Führer's heart." It was not Eva Braun. Whoever the blonde was, she "confirmed my impression that Hitler's misogyny and his 'marriage with Germany' were only a legend."

After the war, Edda was not entirely insensitive to the question of the Holocaust. In those memoirs, she writes that she is being "objective and sincere when I deplore the extermination of the Jews by the Germans." She continues, "It is true that I believed that the Jews, although charming personally and in small numbers, represented a danger since they were eager for power and because at a certain period (and even today) they controlled the levers of command almost everywhere in the world. I was equally convinced, because the propaganda confirmed it and there was nothing to prove the contrary, that the Jews had neither pride nor a sense of humor, and I was delighted to be an Aryan."

There is a "but" coming: "But I shivered in horror when I learned what the Germans had done to them, for such extermination cannot be justified, and my father would have opposed it with all his force if he had known of it."

What can we say about a woman who writes the above passages? That she is repulsive, certainly, but also that she is frank (leaving aside the question of Mussolini's awareness of the Holocaust). Edda herself says that, after the war, an expression arose in Germany: "Hitler?

Don't know him." But she was different. "I myself prefer to say, 'Hitler, Goering, Goebbels? I knew them.' It is more honest."

We will now return to the war, and to February 1943, specifically: Mussolini dismissed his entire cabinet, including the foreign minister. Ciano had been advocating a separate peace with the Allies; he knew the war was lost. He was being demoted to the position of ambassador to the Holy See; Mussolini had decided to be his own foreign minister. The boss said to his son-in-law, "Now you must consider that you are going to have a period of rest. Then your turn will come again. Your future is in my hands, and therefore you need not worry."

Ciano recorded those words in his diary, on February 8. At the end of the relevant entry, he wrote, "Our leave-taking was cordial, for which I am very glad, because I like Mussolini, like him very much, and what I shall miss most will be my contact with him."

The Allies breached Sicily on July 9. On July 24, the Fascist Grand Council, of which Ciano was a member, had a historic and fateful meeting. A motion was proposed restoring powers to the king. This would have the effect of dismissing Mussolini. The motion passed by a large margin, 19 to 7. Voting with the majority was Ciano. The next day, Mussolini woke up and went to work as though nothing had happened. The king (Victor Emmanuel III) had him arrested and imprisoned. One of Edda's sons said to her, "What are we going to do? Are we going to be killed like the czar and his children?" Edda replied that it was possible.

In September, Mussolini was snatched, i.e., rescued, by German commandos. Hitler soon set him up as the head of a rump and puppet government at Salò, on the shores of Lake Garda in northern Italy. This was the "Italian Social Republic." Ciano and several other Fascists who were part of the Grand Council majority were tried and sentenced to death.

Edda was in an agonizing position (to put it far too mildly). She had "always loved and admired my father more than anyone else in the world," as she would write; she also loved her husband, whatever his failings. She fought tooth and nail for him, doing everything she could to spare him. She begged her father to stay the execution, and did so as persistently and passionately as she could. She writes, "I even believe that if he had been informed, toward the end, that I had been killed, he would have heaved a sigh of relief, despite his affection for me." In a desperate gambit, she tried to use Ciano's diary as blackmail against the Fascists and Nazis. That volume included some damning facts and observations.

The hard-core, bitter-end Fascists and the Nazis very much wanted to see the "traitor" Ciano dead. How much leeway did Mussolini have? Was he simply a puppet on Hitler's hand? This has long been a matter of dispute. Vittorio Mussolini—the next of the children we will consider—gives one interpretation, in a memoir: If the dictator had "used his authority to impede the course of justice," Italy's "newly resurgent Fascism" would have been dealt "a mortal blow," and the Nazis would have taken the opportunity to "tighten their grip, already terribly heavy, on our benighted country." In this telling, Mussolini's refusal to spare Galeazzo Ciano was a patriotic act.

Ciano and the others were killed on January 11, 1944. The method of execution was distinctive and meaningful: They were made to sit down in chairs, and then tied to those chairs; then they would be shot in the back. This was supposed to be a humiliating way to die, fit for traitors. Before the bullets flew, Ciano swiveled in his chair to face the shooters. This was a fairly brave death. And Edda was very brave, in her efforts to save her husband, herself, and their children. Indeed, she showed physical courage, on the road and on the run. Eventually, she escaped into Switzerland (where the children had already been spirited).

For a time, she hated her father, and her family more generally. She wrote to Mussolini, "You are no longer my father for me. I renounce the name Mussolini." It must be said, the dictator took it hard, too. Some people contend that he never recovered from the drama of Galeazzo and Edda. Vittorio writes that Mussolini was "the truest and most tormented victim of the whole tragedy." This is the Mussolini-family style—operatic, hyperbolic, and self-pitying—but there must be some truth in the statement.

After the war, Edda served a detention on the island of Lipari, off Sicily. In 2009, a book came out detailing an affair she had in those days: *Edda Ciano and the Communist: The Unspeakable Passion of the Duce's Daughter*. It was made into a movie.

Edda lived out her life in Rome. In a sense, she was a woman without a country, at least for some years. The anti-Fascists hated her, of course, because she had been a true-believing and spectacular Fascist. But some of the Fascists hated her, too, because she was the wife of a "traitor," and a collaborator with him. Eventually, she reconciled with her family. You can see photos where she has her hand tenderly on her mother's shoulder. But there was always some ambivalence in her thinking.

Not until 1974 did she write her memoirs, or speak them to a chronicler. They came out in English under a classically relativistic title: "My Truth." One of the reasons she did not speak out earlier, she says, is that such speaking "would only have served to trample even more on the memory of Mussolini." Addressing the key question of whether she blamed her father for her husband's death, she says this: "Although he was not directly involved at the beginning, he did follow a policy of non-interference, either because of a lack of courage or that sort of fatalistic attitude that makes us say, when faced with a given situation, 'Very well, so be it! The wheels have begun to turn, we shall see what comes of it all.' Therefore, he was partially responsible for what happened." Mainly, however, she makes excuse after excuse for her adored father.

As for Galeazzo Ciano, she says he did not betray Mussolini. No, in voting as he did on the Grand Council, he had been "misled into making an error of judgment." The widow insists not only that Ciano was no traitor, but that "my father knew it too." She calls her father and her husband "the only beings whom I loved and admired with all my heart, and whom I still love today." Edda died in 1995, age 84.

Before moving on to Mussolini and Rachele's second child, Vittorio, I will relate something light. Call it gallows humor. The story is told that Winston Churchill was talking to his son-in-law Vic Oliver—an entertainer who had married the Churchills' daughter Sarah. The prime minister didn't like him in the least. Trying to make innocent conversation, Oliver asked him what figure in the war he admired most. Churchill answered, "Mussolini." Astonished, Oliver asked why. Said Churchill (again, according to legend), "Because he had the courage to have his son-in-law shot." (In reality, Ciano was almost certainly a better man than Mussolini, although that is not much to brag about.)

Vittorio Mussolini was born in 1916, six years after Edda, a year after their parents' civil ceremony. Before World War II, when he was still a very young man, he made a name in the movies. Before that, he was a pilot—like Galeazzo, and like the second Mussolini son, Bruno. Vittorio flew in the Ethiopian war, and in the Spanish Civil War (for Franco and the Nationalists, of course), and in the world war.

He actually appeared on the cover of *Time* magazine, in October 1935, four years before Edda. But he and Bruno were merely adornments, flanking their dictator father, who had just invaded Ethiopia. They are wearing their military finest, looking stern and imperial. Vittorio looks maybe a little less stern and imperial than his father and younger brother—he looks pudgier (historians and chroniclers always nag him about his weight) and slightly awkward.

In 1936, he wrote a book about his Ethiopian experience, *Voli sulle Ambe*, which is to say, "Flights over the Ethiopian Highlands." The book begins excitedly, with Mussolini's Blackshirts darkening—blackening—the bridges of a ship. They are about to sail away to war, and a crowd is hailing them. The air is festive, already triumphal. The Blackshirts sing a chorus, full-throated: "Sing, sing, don't get weary, to Abyssinia we want to go!" The book is replete with happy photos of African children, obviously delighted to be under Italian rule, and heroic Italian pilots, posing in front of their propellers.

It was the film world that Vittorio most relished. The third Mussolini son, Romano, writes, "My father was interested in the Italian cinema and considered it an extraordinary means for spreading propaganda. My brother Vittorio, who was a great fan and connoisseur of movies, had many long conversations with my father about directors and actors and kept him abreast of all the important developments." In a paper on Italian attitudes toward America, Umberto Eco, the novelist and scholar, writes, "Vittorio belonged to a group of young Turks fascinated by cinema as an art, an industry, a way of life. Vittorio was not content with being the son of the Boss, though this would have been enough to guarantee him the favors of many actresses: He wanted to be the pioneer of the Americanization of Italian cinema."

Vittorio did a good deal of writing about film, and edited a journal called *Cinema*. As Eco says, he "criticized the European cinematographic tradition and asserted that the Italian public identified emotionally only with the archetypes of American cinema.... He genuinely loved and admired Mary Pickford and Tom Mix, just as his father admired Julius Caesar and Trajan. For him American films were the people's literature."

In 1937, Vittorio's father sent him to Hollywood, where he struck a deal with Hal Roach, the famed producer. Roach was probably most famous for Laurel & Hardy, the comedy team, and "Our Gang," a.k.a.

"the Little Rascals." He and Vittorio formed a company called "R.A.M.," which stood for "Roach and Mussolini." They were to make movies out of grand operas, beginning with *Rigoletto*. Today, you can go on the Internet and find a film of Vittorio being introduced to the Little Rascals. Darla sits in his lap. Buckwheat shakes his hand. Alfalfa and Spanky express their enthusiastic interest in making movies with him. This all seems rather surreal, with the world war just around the corner.

Immediately, Roach took some heat for collaborating with Vittorio Mussolini, and, by extension, the dictator. He defiantly told a reporter, "Benito Mussolini is the only square politician I've ever seen" ("square" meaning honest, straightforward). But the pressure mounted, and Roach quickly went back on the deal, buying Vittorio out.

In the next few years, Vittorio wrote some movie treatments and did some producing. He used a pseudonym, Tito Silvio Mursino, an anagram of his actual name. Among his collaborators was Roberto Rossellini, who would go on to great fame as a director. During the war, they made war movies, including *Un pilota ritorna*, or "A Pilot Returns" (1942).

Vittorio had a role in the war, in addition to his flying and movie-making: He served as a liaison between Italy and Germany, rather as Edda did, before her husband's downfall. Vittorio writes of shuttling between the two countries. And he says, "It was known that Hitler and the other German leaders liked me and held me in some regard." In the end, he was on the run, like other Mussolinis. He writes, "In the war it had been possible to do one's duty because of the thought that one was fighting for one's country" and might die with honor. Now, however, "there was only fear left, that boundless, cold, useless fear of dying without much hope of resisting with arms or words." And if he died, it would not be "at the hands of a foreigner, but at the hands of men born in my own country, men who would insult me in my own language and—which was worse—would think of me as a real enemy."

He hid out for months, then sneaked out of the country. He went to South America, as more than a few Axis figures did. Wearing a disguise, and carrying a false passport, he sailed to Argentina. When he got there, he told the press, "I never had any interest in politics. I have less now, and you can be sure I have no intention of mixing in Argentine politics. I am just another Italian immigrant."

For a decade or so, he traveled back and forth between his adoptive country and his native country, and eventually resettled in Italy. He became a great defender of his father's legacy, a keeper of the flame. He did this by means of several books, including the one from which I have been quoting—written in 1961 and published in English as *Mussolini: The Tragic Women in His Life.* Those tragic women were Rachele, Edda, and the final mistress, Claretta Petacci. (Ida Dalser was arguably more tragic than all of them.) Whatever else can be said of Vittorio, he wrote well and interestingly, as his remarks about dying may suggest. He died in bed in 1997, at 80.

Bruno was born two years after Vittorio, in 1918. Like his older brother and his brother-in-law, Ciano, he flew. But more than they, he was a very serious and gifted pilot, something of an ace. He began in the Ethiopian war when he was 17. Then he flew for Franco in Spain. The newsreels show him looking the part: dashing, tough, carefree. An American announcer said, "In the wake of squadrons of Fascist planes lie crumbling skeletons of former homes. Destruction rains from the skies on houses that cave like eggshells. Terror rules the land. And the peace of the world hangs in the balance as the red shadow of war lengthens over Madrid." Outside the sphere of war, Bruno set speed records. In January 1938, he and two other Italian pilots made a historic flight from Italy to Brazil. Before he left, his mother said to him, "Please, go slowly." He answered, "Of course, *mamma*, you know I will. I have snails in my engines."

Later in 1938, he married Gina Ruberti. "The bride," reported the Associated Press, "comes from a family of ardent Fascists." A year and a half later, the couple had a daughter, Marina.

In the course of the war—August 1941—Bruno was test-piloting a plane (a P.108 bomber). It crashed, killing Bruno and others. He was 23. His mother later told Romano about the mourning that resulted—her own and others': "What hit me hardest was il Duce's excruciating silence. It was as if he had turned to stone."

Mussolini, in fact, took time to write a little book, *Parlo con Bruno,* or "I Speak with Bruno." As the title indicates, he addressed his dead son personally. He starts by telling him about the funeral procession: There were so many people who wept for him. "Countless people." Young and old, known and unknown. Thousands of arms rose to salute him. Little

country girls knelt down. There was "profound grief, general, spontane-
ous. Why? Not because you were called Mussolini. They called you, and
call you still, Bruno."

The dictator quotes his older son, Vittorio, on the subject of Bruno's
love for music. Bruno enjoyed discussing the merits of this or that
soprano, or this or that tenor, says Vittorio. Most people loved the
tenor Beniamino Gigli, and Bruno did, too; but, in a departure from the
consensus, he preferred Giacomo Lauri-Volpi. During the recent opera
season in Pisa, says Vittorio, Bruno never missed a night. A few days
before he died, he bought a recording of Beethoven's Fifth Symphony,
which he listened to "with joy."

Mussolini declares that his son was a "fascista nato e vissuto."
That is, he was born a Fascist and lived the life of a Fascist. "All that
I have done or will do," says Mussolini, "is nothing compared with
what you have done." He says that he will one day meet Bruno in the
family crypt, to sleep beside him the sleep without end. But first, victory—victory in the war. So that sacrifices of people like him will not
be in vain.

This is a highly sentimental, indeed mawkish book—operatic, hyperbolic. Whatever our judgment or taste, however, perhaps a father, even
a dictator, can be forgiven his reaction to a child's death, whatever that
reaction is. The book is dedicated to little Marina. She was one and a half
when her father died. At six, she would be orphaned. Gina Mussolini
drowned in a boating accident on Lake Como. This was in May 1946.
She was in the company of British officers—apparently friends of hers—
which led to gossip. In any event, Marina was taken in and raised by the
countess, Edda Ciano. Romano cites this as proof that his elder sister
was not estranged from the Mussolinis. It may well be that Edda had a
particular appreciation of Marina's tragic situation.

Romano is the next child, born in 1927—nine years after his predecessor. He was 17 when his father died. The last time he saw him, he
(Romano) was playing the piano. He was picking out melodies from
The Merry Widow. As it happens, Hitler loved this operetta. It may well
have been his favorite work of art, surpassing even Wagner. Hitler saw
it countless times. He bestowed awards on the composer, Lehár, personally. At any rate, Mussolini embraced his son and said, "Ciao, Romano.
Keep playing."

He did, becoming a jazz pianist. For a while, he played under a pseudonym, Romano Full. But he soon discovered that his real name was a draw, not a repellent. He formed the Romano Mussolini Trio, and also the Romano Mussolini All Stars. He played with many of the greats of the day, including Ella Fitzgerald, Duke Ellington, and Dizzy Gillespie.

He married Maria Scicolone, the sister of Sophia Loren, Italy's most famous actress, and one of the most famous actresses of the entire century. They had two daughters. Romano writes, "I admit that I have always been a vagabond, even at the cost of being a terrible husband, or, at the least, a husband deserving of criticism." He left Maria for an actress named Carla Puccini. They had a daughter, who bears the name of her paternal grandmother, Rachele. Later, Romano and Carla married. Maria Scicolone, long after her divorce from Romano, wrote a book called "At the Duce's Table: Unknown Recipes and Tales from the House of Mussolini." (As you may have gathered, the Mussolinis are a book-writing crew. For one thing, Mussolini books are big sellers in Italy.) The book is dedicated "To Donna Rachele, with a daughter's love."

In the main, Romano contented himself with music, not politics or history, until his last years. Then he wrote two books. One of them is *My Father il Duce*. It is from this that I have been quoting. The book is affectionate, meandering, and whitewashing. Romano's father never wanted the world war, you see, and had a secret plan to end it. "At times he seemed to live more for others than for himself," Romano writes. More than once, he mentions the men of the Fascist Grand Council who voted against his father on that pivotal day in July 1943. Why, a Hitler or Stalin would have had them killed forthwith. See how benign Mussolini was in simply going to the king's palace and allowing himself to be arrested?

Romano has a point there, of course. It may be faint praise to call a man better than Hitler or Stalin. But, in the dictator business, as in other businesses, one sometimes grades on a curve. Furthermore, one can learn things from Romano Mussolini, as we have seen. He died in 2006, age 78.

He had a younger sister, Anna Maria, the last Mussolini child. She was born in 1929. And she led what most people describe as a sad life. Anna Maria was the least "public" of the Mussolinis. As a child, she was stricken by polio, and this ailment recurred. Through treatment, Vittorio tells us, she was able to return to "semi-normality." After the war, she worked as a radio host, using a pseudonym. When her real identity was discovered, there was a controversy, and she left, or was driven out. In 1960, she married. Her husband was Giuseppe Negri, an actor and television personality. Stage name, Nando Pucci Negri. They had two children, a daughter named Silvia and another daughter named after Anna Maria's sister, Edda. Anna Maria died in 1968, when she was 38 years old.

Both of her daughters ran for office, and won—not grand offices, but offices all the same. Silvia Negri was elected to the city council of Forlì, where the Mussolini family has roots. Edda Negri was elected mayor of Gemmano, not far away. Later, she ran for parliament, unsuccessfully. She said she was quite proud of her grandfather, and to be his granddaughter. He made some mistakes, she allowed, but did many good things as well. She went so far as to change her name to Mussolini—to Edda Negri Mussolini.

A much older Mussolini grandchild, Fabrizio Ciano, ran for office, too. This was the third Count Ciano, after Costanzo and Galeazzo. He was twelve when his father was executed, thirteen when his grandfather was killed. He did not make it to parliament. In the early 1990s, he wrote a book with a hard-to-beat title: "Quando il nonno fece fucilare papà," or, "When Grandpa Had Dad Shot." The jacket copy explained that Fabrizio had always lived with a "heavy burden"—a statement pretty much impossible to deny.

When it comes to politics or ideology, all of the Mussolini grandchildren have been "neo-Fascists," evidently. And it's sometimes hard to tell the "neo" from the old-fashioned variety.

Vittorio's son, Guido, ran for office: He ran for parliament, and for mayor of Rome. He got very few votes in both endeavors. Running for mayor, he said, "We draw inspiration from Mussolini's principles, but we look to the future." In his view, "Mussolini's ideas were 99 percent good, and 1 percent maybe questionable." After his defeat, he made it clear that his name was not to blame. On the contrary, the Mussolini name "worked in my favor. The Fascists love you, while the others, who aren't Fascist, have to respect you. It has been a beautiful experience."

He led a bid to have Mussolini's body exhumed and his death "definitively" investigated. (That was Guido's word, "definitively.") He did not succeed in this bid. He said, "I'm not looking for anything—not for revenge, not for money, not for anything else. I just want someone to tell me the first name and last name of the person who killed him in such an ignoble way, when they were supposed to hand him over alive to the Americans. Before I die, I want to know whom I must curse."

The real politician in the family—after the dictator, of course—is Alessandra: a daughter of Romano and his first wife, Maria Scicolone; a niece of Sophia Loren. Today, she is a member of the European Parliament, and she has been a member of both houses of the Italian parliament: the chamber of deputies and the senate. Mouthy, outrageous, she is one of the most colorful politicians in a country known for colorful politics. Alessandra Mussolini is the Pasionaria of neo-Fascism. And that is the name she uses: not Pasionaria but Mussolini, though she has long been married to a man named Floriani.

Earlier in her career, she was an actress, singer, and model. She appeared on the cover of *Playboy* (European editions): "The grit of Grandpa Benito, the sex appeal of Aunt Sophia Loren." Among the movies in which she appeared was *The Assisi Underground*, about a priest who rescued Jews during the war. At first, she was cast as one of the Jews. But this caused an uproar—so she was recast as a nun, Sister Beata.

It was in 1992 that she was first elected to her national parliament. She was 29. Her mother warned her that politics was serious and hard work. She replied that it would be less difficult than her prior work: In the entertainment world, "they don't care if you're a good or talented actress, all they want is to see your legs and your breasts. In politics, at least I can say something important and people will believe me." During her campaign, she defended her grandfather, in various ways. For instance, he was "very modern, one of the first ecologically minded politicians." Mussolini did not even want "a real tree at Christmas, because it hurt him so much to chop it down." When she won, she described the victory as "an act of love for my grandfather."

While a new parliamentarian, she completed her academic studies, obtaining a degree in medicine. She has an unusual résumé: *Playboy* model, doctor, leader of neo-Fascism, etc. (This is in addition to being the granddaughter of Mussolini and the niece of Loren.)

Throughout her career, Alessandra has been with several parties and coalitions, in the ever-shifting world of Italian politics. She broke with the National Alliance in 2003, after its leader, Gianfranco Fini, made a visit to Israel. There, he denounced Fascism, referring to "shameful pages in history." Alessandra said she was a keen supporter of Israel, but could not abide this denunciation. With others, she formed a party called "Freedom of Action," later called "Social Action," which then merged into a coalition known as "Social Alternative." Her father, Romano, composed a party anthem for her: a little, dippy ditty called "The Pride of Being Italian."

On the floor of parliament, she has worn tight T-shirts, boasting in-your-face slogans. And she is perpetually quotable. In 2006, the dictator of Libya, Qaddafi, made a threat: Unless Italy paid Libya compensation for earlier colonization, Italians would be attacked. Alessandra said, "If it hadn't been for my grandfather, they would still be riding camels and wearing turbans on their heads. They should be paying *us* compensation."

Ever and always, she is proud of her name, fiercely proud. Not only does she bear it herself—she fought a legal battle so that her children could bear it. When the leader of the National Alliance made his speech in Israel, she reacted pointedly: "Fini attacked my name. It's my family."

There have been a lot of girls in the Mussolini family. In 1996, Guido's son Caio Giulio Cesare Mussolini had a baby boy, Carlo. A headline read, "Baby Carlo Ensures Mussolini Lineage." The new grandfather, Guido, said, "For many years, I have waited for this lovely surprise, without which our family might have gone extinct." He added, "My father Vittorio is in seventh heaven about this bolt from the blue, which will allow the dynasty started by Benito to last well into the 21st century."

The Mussolinis are an interesting lot, you might agree. You might also agree that they can be likable, in particular moments or circumstances. What did Countess Edda say about the Jews? "Charming personally and in small numbers." The Mussolinis have all shown great family loyalty (allowing for the complicated case of Edda and the Ciano children). Family loyalty is a virtue. But I think of something President Kennedy said: "Sometimes party loyalty asks too much." So it is with family loyalty.

Certainly, we might sympathize with the Mussolinis—who, after all, did not choose the circumstances of their birth. (Who does?) They have been instilled with tremendous love for their patriarch. What's more, they have been surrounded by people who love and venerate him—not only family members, but the public, or a slice of it. When Alessandra first campaigned in 1992, people came up to her to give her the Fascist salute. In all sincerity. Twenty years later, she was caught on the floor of the chamber of deputies signing photographs of her grandfather—giving that same salute. A colleague of hers had asked for the signatures. There is an appetite for this stuff.

From what I can ascertain, there has not been a political dissenter in the family. (Again, allowing for the complications of the Cianos.) What did Mussolini say about his dead son, Bruno? "Fascista nato e vissuto." He was born a Fascist and lived his life as a Fascist. All the Mussolinis, at least to a degree, have been *fascisti nati e vissuti*. It was a mercy that they and their Axis partners lost the war.

In one of his books, Vittorio recounts a serious but teasing exchange he had with his mother, Donna Rachele. At the end of it, she says to him, "You Mussolinis, you're all the same."

3

FRANCO

Franco had one child—a daughter, Carmen. She was born in 1926, ten years before the Spanish Civil War. At the end of that war, in 1939, her father was unchallenged dictator of Spain. As with Edda Mussolini, there were rumors about Carmen's parentage. There still are. It is said that she is the offspring of Franco's brother Ramón, a famed air-force pilot, and rake. According to this rumor, Ramón had a child with someone, and the babe needed a home. The future dictator and his wife, unable to have children of their own, took her in. According to a different rumor, the babe was an orphan in Morocco.

One of the alleged proofs that Carmen came out of nowhere, so to speak, is that no proper notice of her birth was published. This is "a complete canard," as Stanley G. Payne has emphasized to me. (Professor Payne is a leading historian of Spain, and Franco biographer.)

Adding to the store of gossip and speculation, a book came out in 2009 alleging that Franco had one testicle. It is true that he was wounded in the lower abdomen while fighting in Morocco. But claims about the result of this wound are unverifiable. It is said, too, that Hitler had one testicle. A single testicle threatens to become known as a dictatorial trait.

The humdrum truth is this, according to Payne and other top Franco authorities: Carmen is the offspring of Franco and his wife, and any rumors to the contrary are to be discounted. So we will discount them.

Carmen's mother, and Franco's wife, was also named Carmen. The mother was called "Doña Carmen," even as Mrs. Mussolini was called "Donna Rachele." The daughter was known in the family as "Carmencita" or "Nenuca." In time, she would be known as "Doña Carmen" (and she, too, would have a daughter Carmen, so we have to be on our toes about which Carmen is in question).

Francisco Franco, the generalissimo and dictator, loved his daughter dearly. In their 2014 biography of Franco, Payne and Jesús Palacios write, "Becoming a father may have been the greatest pure joy of his life." In his old age, he had this recollection: "When the baby girl was born, I almost went crazy" (with delight). Franco was known for reserve and austerity—even coldness—but he poured affection on his daughter. Earlier, I suggested that fathers have a special love for their daughters. Franco's may have been magnified in that Carmen was his only child.

She married in 1950, when she was 24. The wedding was a very grand affair, taking place in El Pardo, the palace in Greater Madrid where the Francos lived. The groom was an aristocrat: Cristóbal Martínez-Bordiú, the tenth marquis of Villaverde. He was a playboy on the Galeazzo Ciano level, if not beyond. He also had a more serious side. In fact, he was a heart surgeon. Among his friends was Dr. Christiaan Barnard, the South African who performed the first heart transplant in 1967. The next year, Martínez-Bordiú performed Spain's first such operation. The patient lived a little more than a day.

Decades later, in 2011, the patient's daughter sued. One of her allegations was this: Martínez-Bordiú had embarked on the operation under pressure from his father-in-law's regime; the operation was not wise medically, but was undertaken in order to glorify fascist Spain.

The dictator and his wife were not rich in children, and sometimes he sighed over this. But daughter Carmen and her doctor-playboy husband were: They had seven children, four girls and three boys. Their first boy was their third child—and he was named Francisco, after his grandfather. (He was also, of course, the eleventh marquis of Villaverde.)

Carmen was just short of 50 when her father died, in 1975. From the newly installed king, Juan Carlos, she received some new titles:

Franco's daughter, Carmen, as bride

duchess of Franco and *grandeza de España*, i.e., grandee of Spain. A great defender and admirer of her father, she is a living symbol of *franquismo* (Franco-ism). She has long been a special guest at ceremonies and rallies meant to commemorate her father. The faithful sing the old fascist hymn, "Cara al sol," or "Facing the Sun." Doña Carmen (meaning the dictator's daughter) is the president of the National Francisco Franco Foundation. She has lived a relatively quiet life.

But she has surfaced in the news now and then. In 1978, she was accused of trying to smuggle jewels—31 gold and diamond-encrusted medals—into Switzerland. A Madrid court found her guilty and fined her the equivalent of $95,000. About a year and a half later, she had the conviction overturned, and the money paid back to her. Her lawyer said that it was important that the Franco name be free of this taint.

In 1988, her mother died. Ten years later, her husband, Dr. Martínez-Bordiú, died. His medical career had come to an unhappy end: In 1984, he was forced to resign his hospital position after a patient died in controversial circumstances. In addition to being a heart surgeon,

Martínez-Bordiú was a plastic surgeon—and this leads me to an aside (and a somewhat rude one at that): Much plastic surgery has been conducted on Doña Carmen. This is not a matter of a nip here and a tuck there—her appearance has been dramatically altered, as can be seen in photos, taken down the years.

She and her family have suffered various indignities (as well as tragedies). In August 2008, one of Carmen's granddaughters was getting married at the Pazo de Meirás, the family's summer estate in Galicia. Protesters massed outside the home, demanding that the house be opened to the public. They yelled "Fascists!" at arriving guests. Later in the year, the family was indeed made to open the home to the public, four days a month. In due course, Doña Carmen won the right to spend August in the house, free of any public visits.

Also in 2008, the town council in Ferrol, Franco's birthplace, acted against the family. It took back the honorary titles the town had bestowed on Francos over the years. For example, Franco would no longer be called a "favorite son"; and Carmen would no longer be a "daughter of Ferrol." One official said that maintaining those titles would be "glorifying an oppressive regime."

At about this time, an interesting and unusual book was published: *Franco, mi padre*, described as "the testimony of Carmen Franco, daughter of the Caudillo." The book is the fruit of a series of interviews given by Carmen to the biographers and historians Payne and Palacios. The cover has a photo, which shows Carmen as a girl, with her father. He is in uniform and has his arm around her. He's wearing a slight smile—uncommon for him, in photos. Carmen herself is beaming. The book made news around the world, particularly Carmen's statement that her father feared Hitler would kidnap him, to force Spain into the world war.

Guido Mussolini, recall, wanted to have his grandfather dug up, so that an investigation could be performed. Some have wanted Franco dug up, for a different reason: They want his body removed from its place of honor in the Valley of the Fallen, a civil-war memorial. Doña Carmen has opposed this, strongly. She is ever on guard against insults to her father. In 2013, an artist made a punching bag out of Franco's face. The work was called, simply, "Punching Franco." The National Francisco Franco Foundation sued, alleging that the work was "grotesque and offensive." Carmen's deputy told the press, "It is low and vulgar, and unworthy of civilization, and of a supposed sculptor."

To say it once more, there are three main Carmens in the Franco world: the dictator's wife, his daughter, and a daughter of hers, her eldest. In 1972, this third Carmen—Franco's grandchild—had her own wedding in El Pardo. The groom was even higher up on the social scale than the marquis in 1950: He was Alfonso de Borbón, a first cousin of the soon-to-be king, Juan Carlos. Alfonso was serving as Spain's ambassador to Sweden. He was also a hard-living, fast-living type—a ski champion, for example. Once he was enmeshed in the Francos, he schemed to be moved up in the royal line of succession. His mother-in-law even entertained the idea that her daughter could be on the throne, queen. But it was not to be. Franco, who had control of such matters, put the kibosh on the whole thing.

Alfonso and Carmen had two boys, Francisco and Luis. In 1982, ten years after their wedding, the couple were divorced. It was Alfonso who got custody of the boys. (Carmen once admitted, "I have not been an exemplary mother.") In 1984, Alfonso had a car accident, in which Francisco was killed. Luis was in the car too, but, like his father, survived. The father was killed five years later in a skiing accident. A friend of his commented, "He liked to ski fast and drive fast."

Today, Luis de Borbón, or Louis de Bourbon, as he is more often styled, is pretender to the French throne. Imagine that: Franco's great-grandchild, a man who would be king—the king of France. Obviously, fascist royalty and royal royalty sometimes mix.

Luis's mother, Carmen (the third Carmen, remember), has had two marriages since her first. Sadly, she is a tabloid figure, the object of mockery. She has some of the flamboyance and outrageousness of Alessandra Mussolini—but not the taste for politics, apparently. Speaking of fodder for the tabloids, one of Carmen's brothers, Jaime, was convicted of abusing his girlfriend in 2009. The woman declared that Jaime was a "good person" except under the influence of cocaine.

So, Doña Carmen, the dictator's daughter, has had problems to deal with, as most people do. And, according to Stanley Payne, she is a remarkably normal person: a woman without many airs, a woman "uncorrupted" by her peculiar circumstances. As I write, she is a year away from her 90th birthday.

Two of the Mussolini sons—Vittorio and Bruno—flew for her father in the civil war. Their younger brother, Romano, did not. For one thing, he was a child during that war; for another, he played the piano. But he met Franco in 1963, as he recounts in a book. The dictator "had never forgotten his rise to power in 1939 thanks to my father's and Hitler's support." Romano found him in a pessimistic mood. Franco said, according to this account, "The Communists will win because there are millions and millions of poor in the world, and the poor will always be Communists."

4

STALIN

Before we get to Stalin, we should have a word about Lenin, the founder of the Soviet state. He had no children. But he did have a wife, Nadezhda Krupskaya. She was his comrade in Communism and life alike. Krupskaya had a medical condition that apparently prevented her from having children. Lenin had a mistress as well: Inessa Armand. She had several children, both by her husband and by his brother. For a while, Lenin, Krupskaya, and Inessa lived at close quarters in a kind of *ménage*. It is said that Lenin liked children, taking a paternal interest in Inessa's. There must have been limits to his liking, however: He sent children to concentration camps.

This is what Richard Pipes, the historian, pointed out when I raised with him the subject of Lenin and children. He cited an interesting source on the matter: Alexander Yakovlev, the Gorbachev-era Communist (about whom Pipes was completing a book).

Lenin's successor, Stalin, was second to none in sending children to concentration camps. He had three of his own, from his two wives. He sired at least two other children as well. This was during his years of internal exile in the 1910s. One of his landladies, Maria Kuzakova, gave birth to a son in 1911. His name was Konstantin. A

Stalin biographer, Robert Service, writes, "There was little doubt on the question of paternity. Those who saw Konstantin as an adult recorded how like Stalin he was in appearance and even in physical movement." Stalin never had anything to do with him, but there are a few curious details.

Konstantin Kuzakov was admitted to Leningrad University. Stalin must have had a hand in this, according to another biographer, Simon Sebag Montefiore. In 1932, the NKVD (a forerunner to the KGB) made Kuzakov sign a statement swearing that he would never discuss his "origin." He worked in the Central Committee apparat under Andrei Zhdanov, a trusted deputy of Stalin's. Zhdanov was also the father of the man who would become Stalin's daughter's second husband. (We will hear more about this later, of course.) Kuzakov went on to be a television official in the Ministry of Culture. He died in 1996, five years after the death of the Soviet Union.

He and his biological father never properly met, but there was an interesting encounter. Montefiore quotes Kuzakov himself: "Once, Stalin stopped and looked at me, and I felt he wanted to tell me something. I wanted to rush to him, but something stopped me. He waved his pipe and moved on."

In 1914, Stalin met an adolescent girl named Lidia Pereprygina. She was 13, and he was 35. He got her pregnant. The baby died not long after being delivered. Stalin got Lidia pregnant again, and this second child lived. Born in 1917, he would bear the name of Alexander Davydov: adopted by the fisherman whom Lidia married. Unlike Konstantin, Alexander never had a glimpse of Stalin. Like Konstantin, he was made to sign a secrecy oath by the NKVD. He later ran a canteen in the mining town of Novokuznetsk—known from the 1930s until the 1960s as Stalinsk. He died in 1987.

Stalin had an adopted son, in addition to his two illegitimate sons and the two sons he had with his wives. This was Artyom Sergeyev, son of Fyodor Sergeyev, a top Bolshevik and ally of Stalin's. The senior Sergeyev died in a notorious accident in 1921: An experimental high-speed train, the Aerowagon, derailed. Lenin himself assigned Stalin to look after Sergeyev's widow and infant son. Artyom would call his adoptive father "Uncle Stalin." He rose to be a major general in the Soviet army. He died in 2008—still devoted to the USSR, and to Stalin in particular. He regarded Gorbachev, the reformer who lost the Soviet Union, as a traitor.

An obituary in the *Guardian*, the British newspaper, told of his final moments: "As he lay on his deathbed, a group of war veterans brought him a medal in commemoration of Stalin." The old general sat up slowly, and as the veterans pinned the medal on his pajamas, he said, proudly, "I serve the Soviet Union." Those were his last words.

Stalin's son Yakov served the Soviet Union, too. He was born of the dictator's first wife, Yekaterina Svanidze, in 1907. His mother died later in the year. Stalin's daughter, Svetlana, was to write in one of her books that Yakov must have taken after his mother—"for there was nothing rough or abrasive or fanatical about him." He was gentle, unassuming, and honest. After Yekaterina, or "Kato," died, Stalin promptly forgot about Yakov. The boy was raised by his grandmother and other relatives. A biographer of Svetlana's, Martin Ebon, writes that Yakov "was a relic of Stalin's past. But he remained on the periphery of his father's life, a goading reminder of Stalin's early personal history, for more than three decades."

One of the things that Stalin denied him was his name: Stalin, that is. The dictator's two children with his second wife enjoyed the glory of the name. But Yakov was always a Dzhugashvili—that being his father's original, Georgian name. Stalin discarded it for himself in about 1910. As Ebon notes, Yakov was "marked for emotional defeat early in life."

He moved from Georgia to Moscow in 1921, when he was 13 or 14. He lived with Stalin and his wife, Nadezhda Alliluyeva ("Nadya"). He had a hard time of it. To begin with, he had to learn Russian, which was difficult for him. Unfortunately, many things were difficult for him. He was a bit slow, or clumsy, or earnest. Stalin thought him a despicable country bumpkin. He scorned and bullied him. "In his eyes," Svetlana writes, "Yakov could do nothing right." Stalin "had no use for him and everybody knew it."

Yakov married a priest's daughter, Zoya. His father disapproved. In despair, Yakov went into the Stalins' kitchen and shot himself, although failing in suicide. The bullet either grazed his chest or pierced a lung (accounts vary). His father snorted, "He can't even shoot straight." According to Svetlana, her father treated her brother even worse thereafter.

Stalin's first son, Yakov Dzhugashvili

The young man worked at menial, or at least humble, jobs. He and Zoya had a baby, who died at less than a year. They soon divorced. In the mid-1930s, Yakov got married again, to Yulia, who was Jewish. Stalin once more disapproved. Svetlana writes, "He never liked Jews, though he wasn't as blatant about expressing his hatred for them in those days as he was after the war." Yakov and Yulia had a daughter, Galina, called "Gulia."

It seems that Yakov had another child too, in between his marriages. A Stalin biographer, Miklós Kun, says that Yakov had a son named Yevgeny with Olga Golisheva, an accountant. Today, Yevgeny Dzhugashvili is proud to be Yakov's son—or, more to the point, proud to be Stalin's grandson. Gulia always refused to accept that he was related. (She died in 2007.) Yevgeny once told the press, "She suggested we do a DNA analysis. I accepted her offer on the condition that she pay for it. Then she disappeared."

Yevgeny became a colonel in the Red Army. He has long lived in Tbilisi, the Georgian capital. In 2006, a journalist, Steven Knipp, visited him at his apartment and found "several huge photos of Stalin staring down from the walls." Yevgeny is a super-dedicated Stalinist. He helped form a political coalition, the Stalinist Bloc. He has sued individuals and institutions for defaming Stalin—i.e., for telling the truth about his crimes. He even sued the Duma, the lower house of the Russian parliament, for acknowledging that Stalin ordered the Katyn massacre (the wholesale execution of Polish officers).

Gulia, incidentally, was no less faithful a Stalinist, even if a less litigious one.

Svetlana Stalina loved her brother Yakov. In a memoir, she says she saw him angry just twice. In both instances, their brother, Vasily, had spoken crudely in front of Svetlana and other girls and women. "Yakov couldn't stand it," she writes. "He turned on Vasily like a lion." But mainly he was gentle, which irritated his ungentle father. They were "too unlike each other ever to be compatible," writes Svetlana, in an understatement. Yakov once said to her, "Father speaks to me in ready-made formulas."

Hitler and the Nazis had a pact with Stalin, which they broke in June 1941. They invaded the Soviet Union. Stalin barked at Yakov, "Go and fight!" He did. In less than a month, he was captured. The Germans discovered they had a plum. Stalin denied to them and everyone else that he had a son named Yakov. He further denied that there was really such a thing as a Russian POW: "In Hitler's camps, there are no Russian prisoners of war, only Russian traitors, and we will do away with them when the war is over." Stalin had his daughter-in-law, Yulia, arrested as the wife of a traitor. She was imprisoned for a year and a half, and was never the same again.

In February 1943, Field Marshal Friedrich Paulus, leading the German army at Stalingrad, surrendered. The Germans proposed a swap: Paulus for Yakov Dzhugashvili. Acting as mediator was Count Bernadotte, the famed Swedish diplomat. Hitler and Stalin were of the same mind (as so often): One was furious at his commander for choosing surrender over suicide; the other was furious at his son for the same reason. But they differed on a swap—which Stalin refused. He is reported to have said, "I will not exchange a soldier for a field marshal." He is also reported to have said, "They are all my sons," meaning that all the boys of the Red Army were dear to him.

The details of Yakov's captivity are murky—like the details of his life in general—but we know two things: He was brutally treated, and he refused to crack. He did not go over to the other side, which would have given the Germans a propaganda victory. The details of his death are, of course, murky. But he seems to have committed suicide by throwing himself on an electric fence, in April 1943.

Svetlana says that her father "abandoned Yakov to his fate." And "it was very like my father to wash his hands of the members of his own family, to wipe them out of his mind and act as if they didn't exist." That is no doubt true. But there are reports that Stalin ordered secret rescue attempts. And the biographer Montefiore adds a wrinkle or two. Those wrinkles are as follows: Stalin was somewhat haunted by Yakov in later years. He was also somewhat proud of him, for his behavior at the end. "A real man," he called him.

With his wife Nadya, Stalin had Vasily and Svetlana. The second son was very, very different from Yakov. Vasily was a classic type of dictator's son: the little tyrant of a tyrant, the little monster of a monster. We will meet more such sons as this book proceeds. Vasily used his privileged position to get everything he wanted: sex, power, riches, thrills. And, as frequently happens, it all ended very badly for him.

He was born in 1921, Svetlana in 1926. You might have thought it problematic enough to be Stalin's son or daughter—but when Vasily was eleven, and Svetlana six, their mother committed suicide. Svetlana was raised by a nanny and other generally civilized women; Vasily was given over to brutish bodyguards, especially to the chief of Stalin's personal security team, General Nikolai Vlasik. They were happy to foster a monstrousness in Vasily.

Stalin essentially ignored Vasily, as he did Yakov. He doted on Svetlana (until he decided to ignore her too). When he did pay attention to Vasily, he was very hard on him. Vasily was 20 when the war came to Russia. Like Yakov, he fought. But he was a pilot, like the Mussolini boys. The pilots were the elite of the military. And Vasily received promotion after promotion.

In no time, he was a major general. Then he was a lieutenant general. For these positions, Vasily was not in the least qualified. He performed appallingly. He was drunken, bullying, physically abusive, incompetent, and reckless. His recklessness endangered lives, and sometimes cost them. "No privilege was denied him," as Svetlana writes. Vasily feared and answered to no one—except to Stalin, of course, before whom he quaked in his boots.

Once, in the war, Stalin actually fired him. The order reads, in part, "Colonel Stalin is being removed from his post as regimental commander for drunkenness and debauchery and because he is ruining and perverting the regiment." He was reinstated after several months and, once more, promoted.

Vasily and Svetlana with their father

Vasily was a satyr, in addition to a drunkard, and the seat of his activities was the family dacha at Zubalovo, 20 miles from Moscow. Drunken orgies were regular. Imagine Vasily and his sidekicks commandeering women and firing pistols at chandeliers. He was not only a little Stalin, he was a little Caligula too. Stalin himself complained that his son had turned the dacha into a "den of iniquity." (When you have been rebuked by Stalin, morally, you have been rebuked.)

Vasily was married either four times or three—accounts vary (as I have said in this narrative before). He was definitely married to a daughter of Marshal Timoshenko; he may have been married to a daughter of Molotov, the foreign minister, too. Though he was the dictator's son, it was no prize to be married to him. "He beat his wives as drunken peasants do in a village," writes Svetlana. He beat whomever he wanted, "even policemen in the street," as Svetlana says, for "in those days everything was forgiven him."

After the war, he formed and directed air-force sports teams. The sports included hockey, basketball, swimming, and gymnastics. When the athletes performed well, he would reward them, lavishly; when they did not, he would punish them, including by having them jailed. In 1950, the hockey team went down in a plane crash. Vasily covered it up, fearing his father's wrath.

Everyone wanted to please or appease Vasily, because he was the czarevitch, so to speak: the crown prince. But it would not last beyond his father's lifetime. In this sense, he was not the crown prince, not a successor, just the dictator's spoiled brat. He knew all this, too. He was highly anxious about his future, as well he should have been. According to Montefiore, he told Artyom Sergeyev, "I've only got two ways out. The pistol or drink! If I use the pistol, I'll cause Father a lot of trouble. But when he dies, Khrushchev, Beria, and Bulganin'll tear me apart. Do you realize what it's like living under the axe?" (These men were deputies under Stalin, who would vie for power in the post-Stalin era.)

Stalin died on March 5, 1953. By the end of April, Vasily was arrested. He was charged with embezzlement, the utterance of "anti-Soviet state-ments" (i.e., criticisms of Stalin's heirs), and myriad other offenses. As Svetlana says, there were "enough charges to put ten men in jail." Nobody came to Vasily's defense now. All the sidekicks and hangers-on and flunkies were gone. Vasily was "just an alcoholic," as Svetlana puts it, whom "nobody needed anymore." He was sentenced to eight years in prison. They even took away his proud, glorious name, imprisoning him as "Vasily Pavlovich Vasilyev." ("Vasilyev" had been one of his father's noms de guerre.)

As time passed, he appealed to Nikita Khrushchev, the new Number 1. After almost seven years' imprisonment, he was taken to see Khrushchev. Another Stalin biographer, Dmitri Volkogonov, tells the story, via Alexander Shelepin, who was the head of the KGB at this time. Shelepin says that Vasily "fell to his knees and begged and implored and wept. Khrushchev took him in his arms and was in tears himself, and they talked for a long time about Stalin. After that, it was decided to release Vasily immediately." This was in January 1960. Vasily went back to his old ways, to the extent he could, hopelessly alcoholic. They exiled him to the (closed) city of Kazan. He died there in March 1962, at the age of 40. The stone of the grave they put him in bore neither the name Stalin nor the name Vasilyev. It said "Dzhugashvili," just like poor Yakov.

There is a coda to this story. In 1999, eight years after the end of the Soviet Union, Vasily was partially rehabilitated by the Russian supreme court. The court overturned the 1953 conviction for anti-Soviet statements and reduced the degree of some of the other convictions. Three years later, in 2002, Vasily's remains were removed from Kazan to Moscow, where they were buried next to those of his mother.

Vasily was a victim, in a sense, like Stalin's other children, and like many of the sons and daughters of dictators whom we are surveying. Needless to say, Stalin had millions more victims, unknown to him personally. And Vasily was victimizer as well as victim. What Dmitri Volkogonov says is true: "Vasily's life was an illustration in miniature of the moral sterility of Stalinism." He was "fine proof that the abuser of power [Josef Stalin, in this case] corrupts everyone he touches, including his own children. The Caesars, having reached the acme of their power, often left behind them children flawed in body and soul, morally dead while the dictator was still living and revelling in his own immorality."

We now get to Svetlana: the most famous of all the "children of monsters," probably, except for the sons who succeeded their father in "office"—a Duvalier in Haiti, a Kim in North Korea, an Assad in Syria, another Kim in North Korea. Why is Svetlana so famous? There are two main reasons, I think, one more important than the other. The less important reason is this: She defected from the Soviet Union to the United States in 1967. This caused a global sensation. But the more important reason is that she got it all down, and superbly. She wrote up her life in three books. The first two have enduring power, and the third is not without interest.

Svetlana was born, as you know, in 1926, when her father was firmly entrenched in the Kremlin. What we have said about other dictators and their daughters, we can say about Stalin and Svetlana: He adored her, and she adored him back. Stalin felt more tenderly toward his daughter than he did toward any other human being. Later, she thought she knew why. She often said, "I reminded him of his mother, who had red hair and freckles all over, just like me." Nadezhda Alliluyeva, Svetlana's mother, was not the maternal type. She was the Bolshevik type: devoted to Party and work, not to "bourgeois" interests such as family. Svetlana could not remember that her mother had ever hugged, praised, or kissed her. Nadya thought that her husband coddled their daughter.

Father and daughter

We might pause to imagine a household in which Stalin is the more loving parent.

Still, Svetlana always cherished the memory of her mother, and this cherishing grew with the years. She dedicated her first book "To My Mother." Later yet, she regarded her mother as a kind of angel, I believe.

She killed herself—Nadya did—in 1932, when she was 31. Svetlana was six. She was told that her mother had died from a burst appendix. She would not find out the truth until later (ten years later). As an adult, she would write that her mother was "driven to despair by a profound disillusionment and the impossibility of changing anything." In her life with Stalin, Nadya was trapped. (Such was the predicament of countless Russians and other people in the Soviet Union, in any number of stations.)

I should pause once more to say that, from the beginning, there have been people who think that Nadya did not kill herself; that, in fact, Stalin killed her. Serious people take this suspicion seriously. But most who have looked into the question believe that Nadya was a suicide, and that is the assumption of this book.

For the next ten years—that is, until Svetlana was 16—Stalin continued to treat his daughter tenderly. She was "Setanka" and "Setanochka" (nicknames derived from "Svetlana"). She was also his "little fly" and "little sparrow." Furthermore, she was his "little Housekeeper": the mistress of the house. Sometimes Stalin rendered this "Comrade

Housekeeper." She was also the "Boss." Even Stalin's underlings, members of the Politburo, went along with this game: "All hail Boss Svetlana!" The real boss had another game, too: He would have Svetlana issue orders to him, in writing. Then he would respond, "I obey." He had a habitual sign-off in his notes to her: "From Setanka-Housekeeper's wretched Secretary, the poor peasant J. Stalin."

You can imagine how Setanka felt about her father: He was not only her own adored father—and it's natural for little girls to adore their fathers—he was the king of the whole wide world. In a memoir, she says that she never heard her father's name except with such words as "great" and "wise" attached to it. This was true at home, at school, and everywhere else. The atmosphere at home was "official, even quasi-military," she says. Home was run by the secret police, to a considerable extent. But Svetlana was not unduly stifled.

She was a bookish child, even an intellectual one. She loved literature, foreign languages, music. She had fine tutors. She went to school with other Kremlin children. In this period, her life was probably as happy and normal as possible, under the circumstances.

Nonetheless, there were shadows. With some regularity, her schoolmates would simply disappear. They would be there one day, and not the next. Their fathers had fallen from favor, being arrested, imprisoned, or killed. Sometimes, a schoolmate would give Svetlana a note to pass to her father. It had been written by the schoolmate's desperate mother, whose husband had been dragged away in the night. Could Comrade Stalin do something? The dictator got sick of these notes, telling his daughter not to serve as a "post-office box."

Worse, much worse, her own relatives disappeared: her aunts, uncles, and cousins. These were members of Nadya's family. Stalin had taken her suicide, quite naturally, as a gross insult and betrayal. He punished her family for it. He also punished the family of his first wife, Kato. Those relatives were killed or imprisoned too. Why? It's usually foolish to ask such questions about Stalin: but he probably wanted to erase signs of the past. Svetlana writes that it was hard to think of her beloved aunts and uncles as "enemies of the people," as the official propaganda had it. "I could only assume that they must have become the victims of some frightful mix-up, which 'even Father himself' could not disentangle." There would come a time, an awful time, when she realized it was all his doing. And he had an explanation for her: "They knew too much. They babbled a lot. It played into the hands of our enemies."

You and I can do our best to slip into the skin of such people as Svetlana Stalina. To be in sympathy with them. But it takes a very big imagination to slip into the skin of a girl whose adored relatives, after her mother's death, were killed by her own adored father.

She was 16 when she found out about her mother—about the way she died. With her gift for languages, and her curiosity about the world, she liked to read English and American magazines. They were available to someone in her privileged position. "One day," she writes, "I came across an article about my father. It mentioned, not as news but as a fact well known to everyone, that his wife, Nadezhda Sergeyevna Alliluyeva, had killed herself on the night of November 8, 1932." She did not want to believe it, but she could. And "something in me was destroyed."

Something else happened when she was 16: She fell in love, with someone who was all wrong. He was 40, married, a playboy, and Jewish. (In her memoirs, Svetlana doesn't mention that he was married, or a playboy, but Simon Sebag Montefiore does.) The love interest was a prominent screenwriter named Alexei Kapler. They met when he was a guest at one of Vasily's notorious parties at Zubalovo. But the romance that ensued between the screenwriter and the schoolgirl was "innocent enough," writes Svetlana (believably). They went to art exhibitions, the movies, the theater, and the opera. He introduced her to books, including novels by Hemingway, which were extremely hard to obtain. They kissed and sighed. Svetlana basked in the intellectual company and the romance.

Kapler was arrested on March 2, 1943. The next morning, as Svetlana was getting ready for school, Stalin did something he had never done before: show up at her quarters unexpectedly. He was in a volcanic rage. "Your Kapler is a British spy!" he said. Svetlana protested that she loved him. And here is how she describes what happened next: "'Love!' screamed my father, with a hatred of the very word I can scarcely convey. And for the first time in his life he slapped me across the face, twice." He also said that a war was on, and all his daughter could do was ... Here he used what Svetlana describes as a "coarse peasant word."

Her nanny, who was present, tried to protect her charge, crying that the accusation was untrue. Stalin dismissed this. Then he said to his daughter, "Take a look at yourself. Who'd want you? You fool. He's got women all around him!" With that, he left. Svetlana was devastated— "utterly broken," she says. Her father's words made her doubt that Kapler had ever loved her at all. Or that anyone could.

In a daze, she went on to school. When she came home, her father summoned her. She found him tearing up the letters and photos that Kapler had sent her. He muttered, "'Writer'! He can't write decent Russian!" Why, his daughter "couldn't even find herself a Russian!" Apparently, says Svetlana, "the fact that Kapler was a Jew" was what bothered her father the most.

He sent him to the Gulag—to Vorkuta, for five years. (A normal person might, for once, sympathize with Stalin.) As Montefiore says, the amorous 40-year-old screenwriter was lucky he wasn't shot. His five years were relatively easy—he was allowed to work in the theater. After his release, though, he broke parole, returning to Moscow, which was off-limits to him. He was rearrested and sentenced to another five years—this time, in a mine. When he was at last out, he and Svetlana had a brief affair, according to Montefiore. And that was that.

After Stalin's confrontation with Svetlana that morning before school—March 3, 1943—nothing was ever the same between father and daughter. He lived ten more years, plus two days, but Svetlana hardly saw him. One might say she knew him only until she was 16. As she would write, "He loved me while I was still a child, a schoolgirl—I amused him." But when she became an adolescent, with some of the problems that often attend that stage, she was less amusing.

Svetlana proceeded to Moscow University. She wanted to study literature, her bent and passion. But Stalin still cared enough about her life to disallow it. "You want to be one of those Bohemians!" he said. He told her to study history instead, after which she could do whatever she desired. That is exactly what she did. At the university, she concentrated on U.S. history, for the Soviet Union's alliance with America had generated interest in that country, and enthusiasm for it.

Before long, she received a marriage proposal from a fellow student, Grigory Morozov. She had been madly in love with a Kremlin prince: Sergo Beria, son of one of the most monstrous of Stalin's sub-monsters, Lavrenti Beria. She had known Sergo since childhood, but their relationship did not blossom as she hoped. So smitten was she by him, she even tried to upend his marriage. (She leaves this vexing business out of her books, but others do not.) In the mid-1990s, Sergo Beria was interviewed by Andrew Higgins of the London *Independent*. Little Beria criticized Svetlana because she had turned against her father. He himself venerated Stalin, as he did his own father.

Anyway, this Morozov proposed to Svetlana. He, like the banished Kapler, was Jewish. In one of her books, Svetlana writes, "I was drawn to kind, gentle, intellectual people. It so happened, independent of any choice on my part, that these lovely people, who treated me with such warmth, both at school and at the university, were often Jews." She went to her father with Morozov's proposal. It was May, and they were sitting outside, on a splendid day. For a long time, Stalin just stared at the trees, saying nothing. Suddenly, he said, "Yes, it's spring. To hell with you. Do as you like." He set one condition on the marriage: that the groom and husband never set foot in his house. Indeed, Stalin never met his son-in-law.

The next year, 1945, the Morozovs had a child, Josef. Was he named after Stalin? Of course. But he was named after his other grandfather too. (This other grandfather would be arrested a few years later.) Eventually, little Josef met his maternal grandfather, the Red Czar. Svetlana writes, "I'll never forget how scared I was" the first time her father saw her son. The child "was about three and very appealing, a little Greek- or Georgian-looking, with huge, shiny Jewish eyes and long lashes. I was sure my father wouldn't approve; I didn't see how he possibly could. But I know nothing about the vagaries of the human heart, I guess. My father melted the moment he set eyes on the child." Stalin saw him twice more.

In 1947, after three years of marriage, Svetlana and Morozov divorced. It is often said that Stalin wanted the divorce, or insisted on it. Or that the couple divorced because Stalin was starting his terror campaign against the Jews. Or that he was about to have his son-in-law arrested. Svetlana, for her part, says this is untrue: that she and her husband divorced "for reasons of a personal nature." The facts are elusive here, as elsewhere. In any event, Stalin would tell his daughter, "That first husband of yours was thrown your way by the Zionists." She could not convince him of the falsity of this belief. As for Morozov, he went on to be a distinguished lawyer and law professor.

Svetlana never wanted for men—for boyfriends, suitors, or husbands. In 1949, she took a husband much more appropriate, from the Stalin point of view. He was, in fact, a Kremlin prince, Yuri Zhdanov—son of the late Andrei Zhdanov, whom we have already met in this story: It was under him that one of Stalin's illegitimate sons, Konstantin Kuzakov, worked in the Central Committee. Svetlana's marriage to Yuri was not a great love match, certainly as she saw it. It was, she writes, "a matter of hard common sense," devoid of "any special love or affection."

The next year, they had a child, a girl, Yekaterina. The pregnancy was difficult, the child premature, and the mother miserable. In her misery, she wrote a letter to her father. He answered, with some of the old tenderness. One or two lines were not especially tender. "Take care of yourself," he said. "Take care of your daughter, too. The state needs people, even those who are born prematurely." Svetlana was glad to have the letter, any letter at all. (It would be the last her father sent her.) "But it made me terribly uneasy to think that the state already needed my little Katya, whose life was still in the balance."

Stalin saw Katya once, when she was two and a half. He "wasn't especially fond" of her, writes Svetlana. "She was funny as a button, with pink cheeks and dark eyes that were big as cherries. He took one look at her and burst out laughing." By Svetlana's count, Stalin had eight grandchildren. He saw three of them: her two kids, and Yakov's Gulia. Vasily did not even attempt to bring his kids by. Svetlana says that Stalin enjoyed his brief encounters with his grandchildren, but "would have just as much enjoyed the children of strangers."

To Morozov, Svetlana stayed married three years, and to Zhdanov, two. He was a chemist and went on to be the longtime rector of Rostov University. Unlike his ex-wife, he was always a Stalinist.

"My father died a difficult and terrible death," writes Svetlana. She was at his bedside for three days. Stalin's regular doctors were in prison—he was purging everyone, in those last days—but there were others, working busily, applying leeches to his neck and head. He died, as I have said, on March 5, 1953—same day as the composer Prokofiev, who received less fanfare.

Svetlana taught Soviet literature and the English language at her alma mater, Moscow University. She later worked as a translator. And she changed her name: to Svetlana Alliluyeva, adopting her mother's family name. This was in 1957. She had wanted to do it before, in the interval between her high-school days and her university days. In fact, she brought up the subject with her father. One look from him suggested that this was a bad idea. But almost 15 years after the impulse, she went ahead and acted on it. "I could no longer tolerate the name of Stalin," she writes. "Its sharp metallic sound lacerated my ears, my eyes, my heart...."

Mussolini women have held on to the patriarch's name, sometimes maneuvering legally to do it. Franco's daughter has long used her maiden name: She is Carmen Franco, not Carmen Martínez-Bordiú. But Svetlana was different (and had a different father, to be sure). People assumed that the authorities forced her to give up "Stalin," in the general, national "de-Stalinization" process. This was not so, according to Svetlana herself.

About the name "Alliluyeva": It is akin to "Hallelujah," meaning "Praise ye the Lord." The name came to fit Svetlana better than it had her mother, whose god was Communism. In 1962, Svetlana was baptized in the Orthodox Church. Explaining this step, she writes, "The sacrament of baptism consists in rejecting evil, the lie. I believed in 'Thou shalt not kill,' I believed in truth without violence and bloodshed. I believed that the Supreme Mind, not vain man, governed the world. I believed that the Spirit of Truth was stronger than material values. And when all of this had entered my heart, the shreds of Marxism-Leninism taught me since childhood vanished like smoke."

She further writes that "my father's whole life stood out before me as a rejection of Wisdom, of Goodness, in the name of ambition, as a complete giving of oneself to Evil. For I had seen how slowly, day by day, he had been destroyed by evil, and how evil had killed all those who stood near him. He had simply sunk deeper and deeper into the black chasm of the lie, of fury and pride. And in that chasm he at last had smothered to death."

In 1963, she met a man named Brajesh Singh, an Indian Communist. She was instantly drawn to him. His manners were European, she would later say. And there was another aspect: His "gentle calm" and "serene smile" suggested "the traditional Hindu virtues of nonviolence and spiritual equilibrium." During their second conversation, Singh asked her, "Has life greatly changed in the Soviet Union since Stalin's death?"

Yes, of course, Svetlana replied—but these changes were perhaps not "deep or fundamental." She then revealed to him her parentage. "Oh!" he said. Oddly enough, he would never question her about her father, in the three years they knew each other.

He was about 20 years her senior—in his mid-fifties, while she was in her mid-thirties. He was from an old, wealthy, distinguished family. He was losing his faith in Communism. More and more, he was feeling himself a Hindu. He and Stalin's daughter fell in love and eventually lived together. They were a household, with Svetlana's children, Josef and Katya. The shadow over this was that Singh was sick. He had been sickly, failing, for years. He and Svetlana wanted to get married—but for this they needed the state's permission. Svetlana was still in a sense the state's property.

In May 1965, she went to see the Number 1, Alexei Kosygin. He received her in her father's old office. "What have you cooked up?" he said. "You, a healthy young woman, a sportswoman: Couldn't you have found someone here? I mean, someone young and strong? What do you want with this old, sick Hindu? No, we are all positively against it, positively against it." If she and Singh got married, Kosygin explained, "he would then have the legal right to take you to India, a poverty-stricken, backward country! I was there. I know. Besides, Hindus treat women badly. He'll take you there and abandon you."

Svetlana and Singh never married, formally. But she always referred to him as her "husband," and we may consider this relationship her third marriage. (There would be one other.) Singh died in October 1966. It was Svetlana's wish to go to India, to spread his ashes on the Ganges. Singh had wanted such a ritual to be performed. But for this trip, as for a marriage, Svetlana would need the state's consent. She went to see Kosygin again. Amazingly, he said yes: He gave his consent. Svetlana would be let out for a month. The only condition was that she not speak to the press.

So, Svetlana Stalina, or Svetlana Alliluyeva, would travel to India, urn in hand. The experience would radically change her life.

Worldly and intellectual though she was, she had never been abroad—except for ten days in East Germany: "I saw nothing but war ruins and frightened, silent people." In India, she contrived to stay longer than a month. She in fact spent more than two months in the Singh family's village, Kalakankar, in Uttar Pradesh. She loved life there. It would also be true to say she loved life outside the Soviet Union, and the Soviet bloc. She was required to attend some functions at the Soviet embassy in New Delhi. And she discovered something interesting: that she had "lost the habit" of a Soviet way of life. "India had set free something in me," she writes. "Here I had ceased feeling like a piece of 'government property,' which in the U.S.S.R. I had been all my life." She started thinking of not going back.

And on March 6, 1967, she walked into the U.S. embassy. She requested political asylum. An American on duty said to her, "So you say your father was Stalin? *The* Stalin?"

She was flown to Rome that very night. From there, she went to Switzerland. She was enchanted by this country, as most people are, and she would gladly have stayed there. But the Swiss government would have required that she not involve herself in politics in any way. And that was unacceptable to her. "To remain silent for another forty years could have been achieved just as well in the U.S.S.R.," she writes. She wanted to explain, to one and all, "why I was cutting myself off forever from the Communist world." On April 21, six weeks after she entered the U.S. embassy in New Delhi, she landed at Kennedy Airport in New York. Upon bounding down the steps from her plane, she said, "Hello! I'm happy to be here!"

But wait a second: Didn't she have two children back in the Soviet Union? She did. This weighed on her mind before she went to the embassy, and it would weigh on her for many years afterward. As on other subjects, she said different things at different times. Often, she reasoned (or rationalized) as follows: *Josef was 21, and married. Katya was 16, and more or less grown up. They could take care of each other, and their fathers loved them. I had done all I could for them. They did not need me in order to succeed.* At other times, she thought she had committed a "sin" against her children.

There in the embassy—the American embassy in Delhi—she had written a statement about her life and intentions. It ended with these lines: "My children are in Moscow and I do understand that now I might not see them for years. But I know they will understand me.... Let God help them. I know they will not reject me and one day we shall meet—I will wait for that."

When she arrived in New York, she said, "I have come here to seek the self-expression that has been denied me for so long in Russia." And she had not come empty-handed. She carried a manuscript: *Twenty Letters to a Friend*, which she had composed in the summer of 1963. She wrote the book at great speed: in just 35 days. It is all about her life, an outpouring of memories and thoughts, a testament. "The free letter form," she writes in an author's note, "enabled me to be completely candid." Published in America, the book became a bestseller.

Authorities in the Soviet Union were not pleased with "the defector Alliluyeva," as the state media had it. Kosygin came to the United States in June 1967—two months after Svetlana's arrival—for the Glassboro Summit in New Jersey (with President Lyndon Johnson). He found time to denounce the defector to the worldwide press: "Alliluyeva is a morally unstable person and she's a sick person and we can only pity those who wish to use her for any political aim or for any aim of discrediting the Soviet state." Kosygin must have kicked himself for letting Stalin's daughter out to spread those ashes—the ashes of the man whom he had forbidden her to marry.

Night and day, the Soviet propaganda machine worked against Svetlana. Stung, fuming, she held a little ceremony at a charcoal grill. She announced to those present, "I am burning my Soviet passport in answer to lies and calumny." When the passport had been reduced to ashes, she took those ashes and blew on them. Away they went on the wind.

In 1969, she had another memoir published, *Only One Year*. This memoir, she wrote in America. Its title was not a good one, as she would admit in her third memoir. The title had worked better as she had conceived it in Russian. What the author meant was, "Look what has happened to me, in just one year!" In any case, the second memoir was a bestseller, like the first. It covered the tumultuously eventful year she had from the time she left the Soviet Union. Its dedication: "To all new friends, to whom I owe my life in freedom."

During that first year outside the Soviet Union, she talked on the phone with a Russian who had been in America for a long time: Alexander Kerensky, the prime minister whom the Bolsheviks overthrew exactly 50 years earlier, in 1917. He had read *Twenty Letters* and liked it. In due course, Svetlana became a U.S. citizen and registered with the Republican Party. Her favorite magazine was *National Review*, she said—the conservative, anti-Communist journal founded by William F. Buckley Jr. in 1955. She donated $500 to the magazine.

A very strange episode, in a life of very strange episodes, took place in the first few years of the 1970s. The widow of Frank Lloyd Wright, the great architect, repeatedly invited Svetlana to visit her at Taliesin West, near Scottsdale, Arizona. I will have to take a little time to explain Taliesin West. Mrs. Wright will take some explaining, too.

There are two Taliesins: the one near Scottsdale and one near Spring Green, Wisconsin. At these places, the architect established his home and studio and school. Wisconsin was for the summer, and Arizona was for the winter, generally speaking. Also, Taliesin (at either location) was a commune, or "fellowship." After the architect's death, his widow, Olgivanna, became the mistress of Taliesin.

Once, she had a daughter named Svetlana. In the 1940s, this Svetlana was a young mother, and pregnant with another child. She was killed in a car crash. Her two-year-old son was killed along with her. Many years later, Mrs. Wright began reading and hearing about a new Svetlana—the famous one, who had defected from Russia. She felt a connection to her. And, as I've mentioned, she repeatedly invited her to come visit her in Arizona. Intrigued, Svetlana finally accepted.

Mrs. Wright was keen for her to meet Wesley Peters, the senior apprentice to her late husband. He was also her son-in-law—the widower of the late Svetlana, and the father of those children. Peters still lived in the Taliesin fellowship, as he always would. Svetlana Alliluyeva was immediately drawn to him. He had "an Abraham Lincoln face," she writes, meaning that it was dignified, sad, and kind. (This portrait comes from Svetlana's aforementioned third memoir.) Mrs. Wright had been hoping she would have a special liking for Peters. She did. They were married three weeks after her arrival in Arizona. Mrs. Wright was introducing her as "my daughter Svetlana."

Stalin's daughter now styled herself "Lana Peters." In 1971, the year after they were married, she and Wes had a baby, Olga. Svetlana was 45 years old; she had had her first child, Josef, at 19.

Initially, Svetlana enjoyed her life with Wes Peters. But she soon disliked life in the fellowship, a "queer institution," she writes. Mrs. Wright ran it autocratically. And Wes had no desire to buck her. Svetlana found Taliesin stultifying and oppressive. It reminded her of a previous life: "After my first three blessed years of American freedom of choice, informality and friendliness, I felt as though I were back in my forbidding Soviet Russia." In addition, the marriage was costing her a lot of money—money she had earned from her books. She paid off her husband's sizable debts, and was happy to do so. But the fellowship wanted money, too: more than she was willing to pay.

Wes cooled on her, according to her account. She was in a state of dismay over her marriage. "He married me because of my name; if I were Nina or Mary he would never have looked at me." They separated when Olga was still a baby, and in short order divorced.

"I seemed to be re-living the strange disastrous pattern of my Russian life," Svetlana writes. In other words, she was bringing up a small child after a divorce. This child would be an all-American girl, Svetlana determined. She would not teach Olga any Russian. And the past would be a foreign country, for as long as possible. In 2012, Olga gave an interview, with an arresting detail: She had always thought of her grandfather Stalin as one of the three men in the historic photographs, taken at Yalta—one of the mighty triumvirate, along with Churchill and Roosevelt. These were the men who beat the Nazis and won World War II. What granddaughter wouldn't be proud of that? But one day her mother sat her down and explained about Stalin's monstrous crimes. That must have been an awful conversation.

Svetlana was restless, moving from place to place. She would do this to the end of her days. She was also a seeker, trying or borrowing from many religions. Among these religions were Hinduism, Catholicism, Quakerism, and Christian Science. (She credits the last of these with freeing her from alcoholism, to which she had been succumbing. Her problem especially alarmed her in view of her brother Vasily's death, and life.)

In 1982, she moved, with Olga, to England. Two years later, she came out with her third memoir, *The Faraway Music*. She got the title from *Walden*, by Henry David Thoreau. Many people know the line about the different drummer: "If a man does not keep pace with his companions, perhaps it is because he hears a different drummer." But the next words are these: "Let him step to the music which he hears, however measured or far away." In her foreword, Svetlana says, "I have always managed to hear a *different drummer.*" Never, she says, "did I 'keep pace' with other Kremlin children" or with the Communist Party. "I kept marching under some individualistic *music of my own.*"

Her first two memoirs had been published by the powerful American firm of Harper & Row. *The Faraway Music* was published by an Indian outfit, Lancer. It made no splash and is virtually unfindable today. Svetlana means it to be the third installment of a trilogy. It is not comparable to the other two books, however, in beauty, depth, or polish. Yet it tells the (highly interesting) Peters saga, doesn't it? It has other value as well.

When she wrote *The Faraway Music*, she was in a changed mood, politically and personally. She was no longer the ardent admirer of America and the ardent critic of the Soviet Union. She positioned herself in between, the representative of a "third way." The USSR and the USA were morally equivalent, two "giants," endangering the world with their arrogance and belligerence. The countries she now liked were gentle social democratic ones, such as Norway and Sweden (which could remain gentle and social democratic because they were protected by American military might).

America had disappointed Svetlana. The country's "intellectual and artistic circles," she writes, "never accepted me in their milieu." After her early splash, she became a "housewife," consumed with the quotidian chores of raising Olga. She sorely missed "those sophisticated intellectuals and artists I used to know in Moscow and Leningrad." She longed to be "amidst such fine minds."

In 1984—17 years after her defection—she went back to the Soviet Union. She had been talking with her son, Josef, on the phone, and this increased her longing. He was now a doctor—a cardiologist—and he was also an alcoholic. He had been hospitalized, and Svetlana thought that he needed her. So, she petitioned the Soviet embassy in London, successfully; yanked Olga out of school; and flew home, if home it was.

When she got there, she was quoted as saying she had never enjoyed "one single day" of freedom in the West. Anything she might have said in favor of the United States or against the Soviet Union was to be discounted. She had been manipulated by other people. This posturing aside, Svetlana's homecoming proved very unhappy. Josef did not welcome her. Mother and son fought bitterly. As for Katya, her daughter, she refused to see her mother altogether. Katya was a die-hard Communist and viewed her mother as a traitor, among other things. Recall the statement that Svetlana had written while at the U.S. embassy in New Delhi. She said of her children, "I know they will not reject me and one day we shall meet—I will wait for that." It did not work out as Svetlana had hoped.

She and Olga spent just two months in Moscow. Then they moved to Tbilisi, where the Stalin name was still strong. Svetlana spoke no Georgian; her American daughter spoke neither Georgian nor Russian. Both of the Peters women were miserable. There was little to eat or wear. People had no idea how to deal with them, and vice versa. And they got out as soon as they could. The new, and final, Number 1, Gorbachev, gave them permission to leave. They spent just 18 months in the Soviet Union.

Landing at O'Hare Airport in Chicago, Svetlana said, "I had to leave for a while to realize, 'Oh, my God, how wonderful it is'"—the "it" being America. All the things she had said against the West after her arrival in Moscow? She had been misquoted or mistranslated. She went up to Spring Green, Wisconsin, to stay with old friends.

But she kept moving around. Over the next 25 years, she went to England, France, America again, many places. She knew poverty. For a while, she was living in a charity home in West London—or so said reports. She also lived in Portland, Oregon, with Olga, who was managing a vintage-clothing store. Svetlana spent her last few years in a nursing home in Richland Center, Wisconsin (some 20 miles from Spring Green). She liked to sew and read books. Pictures show her a beautiful old lady, who had weathered a lot. She was born a Kremlin princess—the princess of the whole, vast USSR—in 1926. She died in that Wisconsin nursing home in 2011, age 85.

Her son Josef predeceased her: dying in 2008. Katya is a scientist, a vulcanologist, apparently living in rude conditions at the edge of a volcano on the Kamchatka Peninsula, in Russia's far east. In 2005, she spoke of her mother to a British journalist, David Jones: "She is such a selfish, cruel woman. She didn't seem to care whether she hurt me."

Olga has for many years gone by the name of Chrese Evans. (The first name is pronounced "Chris.") The 2012 interview I quoted earlier was published in *Paris Match*. Accompanying the article was a photo of its subject. What does she look like? The magazine described her as an

American "au look rock'n'roll." I would put it this way: Imagine that Stalin had a granddaughter who was a Pacific Northwest hipster, with all-black clothing and tattoos, one of which says (it appears) "Momma's Girl." That's what she looks like. And she, like her mother, though different in appearance, is beautiful. She told *Paris Match* that she felt close to Buddhism.

Svetlana deserves to be remembered, not just as Stalin's daughter, but as a writer, a memoirist. Her first two books ought to endure. She partially renounced them, in different moods, but they are true, brave, and beautiful. She ends *Twenty Letters to a Friend* with a tribute to her nanny, Alexandra Andreyevna. The nanny had been "dearer" to her than "anyone on earth." "If it hadn't been for the even, steady warmth given off by this large and kindly person, I might long ago have gone out of my mind."

Her books are teeming with stories and observations. But she is more than a storyteller or observer. She is a Sovietologist (to use a word that now seems antique). Svetlana is enlightening—sometimes profound—on Stalin, the Soviet Union, and totalitarian society at large. She had great material, you might say, truthfully. But no one would have wished the life for himself, just to have the material. Svetlana occasionally said that she wished her mother had married a carpenter.

Her father was the great and haunting theme of her life. "Wherever I go," she once said—it could be some remote Pacific island—"I will always be a political prisoner of my father's name." She could not escape "Stalin," with "Alliluyeva," "Peters," or anything else. I met a Russian lady who accompanied Svetlana one day, during Svetlana's 1984–86 stint in the Soviet Union. It seemed obvious to my friend that Svetlana wanted to be regarded as just a normal person. But my friend couldn't help thinking, "This is Stalin's daughter." So it was with a great many.

About Stalin, Svetlana could be "conflicted," to use modern psychological parlance. She once stayed at the home of David Pryce-Jones, the British historian and novelist (not to be confused with the earlier-mentioned David Jones), and his wife, Clarissa. In a memoir, Pryce-Jones tells us something important about his guest: "Having said point blank that she refused to talk about her father, she would come down from her room and talk exclusively about him, tormented that she couldn't help loving a father who she knew was a monster."

Bizarrely, cruelly, there were some people who blamed Svetlana for Stalin's crimes—or who took out their anguish on her. Her daughter Chrese told David Jones, "There was a period when so many people held her responsible for [Stalin's] actions that she actually started to think maybe it was true. It's so unjust." A friend of Svetlana's was quoted in an American newspaper as saying, "She feels the world's hatred of Stalin is on her shoulders." In 1983, shortly before her return to the Soviet Union, Svetlana said, "My father would have shot me for what I have done." That is true. Her father once accused her of making "anti-Soviet statements." She had barely begun.

I believe that Svetlana did her best, considering the circumstances—the circumstances of her almost unimaginable life. Could anyone have done better? Could anyone have turned out more "normal," less crazy, more productive? She made mistakes—Katya would surely agree—but she had a conscience. And that conscience broke through to see Stalin and the Soviet Union for what they were. That was no great achievement, you might argue: Anyone, even a daughter, could see that Stalin and the Soviet Union were monstrous! That takes no special morality or courage! Oh? Consider a few things.

In *Twenty Letters*, Svetlana writes that the other top men in the Soviet Union—Khrushchev, Bulganin, et al.—were "under the spell" of her father's "extraordinary personality, which carried people away and was utterly impossible to resist. Many people knew this through their own experience—of these, some admit it, though others now deny it."

Gulia Dzhugashvili, Svetlana's niece, would always worship the memory of Stalin—this despite the fact that Stalin's response to her father's capture by the Nazis was to arrest and imprison her mother, who had a three-year-old child (Gulia). Moreover, Stalin had always treated her father, Yakov, abominably. Think of Yevgeny, Gulia's half-brother, or alleged half-brother: He is as great a Stalin defender as there is.

Consider, too, Vladimir Alliluyev, a cousin of Svetlana's. Stalin had his father killed. He sent his mother to the Gulag. In the 1990s, Alliluyev wrote a book advocating the return of Stalinism. In a letter to a Russian literary magazine, Svetlana wrote that the book had aroused in her "feelings of revulsion." It was "a political tract whitewashing 70 years of Soviet history."

Relatives who survived the Gulag could not bring themselves to blame Stalin for what happened to them—or to their loved ones who were killed. The guilty party must have been Beria or some other miscreant beyond the great man's control. "Josef Vissarionovich," as they called him, lovingly, could do no wrong.

This was the sort of effect that Stalin had on people, incomprehensible as it may be. But his lone daughter broke through the mesmerism, or "spell," as she labeled it. Her conscience rose in rebellion against her father and his state. This makes her exceedingly rare among sons and daughters of dictators.

In *Only One Year*, she writes, "Many people today find it easier to think of [Stalin] as a coarse physical monster. Actually, he was a moral and spiritual monster. This is far more terrifying. But it's the truth." She also knew the truth about freedom and unfreedom. Yes, there came a time when she talked moral equivalence: saying that between the United States and the Soviet Union, there was nothing to choose. But how did that make her different from any number of professors on American campuses?

Svetlana could have stayed quiet in Switzerland, enjoying a lovely bucolic and Alpine life. But she went to a place where she told the truth. She was sometimes laudatory of Alexander Solzhenitsyn, the great Russian dissident, and sometimes petulantly critical. But, to a large degree, she followed the Solzhenitsyn maxim of "Live not by lies." This is why we might say—why I maintain—that in Svetlana lay a greatness.

5

TOJO

Tojo had seven children. He had them with his wife, Katsu Ito, whom he married in 1909. It was an unusual marriage for the time and place: a love match rather than an arrangement. Plus, Katsu was a college girl. They had their children well before Tojo became prime minister of Japan in October 1941. (He rose to this position just in time to order the sneak attack on Pearl Harbor, thus beginning the Pacific War.) The general was 56 when he assumed power.

I have used a contentious phrase, "assumed power." Does Tojo belong in a book about dictators (or their sons and daughters)? He was a servant of the emperor, to be sure. And when the palace told him to go, he went, without resistance. (The historian Christopher Szpilman made this point to me.) But, in the course of the war, he assumed dictatorial powers. And, as you know, he used them ruthlessly.

The first of the Tojos' seven children came in 1911. He was a son, Hidetaka. There would be two more sons—Teruo and Toshio; and four daughters—Mitsue, Makie, Sachie, and Kimie. In March 1942, the American magazine *Life* had an article on Tojo, which said, "Hidetaka, having got away with an unorthodox disregard for the family's military tradition, now works for the Oryokko Electric Power Co. in Keijo,

Korea." (Keijo was the Japanese colonial name for Seoul.) A Tojo biographer, Courtney Browne, tells us that Hidetaka "failed to get into the army on medical grounds." In September 1943, an Associated Press report had two of the daughters working in a munitions factory, under assumed names. The source of this information was Berlin radio.

We know a little something—though not so little to the people involved—about the eldest daughter, Mitsue: She chose not to get married, opting to help her mother raise the two youngest daughters, and to help her parents generally.

In July 1944, the imperial palace—meaning, the emperor and his men—forced Tojo out as premier. This was after serious Japanese reversals. A year and one month later, Japan was on the verge of surrender. One man who was distraught at the idea of surrender was Major Hidemasa Koga, the husband of Tojo's daughter Makie. A member of the Imperial Guards Division, he joined a plot to prevent the emperor from surrendering. Before he left on this rebellious mission, he made sure that Makie had locks of his hair and some nail clippings—traditional relics in Buddhism. The plot failed, of course, and Koga killed himself. Tojo knew this before Makie did. He said to his daughter, "His body is being brought here in one hour. Prepare yourself."

Before long, it would be Tojo's turn. He sought a neighbor, Dr. Suzuki, for advice: Where exactly was the heart? The doctor marked it on Tojo's chest with *sumi* ink. When the Americans arrived on September 11 to arrest him, Tojo took the gun that the late Koga had used and aimed it at the marked spot. He did not succeed in dying, however. What might Stalin have said, in the Kremlin? The same thing he had said about his son Yakov? That the Japanese general couldn't shoot straight?

The Americans defied Tojo, nursing him back to health, and imprisoning him. A young Navy dentist, Jack Mallory, was ordered to make dentures for Tojo. More than 50 years later, in 2002, Mallory told an interviewer, "I knew I was going to meet an evil man. It was a shock to see him. He was very humble, and just a meek, little guy." Into Tojo's dentures, Mallory etched a message in Morse code: "Remember Pearl Harbor." When word got out about this classic prank, Mallory's superiors ordered him to efface the message from the dentures. He did.

An international tribunal assembled, trying thousands of Japanese for war crimes (while letting the emperor off the hook). On November

12, 1948, Tojo was one of seven men sentenced to death. In his prison diary, he made note of his sons, or two of them: "When judgment was passed, I saw Teruo and Toshio in the gallery. I am grateful to them for having been present there in the final hours." Tojo and the other condemned were permitted a last visit from up to five persons of their choosing. Tojo chose his wife and four daughters. There are several versions of their conversation, all of them similar. One appears in a novel (*Two Homelands*) by Toyoko Yamasaki. I will draw on the version offered by an above-cited biographer, Courtney Browne.

Tojo was manacled to an American officer who sat next to him. Tojo noticed that his youngest daughter was staring at the handcuff. "Kimie," he said, "you seem to be bothered about my hand. Don't be. They can bind my hands or feet, but no one has ever bound my heart." He then spoke of religion, a topic much on his mind in his last days. "All his life, your father has done his best, but he was so busy that he drifted away from religion.... You don't know what kind of difficulties you may find yourself in later. Take a grasp of some good religion.... Your father finds Buddhism best for him. But it can be Christianity or some other religion that fits your heart. Then, no matter what, you won't be afraid."

On December 23, he and his fellow war criminals swung.

Tojo's second son, Teruo, grew up to be president, then chairman, of Mitsubishi Motors. He started with the Mitsubishi company in 1937, before the war. An engineer, he designed aircraft. Later, it would be buses and trucks. In August 1970, Teruo responded to a press inquiry about that year's anniversary. He said, "I have no special feeling or sentiment to mention about the 25th anniversary of Japan's defeat." August 15 "comes around every year, and I think Japan has completely recovered from its defeat by now." Over the years of his long career, he commented sparingly on public affairs. And when he did, it was with moderation, judiciousness, and conciliation. Teruo Tojo died in 2012, at 98.

His younger brother, Toshio, was a general in the Japanese air force. The eldest daughter, Mitsue, who helped raise Sachie and Kimie, eventually married. When she was 40, she married the top general in the Japanese military, Shigeru Sugiyama. The next year, 1959, Sugiyama received the Legion of Merit from the U.S. Armed Forces. It was in honor of his contributions to American-Japanese defense relations.

Kimie, the youngest, made news during the 1950s. In 1951, when she was 19, she went to a United Nations blood bank in Tokyo. The Korean War was on. Tojo's child was going to make a donation. The *New York Times* reported, "She was shy and sensitive. The sight of a crowd of reporters and photographers sent her blood pressure up and the doctors thought it best for her to go home." The next day, she returned. "This time no crowd waited for her and she made her donation."

The *Times* had more to say: "This girl's gift of blood went, as likely as not, to some American soldier. Most Japanese, in the year 1951, can understand that what the Americans did to Japan was the unavoidable sequel to Japanese aggression in 1941." Here, the paper is probably alluding to the atomic bombing, and subsequent occupation. But Kimie Tojo "had a more difficult task of understanding. No Occidental can know precisely what was in her mind and heart, but viewed across a vast ocean and the barrier between two civilizations what she did had the beauty of a perfect porcelain, a flawless print, a garden exquisitely kept. If this gift was meant as reparation, the soul of Hideki Tojo may rest a little easier."

Kimie went to Ibaraki Christian College and then Hosei University. She earned degrees at them both. An American classmate described her as "a diligent student, the straight-A type." She then went to study in the United States—specifically, to the University of Michigan. In June 1959, an American newspaper showed her on the front page, over a caption headed "Loyal." The caption read, "Pretty Miss Kimie Tojo, 27, arrives in Seattle from Tokyo." Landing on U.S. shores, she commented, "My father was a very sweet, very kind person. I do not dislike America for what happened. I know I will make friends here."

In Ann Arbor (home of the University of Michigan), she lived in the Martha Cook residence hall. A yearbook says, "Memorable and unique this year was a demonstration of the Japanese Tea Ceremony by our Kimie Tojo." Another yearbook notes that she was invited by another hall to "eat and speak" with the young women who lived there. This yearbook describes Kimie as "the daughter of a Japanese general"—true, but gingerly. Another publication shows her smiling with an administrator, and the description of her is more blunt (perhaps rudely so): "Kimie Tojo, youngest daughter of Japan's Word War II premier who was executed as a war criminal, is now enrolled in the English Language Institute and plans to take graduate courses this fall."

Kimie Tojo with her mother, Katsu Ito, and, behind
them, a portrait of the late Tojo

She married an American, Dennis Gilbertson, and lived as Kimie T.
Gilbertson in Honolulu and elsewhere. We might reflect, for a moment,
on the proximity of Honolulu to Pearl Harbor. I might also note that
Mrs. Gilbertson declined, politely, to be interviewed for this book. And
here is a tiny detail, perhaps of interest: The return-address stamp of
Tojo's child featured the Jefferson Memorial in Washington, D.C.

Typically, when the Tojo family made the news, it was with dignity
and measuredness—Kimie and Teruo are perfectly representative. Their
mother, Katsu, visited her husband's tomb every December 23, the day of
his execution. She was very private, declining to give interviews, even to
appear in public. She would say, "I am a person of the past. Please leave
me alone." Katsu died in 1982, age 91. Where the past was concerned,
the Tojo family maintained what some press reports called a "code of
silence." In the 1990s, that code was shattered.

It was shattered by Yuko Tojo, or, as she had long been known,
Iwanami Toshie. She was a granddaughter of Tojo, the daughter of

his firstborn, Hidetaka. She changed her name late in life in order to embrace her grandfather's legacy. The Tojo name "was untouchable for 50 years," she said. (This is false—witness Teruo's corporate ascent—but we can grant that it was her perception.) Now she was reclaiming the name, defiantly, exultantly. She revered her grandfather as a great man and hero. She kept his hair and fingernail clippings, and also the butt of the last cigarette he smoked. She would bring them to interviews. One interviewer, Deborah Cameron, wrote, "In her heart she holds 60 years of accumulated anger."

She wrote several books, including one called "Never Talk" (she was talking, breaking the code). She was, in brief, an extreme right-wing nationalist. An apologist, a revisionist. She denied that Japan had any culpability for World War II, saying that the West had started the war and Japan was merely defending itself. Her grandfather's "greatest crime," she said, "was that he loved his country." She revived a combustible term from his era: "warrior race." That's what the Japanese were meant to be, she said. Moreover, "no Japanese warrior ever committed a crime if his heart's true intent was the expansion of our grand empire."

One might expect a nationalist of Yuko Tojo's sort to be anti-American. She was not, however. An interviewer, David McNeill, asked her, "Do you resent America?" "Not even a little," she answered. "If I resented America, I wouldn't be happy that my daughter was married to a citizen of that country, would I?" Her son-in-law worked for Boeing and served in the Iraq War. "My grandfather admired America and said we could learn from it. And his American lawyers defended him.... Those people treated my grandfather with great respect and he respected them, even as enemies."

She was nine years old when Tojo was executed. In the following years, she told McNeill, she and her family were subjected to terrible harassment. She watched in horror as other children mimicked her grandfather's death by hanging. "We suffered awful discrimination with our name. We weren't allowed to sit in class. Even when we changed schools we weren't allowed into the classroom. My little sister was beaten and came home covered in blood. My brother couldn't go to school, so he was taught by private tutors. That was what it was like at the end of the war in Japan."

What she wanted, above all, was pride and honor: for herself, her family, and the Japanese nation at large.

Like several of Mussolini's grandchildren, Yuko ran for office: standing at the age of 68 for the upper house of the Japanese parliament. Her purpose was to make her points, she told the press. "Even if I am not elected, I won't see that as a defeat." She received very few votes. She did not have the electoral touch of an Alessandra Mussolini. But she made her points, twisted as some of them were. She was the sort who believes that the Rape of Nanking is a Sino-American fabrication. Unlike Svetlana Stalin, Yuko Tojo did not follow the maxim "Live not by lies." She died in 2013, age 74. The Tojo family on the whole, however, has conducted itself with honor (though maybe not the kind favored by Yuko). And Japan, of course, is a country in which honor is unusually important.

6

MAO

Mao had ten children, by most counts. He had those ten by three of his four wives. How many other children he had, it is impossible to say. That is a refrain of this book. Mao's appetite for women was as great as Mussolini's, and his consumption probably greater. He had them at his command, as dictators tend to.

Dictators are not overflowing with the milk of human kindness, obviously. But it was particularly absent in Mao Zedong. Such men as Pol Pot and Idi Amin—even they had affection, sometimes great affection, for their children, if not for others. Mao was a different sort.

In his famous memoir, Mao's doctor writes, "So far as I could tell, despite his initial friendliness at first meetings, Mao was devoid of human feeling, incapable of love, friendship, or warmth." (This is Li Zhisui in his *Private Life of Chairman Mao*.) The doctor then tells a story—very small, relative to Mao's China as a whole, but illustrative: "Once, in Shanghai, I was sitting next to the Chairman during a performance when a young acrobat—a child—suddenly slipped and was seriously injured. The crowd was aghast, transfixed by the tragedy, and the child's mother was inconsolable. But Mao continued talking and laughing without concern, as though nothing had happened.

Nor, to my knowledge, did he ever inquire about the fate of the young performer."

Several of Mao's own children died young and tragically. "But I never saw him express any emotion over those losses," says Li Zhisui. "The fact that he had lived while so many others died seemed only to confirm his belief that his life would be long. As for those who had died, he would simply say that 'lives have to be sacrificed for the cause of revolution.'"

Of his ten children, Mao really knew just four. And those, he rarely saw. He tended to treat his wives with similar indifference. Until his fourth wife, Jiang Qing, known in the West as "Madame Mao," his pattern was to discard them without telling them. He simply moved on.

In the following pages, I will present a blizzard of names, and those names tend to be tricky to the Western eye. I will follow the usual Chinese practice of "last name" first and "first name" last. Sometimes I will use the names together, and sometimes just the "first" or the "last." This gets especially delicate with one of Mao's wives—whose name was He Zizhen. "He" looks like our masculine pronoun, especially at the beginning of a sentence. I will usually refer to the lady as "Zizhen." In any case, the reader will forbear (and the same forbearance will be required in our next chapter, about North Korea).

I will also present, or quote, a blizzard of biographers—as well as other scholars, investigators, and analysts. There are competing versions of Mao's life, including the lives of his wives and children. From them, however, a picture emerges, clear enough. After too many introductory statements and apologies, I'm sure, I will now properly begin.

Mao's first marriage was arranged. At age 14, he was married off to a relative, Luo Yigu, who was 18. This was in either late 1907 or early 1908. According to Mao, he never lived with his bride nor consummated the marriage. Luo Yigu died in 1910, when she was 20.

Ten years later, Mao married a woman named Yang Kaihui. They had three sons together, whose names chime: Anying, Anqing, and Anlong. Shortly after the birth of this third child, in 1927, Mao went off to make revolution, and he evidently put his family out of his mind. Within months, he had married a third woman, He Zizhen.

In 1930, he and his Reds attacked the city of Changsha, the capital of Hunan Province. Yang Kaihui and the three boys were living there. The

Reds failed to hold the city. And the Nationalists arrested Yang Kaihui on October 24—the eighth birthday of the eldest son, Anying. They demanded that Yang Kaihui publicly denounce and renounce Mao, but she refused. She loved him (though she deplored his violent methods). She was a very brave woman. They paraded her through the streets and killed her. She was 29, leaving the three boys behind.

Mao had a role in this horror. In their 2005 biography, *Mao: The Unknown Story*, Jung Chang and Jon Halliday explain. "During his assault on Changsha, Mao made no effort to extricate [Yang Kaihui] and their sons, or even to warn her. And he could easily have saved her: her house was on his route to the city, and Mao was there for three weeks. Yet he did not lift a finger."

Now essentially orphaned, the three boys were moved to Shanghai, where they lived with the Communist underground or simply on the streets. The youngest, Anlong, died of dysentery, age four. Anying and Anqing acquired new names: Yang Yunfu and Yang Yunshou. Another Mao biographer, Ross Terrill, provides a snapshot of their lives: "They sold newspapers in Shanghai. At one point they found a place to sleep in a deserted temple, outside which they posted a sign: WE TELL STORIES— ONE PENNY."

In the Soviet Union, Stalin had one Chinese prince, Chiang Ching-kuo, son of Chiang Kai-shek, the Nationalist leader. Soon he would have the Mao boys as well. Anying and Anqing arrived in 1936 or 1937, and were dubbed Sergei and Nikolai. Chiang Kai-shek's son, too, was called "Nikolai." What was he doing in the Soviet Union? He had gone there in 1925, to study. His father was an ally of the Soviet Union. Then Chiang Kai-shek turned hard against Communism, and was in civil war against Mao's Reds. Back in the USSR, young Chiang was essentially a hostage. And into Stalin's lap fell the Mao boys, too. The presence of these sons—the three of them—gave Stalin leverage in China's chaotic affairs.

The Mao boys spent about ten years in the Soviet Union. In other words, they did most of their growing up there. Their father communicated with them very little, but there is a letter that biographers like to quote, understandably—for Mao was seldom so fatherly. "I have only one thing to suggest to you both," he wrote. "While you are young, study natural science more and talk politics less. Politics needs to be talked about, but at the moment you should set your mind to studying natural science .... Only science is real learning, and will have boundless use in the future." That is not only genuine advice; it is good advice.

The life of He Zizhen, Mao's third wife, was horrifically sad. No one around Mao led an especially charmed life, true. But Zizhen was more tragic than most. She bore Mao six children, and suffered from repeated post-natal depression. She had four miscarriages. Mao quipped, "She has babies as easily as a hen drops eggs." The remark wounded Zizhen, but then so did much else. Her last decades, she spent in and out of insanity.

Her first child was a girl, Mao Jinhua, born in 1929. Moving on with the Red Army, Zizhen left the babe with a peasant family. Mao told her, "We will get her back after the victory of the revolution." (This remark is recorded by the biographical team of Alexander V. Pantsov and Steven I. Levine, in their 2012 book, *Mao: The Real Story*.) Later in life, Zizhen looked obsessively for this girl. In 1973, a woman named Yang Yuehua surfaced, and she may have been the daughter in question. Zizhen never had a chance to meet her.

The second child of Mao and Zizhen was a boy, born in 1932. They called him Xiao Mao, or "Little Mao." Eventually, this boy, too, was left behind, as his parents fought the revolution. In 1952, Zizhen met a young man who may have been Little Mao. She was convinced he was. But the Party ruled that he belonged to some other Red Army mother.

A year or two after Little Mao was born, another son was born, prematurely. He soon died. The fourth child was born in February 1935, on the Long March—the Communists' fabled trek. This child was a girl, but Zizhen declined to give her a name: She knew she would quickly abandon the girl, which she did. The baby was given to an old woman, along with some money and opium. "Three months later," write Chang and Halliday, "boils erupted all over the baby's body, and it died." At about this time, Zizhen was badly wounded in a bombing attack. Her body was laced with shrapnel.

She continued to have babies, however. Mao had affairs with any number of women, openly—but he kept impregnating his wife. Zizhen had the burden of pregnancy without the joy of motherhood. A girl, Jiaojiao, was born in 1936 or 1937. Then Zizhen went to Moscow (without Jiaojiao). Why did she go? There are competing theories. One says that Zizhen chose to go, tired of Mao's philandering. Another says that Mao sent her away, tired of her. In any event, she arrived in Moscow pregnant—and in the spring of 1938 gave birth to a boy. He was called "Lyova." His mother wrote to Mao to say that the baby looked just like him. The father never replied. Lyova contracted pneumonia and died within a year. Zizhen was grief-stricken (again).

The next year, she learned, by chance, that Mao had taken another wife. This was yet another heavy blow. Meanwhile, daughter Jiaojiao was growing up a virtual orphan in China. When she was four, she was sent to live in the Soviet Union with her mother. "Tanya Chao Chao," she was called. But her mother was probably in no mental shape to care for her.

Did Zizhen suffer from schizophrenia? Many thought so and think so. But here is a summation from Sue Wiles, writing in the *Biographical Dictionary of Chinese Women*: "The wounds received during the Long March caused her lifelong pain, and the unsubstantiated diagnosis of schizophrenia that dogged her from the time she was thirty reeks of expediency." Zizhen was inconvenient to many people, including her husband. If she was mad, he and events probably made her so. She returned to China from the Soviet Union in 1947. (Her daughter was with her.) Zizhen lived a fairly long time, in her fragile condition: till 1984.

Anqing, the second of Mao's sons with Yang Kaihui, was evidently a schizophrenic. Some attribute his mental troubles to beatings he suffered while a street urchin in Shanghai. Others point to an earlier trauma: the arrest of his mother, during which the boy was rifle-butted by a soldier. His older brother once remarked, "Anqing has hearing ailments and his nerves are wrecked."

That older brother was Anying, recall. He returned from the Soviet Union in 1946. Another way of putting that is, Stalin decided to release him then. Before Anying's departure, Stalin presented him with an inscribed pistol. Anying was now 23, and he had not seen his father since he was four. At the airfield, Mao greeted him with, "How tall you have grown!" But he was eager to cut his son down to size. He often belittled him in front of others. He also sent him to a farm, to do hard labor. This was supposed to make Anying a better proletarian man.

Anying harbored some rebellious or doubtful thoughts, and went so far as to express them. He noted a "cult of personality" around Mao. That was a very bold, or reckless, thing to do. Anying was made to write a self-criticism. He also wrote a letter to his father. He avowed that his "proletarian stand" was "firmer now." Nevertheless, the brutality he saw around him, organized by the Communists, troubled him greatly. And this was a man, remember, who had come of age in Stalin's Russia. Anying seems to have had a conscience.

Late in 1948, he wanted to marry a girl he loved: Liu Songlin. But his father objected. (He may have desired her, too.) Eventually, though, he relented, and the young couple were married in October 1949. They had little time together—because, the next year, Anying went to Korea as a volunteer, aiding Kim Il-sung's Communists in the war. He worked as a Russian-language translator. In November 1950, he was killed in an American airstrike. Mao's eldest child was 28 years old. Mao himself is recorded as saying, "In war there must be sacrifice. Without sacrifice there will be no victory. There are no parents in the world who do not treasure their children."

Anying lies buried in North Korea, at the Chinese People's Volunteers cemetery. There is a modest though handsome statue of him. Kim Il-sung sent a wreath to the site every year. Whether his successors have continued the tradition—we're talking about his son and grandson, of course—is unclear.

Anqing, the younger brother, returned to China from the Soviet Union in 1947. Despite his mental illness, and frequent hospitalization, he was able to do some work—as a Russian translator in the propaganda department of the Central Committee. He was also able to marry. He did not necessarily have a free choice, however. Mao's doctor, Li Zhisui, gives us an inside story. Sometime in the 1950s, Anqing stayed in the seaside town of Dalian, in China's northeast. "He lived in a private home," writes Li, "where he was cared for by a full-time nurse. Anqing and the nurse fell in love, but the family had arranged a marriage for him ... and the disappointed, heartsick nurse was forced to return to Beijing."

The chosen bride was Shao Hua, the half-sister of Liu Songlin, Anying's widow. The arranged marriage is interesting in light of Mao's reputation as a great foe of arranged marriage. He had detested his own arranged marriage, and thought this practice a scourge of the land. He is often portrayed as the Great Liberator of Chinese Womanhood. At

The dictator flanked by his daughters
Li Na and Li Min

any rate, Anqing married Shao Hua. They had a child, a son, whom we will meet before long. Anqing died in 2007 at the age of 83.

We will now go back in time, to the late 1930s, when Mao married his fourth and final wife, Jiang Qing—later to be known as the notorious "Madame Mao." We will also be faced with a mini-blizzard of names, amid the larger one. In 1940, Mao and Jiang Qing had a daughter, Li Na. She was Mao's tenth and final child (official child). There are several explanations for that surname, that "last name," Li. One is that it was a pseudonym or nom de guerre of Mao's. Another is that it was Jiang Qing's family name. Neither of these explanations excludes the other. Mao could have thought "Li" serendipitous.

At some point, Mao's surviving daughter with He Zizhen came to live with them—with Mao and Jiang Qing. She had gone through two names already: "Jiaojiao" and "Tanya Chao Chao." Now she would have a third one (and final one): "Li Min." So, there were two girls named Li in the family.

Mao did not have what we could call a regular household, but, to the extent he did, it consisted of five members: Mao and Jiang Qing; the daughters, or half-sisters, Li Min and Li Na; and Mao's nephew, Mao Yuanxin, son of his brother Mao Zemin (executed by a warlord in 1943). According to Dr. Li Zhisui, "neither Mao nor Jiang Qing took much interest in their children, and they rarely saw them." The girls were away at boarding schools, and "even when they came home for vacation they only occasionally joined Mao or Jiang Qing for dinner—never more than a few times a year."

Yet the girls loved their father, the ruler of China. Did he love them? This is a hard question to answer. They amused him when they were quite young, as Svetlana had done for Stalin. But, like Svetlana, they were less amusing to their father when they got older. Jiang Qing clearly favored her own daughter, Li Na, over her stepdaughter, Li Min. But she was not overly maternal toward either. In his biography of Jiang Qing, Ross Terrill writes, "It was not the style for a mother in revolutionary Yanan to coddle her child, and Jiang by nature was less inclined to do so than most women." (Yanan was the Communist capital in China, until Mao and his forces took the whole country.) "Charming with adults, she was not one to dote on children, her own or others'. She had a sincere belief that a child was better served by having to fend for itself than by a fussy protectiveness, and this harmonized well with her self-preoccupation."

In her own biography of Jiang Qing, Roxane Witke quotes a speech that her subject gave on the art of motherhood, or parenting at large. Said Mao's wife,

> I think parents should treat their children as equals. They should not treat them in the feudal way, by regarding themselves as lords of the households. One should follow the example of Chairman Mao, who is utterly democratic at home. Our children are allowed to talk back to their father; sometimes we even make them talk back on purpose! ... But most of the time they don't, because they respect their parents. It is good for them to argue. Let them rebel a little!

As Dr. Li Zhisui tells it, Li Na was a spoiled brat, a little Red diva. Li Min was different: humbler, gentler, perhaps because of the hardships of her childhood. Li Min went to Beijing Teachers College, and worked in a military bureau. In 1958, she married an air-force man, Kong Linghua. They would have two children, a boy and a girl.

Li Na went to Beijing University, studying modern Chinese history, because her father wanted her to be a proper Red historian. She graduated in 1965—just in time for the Cultural Revolution, that orgy of incitement, torture, and murder, which began the next year. In his biography of Mao, Jonathan Spence writes that Li Na "was to be a key link between Mao and the student community in 1966." The students were particularly fanatical in this revolution. Li Na became editor of a major organ, the People's Liberation Army newspaper. The previous editors were hauled off to prison. Li Na conducted herself with great imperiousness, her father's daughter. She turned hard on anyone deemed insufficiently obedient. In their biography, Chang and Halliday record a simple, solemn fact: "Among the many who were tortured was a former personal friend who had expressed disagreement with her over some minor matter."

But as the Cultural Revolution wore on, even Li Na was subject to discipline. "In 1970," writes Spence, "she was sent—perhaps on Mao's instructions—to one of the rectification institutions, known as 'May 7 cadre schools,' where hard agricultural labor was combined with ideological study." (The term "May 7" came from the date of a Mao directive in 1966.)

Li Min, too, was subject to discipline. The way Spence puts it is, she "came under harsh criticism for at least five months." Mao "refused to help her in any way," and she and her husband "had a difficult time." Ross Terrill says that the couple were branded "counterrevolutionaries" and imprisoned. Those involved in this drama, as victims or victimizers, have never been very willing to clarify.

According to Chang and Halliday, Li Na recoiled from the savagery of the period and broke down. She married a young servant or guard, with her father's consent (of course). Jiang Qing was fiercely opposed to the marriage. Her daughter was marrying beneath herself, she thought. Neither she nor Mao attended the wedding. But Mao made a gift to the couple of the collected writings of Marx and Engels. In a few years, the marriage collapsed. A son came out of it, however. "Jiang Qing disliked the baby because she despised its father," write Chang and Halliday, "and never once held it in her arms." As for Mao, he "showed zero interest in this grandson, as in his other three grandchildren."

Stalin-style, Mao ignored Li Na and Li Min till the end of his days. (He died in 1976.) Li Min went to the gates of her father's compound several times, say Chang and Halliday, but "he refused to let her in. She had a nervous breakdown, and was in and out of depression for years."

Li Na married again in 1984. Her mother, who had rejoiced in the killing of so many, killed herself in 1991. In her suicide note, Jiang Qing regretted that her husband had not "exterminated" Deng Xiaoping, the reigning Number 1. And she wrote, "Chairman, your student and co-fighter is coming to see you now." In later years, Li Na became a member of the CPPCC, or Chinese People's Political Consultative Conference. Li Min did the same. At the end of 2003, Li Min came out with a book in celebration of her father, at the 110th anniversary of his birth.

So, there you have Mao's children—or at least glimpses of them. We will now look at his grandchildren, some of them. Like Stalin's, most of them, they revere their grandfather, no matter how he treated their parents, or anyone else. Mao Xinyu, the son of Mao Anqing and Shao Hua, gave an interview to a Chinese newspaper in 2008. One question went, "You have said that your grandfather is God. Is he a perfect man to you?" Xinyu answered, "Yes." (Mao was responsible for the deaths of something like 70 million people.)

Xinyu was born in 1970, six years before his grandfather died. In 1989, he was a student at the People's University in Beijing, when the Tiananmen Square demonstrations broke out. (These were the demonstrations for democracy, crushed by the Party in a massacre.) Some classmates evidently asked Xinyu to lead a hunger strike. He later explained, "I resolutely refused. I would have approved if it had been in support of Chairman Mao, but I would never agree to anything that negates socialism and promotes bourgeois liberalism." In 1991, he had a turn upon the stage, portraying his grandfather in an opera. To enhance the resemblance, they shaved some of his head and placed a mole on his chin. Audience members were delighted with the result. Two years after that, on the eve of the Mao centenary, Xinyu was formally inducted into the Communist Party. The Number 1 of the day, Jiang Zemin, congratulated him personally. Xinyu said, "I will continue to grow under the leadership of the General Secretary."

There is a revived cult of Mao in China, and the grandson Xinyu is a figure and a symbol in it. In fact, the above details come from Geremie R. Barmé's book *Shades of Mao: The Posthumous Cult of the Great Leader*.

At the time of the centenary, there was a startling headline in the Western press: "Mao's Grandson Regrets Heritage." The grandson in question was Wang Xiaozhi, son of Li Na. He was 21 years old at the time. Interviewed by *China Daily*, he said, "I wish I had been born into a different family. That way I would have had more freedom and no worries about what other people say." Yet he was determined to do the family proud. "I won't let my grandpa down." (Wang Xiaozhi did not go on to have any success of a public variety.)

His cousin Xinyu was even more determined not to let his grandfather down. He studied Party history, and in fact obtained a Ph.D. in the subject. He has written several books in praise of Mao, including one entitled "Grandpa Mao Zedong." In 1997, he married a woman named Hao Mingli. She died in prison in 2003, age 31. Pantsov and Levine say in their biography of Mao, "She had been imprisoned in May 2002, when she began to quarrel with Mao Xinyu after learning that he wanted to divorce her." How and why she died is a dark mystery. Sometime in 2002, Xinyu married Liu Bin, with whom he has had two children, a son and a daughter.

In 2010, the Chinese public received some news: Xinyu had been made the youngest major general in the army. This did not sit well with much of the public. People decried favoritism, and made fun of Xinyu's weight (considerable). He did not look like a military man. It was also noticed that Xinyu had two children, not one, contrary to national policy. But he has long had fans as well. In 2008, he began blogging for the *People's Daily*, the Party newspaper. The next year, readers voted his blog the most "attention-grabbing." Xinyu wrote such lines as "The essence of Mao's thought is the people's war." In 2011, he joined Guangzhou University to teach—what else?—"Mao Zedong Thought."

Earlier, I quoted from a 2008 interview with Xinyu. One of the questions was this: "You were born into an 'emperor's family,' and your life has always been the focus of public attention. Is there anything that makes you feel bad about it? Given the choice, would you like to live this kind of life again?" This was essentially the question addressed by the other grandson, Wang Xiaozhi, in 1993. Xinyu replied, "As a descendant of the leader, I do have a lot of stress. I feel that people are always watching my behavior. So I must do good. . . . If I could choose, I would be born into such a family again. I feel very privileged."

He was also asked about the benefits of being a "Red Descendant." Specifically, "Do the incumbent leaders of the country give you any special attention or favors?" With notable candor, Xinyu answered,

"Yes, they do." He cited his election to the CPPCC National Committee, "authorized by General Secretary Hu Jintao himself." Later in the interview, he was informed that some of Chiang Kai-shek's descendants had gone into business. What did Mao's grandson think of that? "Our family has been keeping our good tradition by studying Chairman Mao's theories, which are more important." Xinyu has always expressed disdain for the world of money and business.

His cousin Kong Dongmei struck it rich. The daughter of Li Min, she appeared in 2013 on a list of the wealthiest people in China. The money came through her husband, Chen Dongsheng, the owner of an insurance company and other businesses. Dongmei's financial status caused some consternation in China—as did a report that she and her husband had had three children. A typical remark was quoted in the London *Daily Telegraph*: "The offspring of Chairman Mao, who led us to eradicate private ownership, married a capitalist and violated the family-planning policy."

Kong Dongmei was born in 1972, meaning that she was four when Mao died. In 2010, she told an interviewer from *China Daily*, "Grandfather chose the name Dongmei—*dong* from his own name, and *mei* from his favorite flower, the plum blossom." She never met her grandfather, though. Or rather, he never troubled to meet her. At the Beijing University of Aeronautics and Astronautics, she studied neither of those things, but English literature. She went on to earn a master's degree in America: at the University of Pennsylvania. When she came home, she established a bookstore in Beijing, dedicated to promoting a "new Red culture." In 2010, *China Daily* found her surrounded by portraits and quotations of Mao, as well as posters of Lenin, Gandhi, and Che Guevara. (This décor was not so different from that of a typical American dorm room, once upon a time.) Like Mao Xinyu, she has written several books hailing her grandfather, and putting him in a soft familial glow.

You might say, and I might say, that every person is entitled to his own view of his grandfather or father—also of his family at large. People are even entitled to their own myths. But the Mao family has resoundingly chosen to "live by lies." The family gathers to celebrate Mao on his birthday (December 26) and death day (September 9). They are not alone. What I mean is, they are joined by millions in love and reverence for

Mao. Once, General Mao Xinyu spoke of his life and the reflected glory he enjoys. "All the people take their love and respect for Mao Zedong," he said, "and transfer it onto my person."

7

KIM

Kim Il-sung had six children by two wives. The unofficial count is unknowable, but high—some people speak of "hundreds." Consider the following: Kim was the absolute dictator of North Korea, the "Great Leader." He was also called the "Sun of the Nation," the "Sun of Mankind," and the "Red Sun of the Oppressed People." He was the object of a cult of personality almost unimaginable in its extent. He was no less than the godhead of the nation. Picking up girls was a snap.

I joke, but this is gallows humor. North Korea is a "psychotic state," as Jeane Kirkpatrick said. (She was a renowned American political scientist and diplomat.) And, as she went on to say, a psychotic state is something very rare in history. North Korea is also the first Communist dynasty: Kim Il-sung passed absolute power, and a cult of personality, on to one of his sons. That son did the same.

The official doctrine of North Korea is *juche*, which is generally translated as "self-reliance." But North Korean "self-reliance" is different from the good old-fashioned virtue: It means that North Korea is sealed off from the rest of the world. Not for nothing is the country known as the "Hermit Kingdom." And, as I said in our foreword, it is hard to glean facts from a hermit kingdom—even elementary facts. For example, whom did the head of state marry and when? North Korea may well require more guesswork than any other place.

Still, this country has been studied for almost 70 years now, and we know some things. We have driblets from defectors and other informed parties. I will provide as accurate a sketch of the Kims as I can. We must bear in mind, however, that North Korea is a "black hole," as so many say.

Kim Il-sung married a woman named Kim Jong-suk. The first of their children was Kim Jong-il, born in 1941, probably. According to North Korean legend, or propaganda, he was born on Mount Paektu, the highest point on the Korean Peninsula. A double rainbow appeared at this momentous birth. In reality, Jong-il was born in the Soviet far east, where his father was leading a battalion. The boy had a Russian nickname, Yura.

His parents had another son, Man-il, called "Shura." Back in Korea, after the war, they had a third child, a daughter, Kyong-hui. In 1947, when he was just three, Shura died in an accident: He drowned in his parents' swimming pool or pond. (This is unclear.) Jong-il, or Yura, age five or six, was apparently present. Many say that he played some mischievous, terrible part in his brother's death. Shura has always been omitted from official biographical accounts. His death weighed on Jong-il's conscience, goes the theory.

In 1949, their mother died while giving birth (to a stillborn girl). Again, there is gossip or speculation: Was her death actually a violent one? Did her husband do her in, as he did in so many? Probably not. In any event, Kim Jong-il, the future dictator of North Korea, had seen a lot by the time he was ten.

Kim Il-sung and his fellow Communists declared their new state in 1948. They called it the "Democratic People's Republic of Korea." Thus are lies embedded in the very name. During the Korean War, Kim's two surviving children were evacuated to China. At some point, the dictator married a clerical worker, Kim Song-ae. He had taken up with her before his wife Jong-suk died. He and Song-ae had three children together: two boys and a girl.

Of Kim's many illegitimate children, we seem to know about one: a son named Hyon-nam. He was born sometime around 1972, when his father was about 60. His mother was a young nurse to the dictator.

Kim Jong-il

What is not known about Hyon-nam is what became of him: Was he taken under the wing of Jong-il and given power? Was he executed by Jong-il? Both?

Jong-il may have trained as a pilot in East Germany. He seems certain to have studied English in Malta. In his home capital, Pyongyang, he studied at Kim Il-sung University. Early in his rise through the political ranks, he said that *juche* ought to be renamed "Kimilsungism" (the North Korean equivalent of Mao Zedong Thought). "To Kimilsungize the whole society," he said, "is to train all its members into Kimilsungists infinitely loyal to the president, transform it thoroughly in a way required by Kimilsungism, and capture the ideological and material fortresses of Communism."

He was the eldest son, but his succession to the throne was not automatic. He had to maneuver for it. He was good at it, cunning. His main rivals probably came from his own family. One of them was a half-brother, Pyong-il. He looked much like his father, which was an advantage. But he was maybe too openly ambitious, and his father removed him from the scene by sending him abroad as a diplomat. Year by year, he promoted Jong-il. And in 1980, Jong-il was anointed the successor.

Michael Breen and other Korea experts make an important point: Kim Il-sung did not necessarily dream of dynasty. But he had seen the cult of Stalin fall in the Soviet Union, and he did not want to see the same happen to his cult. A son for a successor seemed a smart bet.

The son's primary interests, apart from dictatorial control, appear to have been three: movies, women, and basketball. He was obsessed with movies, a collector and connoisseur. He might have enjoyed talking to Vittorio Mussolini. Jong-il went so far as to kidnap two South Koreans, a director and an actress, in order to further North Korean filmmaking. As for women, he was served by what were called "pleasure teams." In fact, these teams had been set up by his father—no amateur as a pleasure-seeker. From basketball, Jong-il took immense pleasure. He followed the NBA in America fanatically. Michael Jordan, the best, was his favorite player.

In 2000, the U.S. secretary of state, Madeleine Albright, made a visit to North Korea. She bore a gift for Kim Jong-il: a basketball signed by Jordan. It wound up in North Korea's International Friendship Exhibition Hall, along with other gifts: a crocodile briefcase from Cuba's Fidel Castro, for example. Or a gem-encrusted sword from the Palestinian leader, Yasser Arafat. Or a bear's head from the Romanian dictator, Nicolae Ceauşescu.

But I have moved too far ahead in this story. In 1994, the "Great Leader," the founder of North Korea, Kim Il-sung, died. So the "Dear Leader," Jong-il, took over. Kim Il-sung became "Eternal President of the Republic." Jong-il was also known as "Unique Leader," "Our Father," and "Morning Star of Paektu."

How many children did he have? Counts vary, but quite possibly six, by four women. A daughter named Hye-kyong seems to have been born in 1968. Her mother was Hong Il-chon, a former classmate of Jong-il. He then took up with an actress, Song Hye-rim, who was married to someone else and had a child. With Jong-il, she had a son, Jong-nam, born in 1971. Jong-il kept his relationship with Hye-rim, and the existence of their son, absolutely secret. He ordered her friends sent to a concentration camp. No one with knowledge of the situation could be in a position to blab. Almost none of them survived the camp.

Hye-rim died in 2002, an exile in Russia, and mentally ill. She is buried in Troyekurovskoye Cemetery, quite close to Vasily Stalin.

Around 1973, Kim Il-sung decided that his son Jong-il should marry. He selected the bride for him: Kim Yong-suk, the daughter of a high-ranking military official. They had at least one child, a daughter named Sol-song. The name means "snow pine." As Mao bestowed a name on a granddaughter—Dongmei, or "plum blossom"—Kim Il-sung gave Sol-song this name.

In fairly short order, his son Jong-il, the future dictator, roamed to another woman. She was Ko Yong-hui, a dancer. In the 1980s, they had three children together: two sons, Jong-chul and Jong-un, and a daughter, Yo-jong. Of all his consorts, Jong-il liked Yong-hui best. But she died in 2004, and he had one more consort, Kim Ok, his personal secretary. It is thought they had no children.

To repeat, Kim Jong-il became dictator in 1994. And in the 2000s, he faced a question—a question his father had faced: Who would succeed him? By all accounts, he was very fond of his daughter Sol-song, who worked alongside him. She was capable and beautiful. But surely the successor would be a son.

The eldest was Jong-nam, the son who was once secret. He was probably the frontrunner for a while. But he fell from favor. Why? Many people point to an incident in 2001: Jong-nam attempted to enter Japan on a false passport (from the Dominican Republic). With a few family members, he intended to visit the Disneyland outside Tokyo. He had apparently visited Tokyo several times before, having a particular liking for "gentlemen's clubs." The passport incident made news everywhere, causing a sensation. Jong-nam's father was livid. Was this the reason he was passed over? Almost certainly not, but it could not have helped.

Bradley K. Martin, among other Korea experts, says that Kim Jong-il must have found Jong-nam unsuited in some fashion. Perhaps the young man was reform-minded (which his father was not). Perhaps he lacked the dictatorial appetite.

Next in line, where sons were concerned, was Jong-chul. This one was most unsuited, apparently. They say his father found him too feminine, too soft. Some contend that Jong-chul suffers from a hormonal imbalance. One fact that seems firm is that he likes Eric Clapton, the English rocker. Jong-chul has been spotted at more than one Clapton concert.

Kim Jong-il settled on his youngest son, Jong-un. As Jong-il himself had been a chip off the old block, so was Jong-un. There was no softness in *him*; he had the appetite indeed. In 2009, Jong-un was put forward as the "Great Successor." He was also dubbed "Brilliant Comrade." In 2010, he was made a general, with four stars. He was promoted at least as far and as fast as Vasily Stalin and Mao Xinyu.

It seems clear that Jong-un went to school in Switzerland. He then studied at two of the (many) institutions in North Korea named after his grandfather: the war college and the university. His greatest extra-curricular interest, so to speak, seems to have been basketball. In this, too, he was like his father.

While a student in Switzerland, he was chaperoned by an aunt, his mother's sister Ko Yong-suk. From the dictatorship's point of view, it was she who turned out to need the chaperoning. Yong-suk and her husband sought political asylum in the United States. Apparently, they worried that they knew too much about the Kim family and would pay for it (with their lives). According to reports, they have had plastic surgery to alter their appearance and are living under protection in America.

Kim Jong-il, the second of the North Korean dictators, died in 2011, age about 70. As planned, Jong-un took over. He was probably 28 at the time. Some speculated that an uncle and an aunt would serve as co-regents of a kind. The uncle was Jang Song-taek, who had occupied a very powerful position under Jong-il; his wife was Kim Kyong-hui, Jong-il's sister (and a four-star general herself). They had a daughter, but she was dead: a suicide in Paris.

In December 2013, Kim Jong-un left no doubt about who was in charge: He had his uncle arrested and executed. He then killed all the Jang relatives he could get his hands on, no matter how old they were or where they lived. Yes, a chip off the old block, or blocks: None of the three Kim dictators has hesitated to employ murder. It is vital to the ongoing project.

One interesting member of the family is Jong-nam, Kim Jong-il's first son: the one whose visit to Disneyland was aborted. He has been living abroad, in Macau, Singapore, and elsewhere. He speaks out from

Kim Jong-un

time to time. By his own testimony, he has never met the current dictator, Kim Jong-un, his very brother, or half-brother. Such is the bizarre
world of North Korean politics. He has argued for reform, saying, for
example, that the Kim dynasty should be abolished. That would make
him a major family dissenter. But this could be a matter of sour grapes
rather than conscience or conviction: He was passed over for the leadership, after all. In recent years, he has dodged assassination by Jong-un.

His son Han-sol is interesting, too. He was born in 1995, and has
had most of his life outside of North Korea. Via the social media, he has
expressed concern over the widespread famine in his home country. "I
know my people are hungry."

In 2012, when he was a student at the United World College in
Mostar, Bosnia and Herzegovina, he was interviewed by Elisabeth
Rehn, a Finnish politician who was a founder of the college. This interview was filmed for television. Han-sol proved a winsome young man,
speaking American English, complete with slang. He wore two earrings
in his left ear. He told his interviewer that he had spent his first years

in North Korea, kept largely isolated from society. He never met his grandfather, Kim Jong-il. He is not sure his grandfather ever knew of his existence. His mother was not a North Korean "royal," just an ordinary citizen. Visiting her family, he could glimpse the lives of ordinary North Koreans. He said, in the interview, that he dreamed of a united Korean Peninsula.

Han-sol was a student in France when Kim Jong-un executed Jang Song-taek, and then "liquidated" the man's extended family. Han-sol was put under police protection. He is a Kim, not a Jang, but he has been a loose cannon, a virtual Westerner, an offender against *juche*.

The dictator, Kim Jong-un, has a wife, Ri Sol-ju. And they have a daughter, Kim Ju-ae. We know this girl's name because Dennis Rodman, a former basketball star, reported it. Rodman has formed a bond with Jong-un, giving the young ruler a link to the basketball world. Whether Jong-un will be the last dictator from his family, no one can know. It seems unlikely the dynasty can continue. Then again, it seemed unlikely that it could endure, strangling North Korea, for as long as it has.

8

HOXHA

Hoxha had three children. He had them with his wife, Nexhmije—a fellow Communist and "co-fighter," to use Jiang Qing's word. Enver Hoxha ruled Albania from 1944 until his death in 1985. His Communism was practically on the North Korean level: total, crushing, absolute. Life in Poland or Hungary was easy by comparison. Hoxha's Albania was very much a hermit kingdom: No one entered the country, and no one left it.

We should pause for a matter of pronunciation: "Hoxha" is pronounced approximately "HO-djah." Also, "Nexhmije" is pronounced approximately "Nedge-MEE-yeh."

Hoxha idolized Stalin, whom he imitated. Like Stalin—and like the Kims and many others—he imprisoned, tortured, and killed his political opponents. Nothing was left to chance, no crease was allowed. Religion in Albania was banned. One of Hoxha's titles, bestowed by the Party, was "Sole Force."

In the early 1960s, he broke relations with the Soviet Union, deeming the Kremlin under Khrushchev too liberal. He broke relations with China after the death of Mao, on the same grounds. Albania had its own style of *juche*—its own expression of insane isolation. Hoxha spent precious government funds on concrete bunkers. There were 750,000 of these, in a nation of 3 million. The bunkers were supposed to defend against invaders whom Hoxha was always warning about. Private ownership of cars was banned. In the last years of Albanian Communism, there was famine.

Enver and Nexhmije Hoxha were a match made in heaven, or somewhere. Nexhmije liked her luxury, and she was one of the few people in Albania who could have it. But, ideologically, she was very serious. She headed Albania's Institute of Marxist-Leninist Studies.

The Hoxhas had two sons and a daughter, born in the late 1940s and early '50s. The sons are Ilir and Sokol. Those names are traditional. "Ilir" relates to ancient Albania, i.e., Illyria. "Sokol" means "falcon." The daughter's name is traditional, too: Pranvera, "spring." Those are attractive names, and the Hoxhas were an attractive family, physically.

With their father on top, the children prospered, of course. Sokol, for example, was the head of the Post, Telephone, and Telegram Department; his wife, Liljana, held a similar position. Pranvera is an architect. So is her husband, Klement Kolaneci. A team headed by Kolaneci, and including Pranvera, designed the Enver Hoxha shrine in the Albanian capital, Tirana. For a time, it displayed such relics as the great man's toothbrushes. After Communism, it fell into disrepair and disuse, a symbol of a personality cult and dictatorship.

The dictator died in 1985, age 76. Communism in Albania had about six more years to go. Hoxha was succeeded in power by Ramiz Alia—but Nexhmije, the widow, still loomed. She guarded against any reform, any softening. She was much feared throughout the country. Once—almost charmingly, I would say—she described herself as "a hard-line Communist."

In early 1991, a democratic revolution broke out, or, as Pranvera Hoxha is alleged to have put it, "animals woke up." Animals elsewhere in Central and Eastern Europe had been toppling statues. Now they toppled the Hoxha statue in Tirana's Skanderbeg Square. At the end of that year—in December 1991—Nexhmije was arrested.

She was not charged with any crimes committed during her husband's rule. She was charged with crimes committed from his death in 1985 to 1990: corruption. People such as Nexhmije Hoxha equate government funds and property with their own. She had a three-week trial, during which she maintained a posture of defiance. As she went to and from the courtroom, Albanians heckled her. They had been stifled for some 45 years. Nexhmije was sentenced to eleven years in prison.

From her cell, she sent a note: "My children: Do not be upset by my sentence. My only concern was not to discredit Enver, my husband and your father, and this was achieved. It was really we who won in court. I embrace you."

As it transpired, Nexhmije served just five years of the eleven-year sentence. Prison conditions for her were very unlike those for her husband's prisoners. She experienced some isolation and misery—but for the most part, she had regular visits from her family. She got news from the BBC. Later, she would complain that this had been her only news source. She seemed completely unaware of how fortunate she was, as a prisoner, by contrast with Hoxha's.

After the statue fell, and Communism with it, the Hoxha children lost their privileges. They had a difficult few years (relatively difficult). In 1993, Ilir and Sokol gave interviews to the Associated Press. They were in their early forties at the time. The AP report began, "Society's rejection of their father, Albania's long-time Stalinist dictator, has left the two sons of Enver Hoxha jobless and bitter, but unrepentant." They were subsisting on welfare, or so they said. Ilir was still driving a Mercedes. Asked to comment on the mass killings, torture, and imprisonment during the Hoxha era, he had just one thing to say: "There was no infringement of laws." That may well have been true, to the extent Hoxha made the laws. Ilir disclaimed knowledge of the infamous prison camps. And he said, "The worst evils of the capitalist society are coming to Albania: unemployment, prostitution, corruption, high prices, and inflation." There, he had a point.

The younger brother, Sokol, took a slightly softer line. He acknowledged that the Hoxhas had lived in high style while the rest of the country suffered, but noted that "even in the West" there were differences between rulers and ruled. He also admitted that his father had made a mistake—in forbidding foreign investment in Albania. Ilir, however, would not acknowledge any mistakes at all.

In April 1995, Ilir was placed under house arrest. His crime? He had given an interview to a newspaper, *Modeste*, in which he said that his father's statue had been toppled by a fascist mob. "It was not the

Ilir Hoxha

people who toppled the monument of my father, but the mob. The people were the ones who went out into the streets to protect him." This was fantasy, of course. Ilir also said that the current government was "a pack of vandals and dark forces." He had a warning: "The day will come when those who betrayed my father have to answer for their actions."

The government charged Ilir with inciting hatred and encouraging violence. In response, he said that his arrest was nothing more than "political revenge." He observed, "No one has the right to accuse me simply because I defend my father, in a country that pretends to be democratic." That was not a fantasy; that was a point beyond argument.

Ilir appealed to Amnesty International and other such organizations. It seemed not to occur to him, or bother him, that people in his father's time never had any such recourse. At his trial, he emphasized, "It is my duty to defend my father." He also called for "tolerance rather than vengeance." Ilir was found guilty and sentenced to a year in prison (starting from the time of his house arrest). He appealed twice, losing out at each level.

How did his time in prison go? He would tell us, in a memoir: "I found life in prison very boring and frustrating, and was impatient to have a visit from Teuta and learn how the children were bearing up." (Teuta is his wife, about whom, more later.) "Two days after my arrival," writes Ilir, "a warder came and told me to prepare for the meeting," i.e., the first visit from Teuta. "He warned me that I would have to wear handcuffs, because the regulations required this. But he did not lock them properly and they fell to the ground. He winked at me. We understood each other."

Again, it did not go this way in Enver Hoxha's time. His prisons were places of scarcely imaginable terror.

What was the reaction of fellow inmates to Hoxha's eldest child? "When it became known who I was, despite their varied political views, they treated me with kindness and friendliness, saying, 'Everyone has the right to stand up for his father!'"

In April 1996, a year after his house arrest, Ilir was released. In the meantime, he had written the above-quoted memoir. It is called "My Father, Enver Hoxha." Ilir explains that he wanted to write "a defense of a greatly loved human being."

According to the author, Hoxha was "a model parent who loved us, reprimanded us, advised us, and taught us social morality. He was the same as a grandfather to our children, his grandsons and grand-daughters." Furthermore, he was "a leader who worked all his life for Albania and its people." Ilir hails this leader for an array of achievements, including "the placing of agriculture on a scientific basis," "the development of art," and "the emancipation of women." Also on his list is "the honored place which Albania gained in the world." That is maybe the most fantastic claim of all.

For Ilir, Hoxha was "a true democrat." People may call Hoxha a dictator, but "he was no such thing." People may call the author himself the son of a dictator, but this makes "not the slightest impression on me."

In the course of his memoir, Ilir describes "the most painful event in my life": namely, the exhumation of his father's body at one cemetery and its removal to another. Initially, the body was buried in the Cemetery of the Martyrs of the Nation; but then it was removed to a humbler abode, the People's Cemetery. Throughout his memoir, and in his conversation at large, Ilir talks a lot about "the people." Communists are conditioned to use this phrase. Ilir portrays his father as a great champion and friend of the people. Yet it is a gross insult, certainly to Ilir, for Hoxha to be stuck in the People's Cemetery.

In 1997, a few months after she was released from prison, Nexhmije was visited by an extremely sympathetic reporter from Toronto's *Globe and Mail*. He said, among other things, that "Mrs. Hoxha hardly deserves the nickname the Crow thrust on her by a society with little capacity for forgiveness." Before he left, Nexhmije said to him, "I ask that you pray for Albania"—a curious request from the first lady of a ruthlessly atheist state.

Eleven years later, in 2008, she and other die-hards celebrated the hundredth anniversary of Hoxha's birth. "Enver was a comrade and an ideal leader," she said. Like Ilir, she denied that Hoxha had been a dictator. "The existence of Albania was threatened by both exterior and interior enemies. He had to react." In another Hoxha-family line, she said, "I do not regret anything, and there is nothing I should feel guilty for. We only respected laws in force at the time." Then, there was this ringing declaration: "I continue to have confidence in the Communist ideal that will never die."

The widow herself is not dead either, as I write. In her mid-nineties, she lives with Ilir and Teuta. She still gives television interviews, hailing the Hoxha dictatorship as a golden age. She is widely despised by Albanians, many of whom remember her husband's rule. They might be forgiven for calling her "the Crow," or worse.

Her daughter-in-law Teuta, incidentally, is the niece of Ramiz Alia, the dictator who succeeded Hoxha. Nexhmije's other daughter-in-law, Liljana, the wife of Sokol, spilled some family beans in a 2012 interview. At a minimum, she related some gossip. Ilir had really been in love with Alia's daughter, she said. But the dictator blocked that marriage, choosing Teuta for Ilir instead.

Liljana is the "bad" daughter-in-law, a bit of a rebel, at fierce odds with Nexhmije. She blames her mother-in-law for the horrors of the last years of Hoxha's rule. She says that the dictator was incapacitated by illness, leaving Nexhmije in a position to call the shots. She further alleges that Nexhmije's people—her handpicked functionaries—are still lodged in the government. Liljana is quite outspoken about all this, fracturing the Hoxha-family unity.

Yet the Hoxha family is doing pretty well. Some of them are succeeding in business, benefiting from long-ago ties to China. The dictator's grandchildren have married advantageously. For instance, Sokol and Liljana's son married the daughter of a top businessman: the head of the Albanian Chamber of Commerce. The couple had a grand wedding at Villa No. 31, the old dictatorial residence. Thus do Communist elites and a new business class blend. The Hoxhas cut figures in Albanian society.

Ermal Hoxha, son of Ilir and Teuta, is a particular case. He married a popular Albanian singer, Rezarta Shkurta. A hot tamale. Evidently, he also found a very, very lucrative line of work: illegal drugs, and in particular cocaine. In January 2015, when he was 40, he was arrested, along with a dozen other people, including two Colombians. The bust took place in a village called Xibrake, near the city of Elbasan. The police seized 264 pounds of cocaine, worth about $33 million. In Ermal's car was $347,000 in cash. Another $38,000 was in his apartment.

Immediately, his parents, Ilir and Teuta, said that he was a victim—of people wanting to discredit the name "Hoxha." As of this moment, Ermal faces 20 years in prison.

During election seasons, the Hoxhas campaign for the "Enverists," who are a kind of Hoxha remnant. The Enverists do not command much support. Like other dictators' children, the Hoxhas bask in the approbation of elderly die-hards. They dismiss and blast critics of the dictatorship as fascist collaborators in World War II. Alternatively, these critics are Titoist agents—agents of Hoxha's Communist rival in Yugoslavia, Josip Broz Tito.

A great day for the family occurred in 2003. Ilir and Teuta got a grandson, Rei—born on October 16, the dictator's birthday. For the family—the truest Enverists of all—October 16 is a holy day.

9

CEAUŞESCU

Like Hoxha, Ceauşescu had three children. Also like his Albanian counterpart, he had them with his wife and "co-fighter"—Elena, who was even more powerful than Nexhmije. Indeed, Elena was not just a co-fighter but a virtual co-ruler with her husband. He had a massive personality cult; hers was not far behind. He was "The Genius of the Carpathians"; she was "The National Heroine." Together, they were "The Father and Mother of the Nation." Both their birthdays were national holidays.

The name of this dictatorial couple, by the way, is pronounced "Chow-SHESS-coo."

Nicolae Ceauşescu ruled Romania from 1965 until 1989—until Christmas Day of that year, when he and Elena were put to a wall and shot. His Communism was almost as thorough and suffocating as Hoxha's. His system of internal security was probably second to none: The Securitate, the secret police, spied on practically the entire citizenry. Ceauşescu was a great fan of Mao and Kim Il-sung. The latter's books on *juche*, he made sure to have translated into Romanian. He departed from Kim (and Hoxha) in one respect, however: He liked to have relations with other countries, and to swan around the West.

He paid high-profile visits to Queen Elizabeth and President Jimmy Carter, among others.

Like the Hoxhas, the Ceauşescus had two sons and a daughter. They were born at the same time as the Hoxha kids, too: the late 1940s and early '50s. The older son was, and is, probably as normal as a person in his circumstances can be. The daughter (who was born in the middle) was a tragedy. The younger son was a little monster, prevented from becoming a bigger monster only by the death of his father's regime.

Ceauşescu wanted to be president for life, but that was a relatively modest goal: He also wanted to build the first Communist dynasty in history (though he was having competition from Kim Il-sung in North Korea). We have solid testimony on this, including from Ion Mihai Pacepa, a general in the Securitate and a top adviser to Ceauşescu. Pacepa defected to the United States in 1978, and wound up the highest-ranking intelligence official ever to have defected from the Soviet bloc. In the mid-1980s, he wrote his famous memoirs, *Red Horizons*.

In correspondence with me, he writes, "Ceauşescu envisioned his younger son, Nicu, as his hereditary heir to the future Communist Kingdom of Romania. His older son, Valentin, would be the brains of the government. His daughter, Zoia, would run foreign policy." None of it was to be.

Valentin decided at an early age that he wanted nothing to do with government or politics—with the dictatorship and his parents' world. He studied physics, and would make a career in that field. In 1970, he married a girl named Iordana, or Dana, but not just any Dana: Dana Borilă, the daughter of Petre Borilă, an old rival of Ceauşescu's within the Party. The Ceauşescus hated the Borilăs, for several reasons. One was, Dana's mother was Jewish. After he married Dana, Valentin had virtually no relationship with his parents. He and Dana had a child, Daniel. Eventually, Ceauşescu exiled his daughter-in-law and grandson. Later, Valentin married someone else.

Yes, he wanted nothing to do with the dictatorship, but he did indulge in one or two perks. Very rare would be the dictator's child who denied himself all perks. Valentin acquired an impressive art collection, including Goyas. Also, he assumed an administrative role with a Bucharest soccer team, Steaua. That is a typical perk of a dictator's son:

involvement with a soccer or other sports team. But Valentin was not like Vasily Stalin (or Uday Hussein, as we will see). He did not rule or terrorize his team. On the contrary, he was modest.

In a 2011 interview with the *Guardian*, a star player, Miodrag Belodedici, remembered Valentin and his role: "He was an example to the players. He was very polite and spoke pleasantly to everybody. He wasn't involved in the tactics or teaching the players how to play or telling us we played good or bad." Moreover, there was this benefit: "When Valentin was in the stands, we felt sure that the referee wouldn't cheat Steaua, especially when we played against Dinamo"—another Bucharest team, and Steaua's big rival. Dinamo "had a bad reputation in the country because they were involved with the Securitate."

You will occasionally see, in articles about Valentin, that he was adopted. That he was not Ceauşescu and Elena's natural son. General Pacepa writes to me, "To the best of my knowledge, it's not true. But with the Ceauşescus, one never knew what was truth and what was lie. What I know for a fact is that after Valentin married the daughter of Borilă, the Securitate was ordered to spread the rumor that Valentin was not Ceauşescu's natural son."

Pacepa knew the Ceauşescus' daughter, Zoia, quite well. Like her older brother, she wanted nothing to do with politics or dictatorship. A woman of considerable intellectual gifts, she became a mathematician— a real mathematician, providing a contrast with her mother, who claimed to be a chemist, and a great one, but was a fraud. Elena liked to have scientific organizations around the world honor her. It was a strange conceit of hers. She was no chemist, but Zoia, again, was a real mathematician, and Valentin is a real physicist.

Zoia earned a Ph.D. in math, then worked at the Institute of Mathematics in the Romanian Academy. This made Elena furious. Envy? In any event, she simply had the institute dissolved. "That unleashed a quiet war between Zoia and Elena, which lasted to the end of Elena's life," says Pacepa. Zoia then moved to the Institute for Scientific and Technical Creativity (INCREST), whereupon Elena booted her from the presidential palace and into an apartment. "To get revenge on her mother," writes Pacepa, "Zoia started a new department of mathematics at INCREST, and she became its head. She also became a heavy smoker to further antagonize Elena, who never smoked."

Aside from being an intellectual, Zoia was—how to put this?—a party girl. She drank like a fish ("Vodka, in industrial quantities," Pacepa specifies). And she did not lack for male company. After the fall of Communism, newspapers in Romania described her as a "nympho-maniac" and "sex-crazed." Those labels may have been sensationalistic, but they were not far from the mark, if off the mark at all. Picture a hedonistic, pretty, and brainy Zoia, darting around in her convertible white Mercedes, an auto that was "the dream of all Bucharest," says Pacepa.

The Ceaușescus made it difficult for Zoia to marry, even as they made her life in general difficult. This was especially true of Elena. In her eyes, no one was good enough for her daughter. (At the same time, Elena was interested in cutting Zoia down, as we have seen.) Communist though she was, Elena was a terrible class snob. Through the Securitate, she spied on her daughter incessantly. If she disapproved of a boyfriend or suitor of Zoia's, she put an end to the relationship, without delay. Ultimately, Zoia married an engineer and professor named Mircea Oprean.

As Pacepa tells us in *Red Horizons*, Zoia experienced a kind of crisis when she was a student—for she met other students and saw how they lived. She discovered how bad and scarce their food was, for example. The Ceaușescus lived in opulent style, with Elena leading the way (dia-monds, minks, etc.). Zoia had a boyfriend who went to the hospital for an appendectomy—and the dictator's daughter saw for the first time a hospital for ordinary people. Patients had to share beds.

In due course, she got interested in a group of dissident students. "When the Securitate started arresting them," writes Pacepa, "she herself became an outspoken critic of her father's personality cult and of her mother's machinations for power. In the end, she refused to bear her father's name and would answer only to *Mademoiselle*. 'The name Ceaușescu has become a dirty word,' Zoia repeatedly told all her friends."

So, the first two Ceaușescu children, Valentin and Zoia, were big disappointments to their parents. They would not be taking part in a dynasty (though they would prove loyal at a later stage in life, as we will soon find out). All hopes rested on the youngest child, the younger son, Nicu.

Nicu Ceaușescu

He was very different from his siblings. For one thing, he had a great thirst for power. For another, he was no student. He was bright, but he disliked school. Says Pacepa, "It was much more fun to spend his time with the bodyguards and security officers swarming around the presidential residences and to imitate their manners and vocabulary." This should remind us of someone: Vasily, who was raised in essentially this fashion. And Nicu was like Vasily—and Uday and others we will meet—in character: utterly depraved.

I could fill pages with appalling details, but a few lines will suffice. From his mid-teens, Nicu was an out-of-control drunk and a rapist. He raped at will, and his will was ferocious and unopposable. He had complete license. He was the kind who could run red lights and kill people in the process—with total impunity. He was a picture of almost comic-book evil. So were his parents, and they were quite a trio. They were a dictatorial family out of a comic book (although, I hasten to say, they were no laughing matter for Romania).

To begin his son's career, Ceaușescu made him head of the Party's youth league. In this capacity, Nicu traveled to North Korea in 1977.

Chinese state media said that Kim Il-sung "had a conversation with him in a cordial and friendly atmosphere." Nicu went on to Beijing, where again the atmosphere was "cordial and friendly."

The United Nations decided that 1985 would be International Youth Year—and none other than Nicu Ceaușescu would preside over it. At the end of that year, the U.N. gave him a medal, in honor of his leadership. Accepting the bauble, Nicu called for nuclear disarmament and, in the words of one news report, "a more equitable world."

At about this time, other news reports said that the health of Nicu's father was failing, meaning that a succession would have to take place. Would the new boss be Nicu? Or Elena? Would Elena rule for a while, giving place to the prince in the fullness of time? In any case, Romania was "set to be next for a Communist dynasty," as one headline had it. (Next after North Korea, where Kim had his son Jong-il waiting in the wings.)

And yet the old man hung on, until the revolutionaries determined otherwise. If he had been able to die in bed and bequeath his dictatorial rule, he would have designated Elena, according to General Pacepa. Nicu had proven too drunk and unstable to rule. Maybe he could have served as foreign minister under Elena, maturing to the point of readiness for the No. 1 slot.

Nicu was not the marrying type, as you may have gathered: He preferred to rape his way through Romania. But Ceaușescu insisted he get married. He demanded that all the top Party personnel be married, his son included. Elena chose the bride for him. The lucky gal was Poliana Cristescu. Many years later, Dumitru Burlan, another former Securitate officer, was interviewed for a BBC documentary. He recalled the big day: "After the ceremony, having signed the marriage certificate, Nicu said to Poliana, 'Now go live with my mother. She should f*** you because she chose you.'" Nicu and Poliana soon divorced. Ceaușescu did not prohibit this rupture, for reasons he himself would have to explain to us.

In 1987, he promoted Nicu, to boss of the Sibiu region. By the end of the decade, democratic revolutions were breaking out in Central and Eastern Europe, with the Berlin Wall falling on November 9, 1989. Later that month, Romania held a Party conference. The Communists went through the formality of affirming Ceaușescu's position. Nicu said, "The genius of the nation should be reelected." He told his comrades that his father had marked out "the bright path that leads to a magnificent future."

Other Communist states might be tumbling, but Ceauşescu was determined that his would hold firm. In these turbulent weeks, he said there would be no change until "the beech tree bears apples, and the reeds bear flowers."

It happened in December, when Ceauşescu was toppled, arrested, tried, and executed. He and Elena were shot on Christmas Day. Ceauşescu went rather bravely, or at least cheekily, singing the Communist hymn, "The Internationale." Elena went more coarsely, cursing her executioners as "motherf***ers."

The three Ceauşescu children were in varying degrees of trouble. Valentin, the eldest, was arrested, and he watched his parents' trial and execution on television, from a military compound. He later told an interviewer, "I tried to understand, to accept the necessity of the end. But when I saw the way it happened, I was shocked, and not for them. They were dead anyway. But for Romania, for the image." In another interview, he said, "I just watched it, and I felt ashamed I was Romanian. I didn't feel they were my parents."

Zoia, too, was arrested (along with her husband). She was no longer the quasi-dissident student. On Romanian television, she was a most unsympathetic figure, an Elena Jr., whose home was stuffed with luxury: jewels, art, and so on. There was also $100,000 in cash. As she was taken away, Zoia said to the policemen, "Do you have room in the police truck for my poodles?" This disgusted a nation that had long suffered in extreme privation.

Nicu—the child who was complicit—tried to escape. A man named Ivan Maru apprehended him at a checkpoint. Maru told the press what happened: "A very elegant woman was driving the car. The scent of fine perfume poured out of the car when she pulled down the window. Her papers were in order, but we saw that a man was sitting behind her, his cap completely pulled down. We could barely see his face." They asked the woman who the man was. She said he was her lover. Maru reached in and pulled off his cap. "I saw it was Nicu. He got out of the car and pretended to search for his papers. Then suddenly he ran away. I ran after him and jumped on him. I twisted his arm behind his back. My buddies got there too and helped."

The disgraced and captured prince was made to appear on television. A subsequent Reuters report contained a striking sentence. When Nicu "appeared in ignominy before the people," the report said, "his beautifully blow-dried hair seemed a bizarre frame for his bloodied brow." The headline over the report was "Ruling clan held people in grip of fear." Another headline said, "Ceausescu children lived it up while people suffered." Another one said, "Nation vents its hate for family."

Valentin and Zoia—and Zoia's husband Mircea and Nicu's ex-wife Poliana—were jailed for "undermining the national economy," i.e., corruption. In January, news came that Zoia was having a hard time adjusting to life in prison. A UPI report quoted the general prosecutor, who said, "In the very first days, she made a lot of demands regarding her comfort. She just wanted to drink coffee and smoke." UPI addressed the particular matter of smoking: "When the imported Kent cigarettes Zoia brought to prison were gone, she was allowed to smoke only harsh domestic brands, which smell like burning industrial waste. So coveted are Kents that they are traded like currency in Romania." The prosecutor said that Zoia "was told that she is living in the same conditions the Romanian people used to live in."

She was released in August, after about eight months in prison, along with Mircea, Valentin, and Poliana.

Nicu was a different story: charged with deadly violence against anti-government protesters, and sentenced to 20 years. That was a relatively light sentence, given the crime. And Nicu wound up serving less than three years, released in 1992 on health grounds. He had cirrhosis of the liver, and would die of that disease in 1996, age 45. Again, we see the similarity to Vasily Stalin: jail after the death of the father-dictator; early release; heavy drink and an early grave.

Zoia spent some of her time suing. She wanted her stuff back: the jewelry, art, and other goods that had been confiscated from her in December 1989, when her parents were executed and the children sent to jail. In 1997, she got some satisfaction: the return of the jewelry and other items. She did not get the paintings, however—these were judged to be Romanian property, not personal Ceauşescu property.

There was also an exhumation issue (as there often seems to be, where dictators and their heirs are concerned). Nicolae and Elena Ceauşescu were buried in a Bucharest cemetery, Ghencea, though not adjacently: They were buried some distance apart from each other. Furthermore, the graves were marked with false names, because the authorities wanted to prevent the profanation of those graves by furious, revenge-seeking citizens. But people eventually learned about the graves—and Ceaușescu supporters honored them with crosses, which seemed un-Communist.

What Zoia wanted to know was whether the remains in those graves were indeed those of her parents. She sued to have the bodies exhumed and DNA-tested. In life, her parents had treated her terribly, but she was devoted to their memory. Zoia died in 2006, with some of her legal issues unresolved. She had suffered from lung cancer and colon cancer. She was 56 years old. A onetime boyfriend, Petre Roman, who became the first prime minister in post-Communist Romania, said, "It was not easy to be the daughter of a dictator and of a mother like Elena Ceaușescu. Children should not be blamed for their parents' deeds."

Valentin carried on the legal battles. He had his own paintings to get back, in addition to those of other family members. He won. He also won on the issue of exhumation: In 2010, the bodies were dug up and confirmed to be the Ceaușescus'. Valentin said he had never visited the graves before, because he was unsure that his parents were really buried there. Now he would visit. In an act that made news, he performed some wreath-laying on Christmas Day, the 21st anniversary of his parents' death.

When people talk about dictators' children, particularly their sons, they often cite Valentin as the poster child for normality: He seems a regular, decent guy. He works at the Institute of Atomic Physics in Măgurele, outside Bucharest, as he has for the whole of his adult life. He is said to be bookish and quiet, with a close circle of friends. He and Nicu are about as different as two brothers can be. Valentin had the same opportunities for monstrousness that Nicu had. The same license was available to him. You could say that he was wired differently, or you could say that he made different choices. We are in murky and contentious realms.

Valentin's parents treated him terribly, as they did Zoia. Like Zoia, Valentin is loyal to them. Consider a legal episode (another one). In December 2009, the twentieth anniversary of the Ceaușescus' demise, a play opened in Bucharest: *The Last Hours of Ceaușescu*. Valentin and his

Valentin Ceauşescu

brother-in-law, Mircea, sued to get the play stopped—because, the year before, they had registered the name "Ceauşescu" as a personal trademark. After the play opened, Valentin said, "We just want to stop people from exploiting the name." His lawyer said that his client's motive was "to prevent his father's name from being ridiculed."

Over the years, the toppled dictator, Ceauşescu, had figured in Romanian advertisements. This was only natural. Free Romanians could hardly help themselves. One of the ads was for condoms. It showed Hitler, Stalin, and Ceauşescu, and suggested that the world would have been better off if their fathers had used condoms.

Valentin freely admitted that he did not expect to win the case against the theatrical producers—artistic expression and all that. And yet, incredibly, after a protracted battle, he won. A court ruled that the name "Ceauşescu" could not be used for any commercial purposes whatsoever, including a play. Valentin seems to have a golden touch in court. He is benefiting from a legal system that his parents would have been appalled by, or snorted at.

We can probably all agree that Valentin is a loyal son. Is he a good son? An admirable person? A less than admirable person, given that his loyalty lies with a dictator who immiserated, imprisoned, and killed a great many?

At the beginning of 1991, when he was just a few months out of jail, Valentin gave an interesting interview to the *Independent*. He said that his father had been a convinced Communist, "perhaps the only one in the government. I'm sure he believed. It was a faith to him." Valentin himself could not believe, he said. He further objected to a description of his father as "cruel." "My father was tough," he said, and "he could even be ruthless at some moments, but not cruel, not deliberately cruel." As for his own place in Communist Romania, Ceauşescu's Romania, Valentin said, "I do not feel any guilt."

As there are Enverists in Albania, there is a remnant in Romania: die-hard supporters of the dictator. There are also nostalgists, or fantasists, of various ages. In 2011, Valentin said, "People have started coming up to me and saying, 'Why aren't you running for president?'"

10

DUVALIER

Duvalier had four children—three girls in a row, then a boy. The son succeeded him as dictator of Haiti. Together, they ruled, and brutalized, that country for 29 years. *Père* ruled for 14; *fils* ruled for 15. The former was called "Papa Doc," the latter "Baby Doc." The first of these nicknames came from respect or fear or both; the second came from mockery, at least initially. The Duvaliers conducted an almost unrelieved reign of terror. Papa Doc killed something like 30,000 (in a country of maybe 4.5 million); Baby Doc killed not as many, but he contributed his thousands. Beyond the killings, there was the perpetual terror.

François Duvalier, the father, was elected president of Haiti in 1957, in an election less corrupt than subsequent ones would be. He was a medical doctor and a devotee of voodoo. He and his comrades stood for *noirisme*, or "blackism"—a kind of black nationalism, aimed at ending the power of Haiti's mulatto elite. (*Noirisme* did not stop *noiriste* politicians from preferring mulatto women.)

When he got into office, he denuded the army, neutralizing a threat to his power. He built up the "National Security Volunteer Militia," popularly known as the "Tonton Macoute." The name comes from Creole dialect and refers to a bogeyman in Haitian folklore. The Macoutes were Duvalier's personal goon squads—his Brownshirts, in short. They murdered and raped and plundered. Eventually, they outnumbered the army by at least 20 to 1.

Duvalier developed a cult of personality, considering himself semi-divine. He once spoke of "my theocracy." His special tool for control was torture—rape and torture. Much of this cruelty took place in Fort Dimanche. Those words, "Fort Dimanche," were terrifying to all Haitians. The fort was the Duvaliers' dungeon. Also, Duvalier kept a torture room in the presidential palace. He himself liked to watch, through peepholes.

In 1961, he ran for reelection, so to speak: He declared a referendum, asking for six more years as president. The vote turned out to be 1,320,748 to zero (in Duvalier's favor). Humbly, the president said, "I accept the people's will. As a revolutionary, I have no right to disregard the will of the people." Not waiting for the expiration of his "term," he declared another referendum in 1964, this one to make him president for life. He did less well this time around—winning by an even 2.8 million votes to 3,234.

Duvalier was devoted to his work—his rule, his power—but he did have a family life. His wife was Simone, whom he married in 1939. She was the daughter of a mulatto businessman and a maid in his household. The Duvaliers had three daughters, as you know: Marie-Denise, Nicole, and Simone (sharing a name with her mother). The baby, Jean-Claude, came along in 1951, six years before his father rose to power. Did Papa Doc love his children? It seems he did. Whatever tenderness or humanity was within him, he reserved for his children. Like other dictator fathers, and fathers in general, he had a special affection for his eldest daughter, Marie-Denise (sometimes called just "Denise").

The Duvalier kids were the most privileged kids in Haiti, of course. In the palace and outside it, they could have whatever they wanted. Yet there were dangers. In 1963, Jean-Claude and his sister Simone were the targets of an assassination attempt as they arrived at school. They were unharmed. Their chauffeur and bodyguards were killed. Papa Doc and his Macoutes killed a great many—a great many innocents—in the aftermath of this event.

Marie-Denise was a sexy young woman, accustomed to getting her way. She had a long parade of men. One day, she set her sights on a captain in her father's palace guard. At 6 foot 7, he was hard to miss. His name was Max Dominique, and he was married with children. But he junked his family to marry Marie-Denise. Duvalier objected to the marriage, but Marie-Denise got her way. Just possibly, no one else could have defied Duvalier. The dictator promoted his new son-in-law to colonel, and gave him an important command.

Another of his daughters, Nicole, also married. The groom was a mulatto named Luc Albert Foucard, the brother of Duvalier's private secretary. The secretary played other roles as well: She was Duvalier's voodoo medium and mistress. The dictator made Nicole's husband the minister of tourism.

A rivalry developed between the brothers-in-law, which split the Duvalier family. The Haitian upper crust was dizzy with palace intrigue. Duvalier began to suspect that Colonel Dominique was plotting against him. And this suspicion led to a dramatic, bloody chain of events. In describing them, I borrow from Elizabeth Abbott and her enthralling *Haiti: The Duvaliers and Their Legacy* (1988). This is an insider's account of that ghastly period.

In the spring of 1967, Duvalier arrested 19 young officers in the palace guard. These were Dominique's friends. They were all fierce Duvalierists—total loyalists—but that made no difference to the dictator: He was often in the grip of paranoia. The men were thrown into Fort Dimanche. Then Duvalier summoned Dominique and other senior officers to the palace. From there, he led a convoy to Fort Dimanche. What would happen? No one knew (except for Duvalier). Marie-Denise followed the convoy in her Thunderbird. When she reached the road leading to Fort Dimanche, a road that was heavily guarded, she stopped and sat waiting. "If she did not see her beloved husband return alive," writes Abbott, "she had vowed to blow her father to smithereens with the machine gun she had slipped under the front seat."

What Papa Doc did was have Dominique and the other senior men shoot the 19 arrested officers. Behind the senior men stood Macoutes, just in case any of the illustrious firing squad hesitated. Papa Doc yelled, "Fire!" and his officers obeyed, killing their 19 confreres. One of the dead, incidentally, was Major Harry Tassy, who had made the mistake of refusing to marry the Duvaliers' youngest daughter, Simone. She was in love with him. She aborted the child they had conceived.

Max Dominique was spared that day: He was executioner, not executed. But almost immediately afterward, Duvalier had a change of mind. He decided he could not live with Max alive. Marie-Denise and her mother swung into action: They begged for Max's life. And the dictator softened. He decided to send Dominique into exile. So Dominique left for Spain, with his wife and his sister-in-law Simone. "As their plane took off," writes Abbott, "Duvalier gave a signal, and Macoutes shot and killed Dominique's chauffeur and two bodyguards. Later his father was arrested and thrown into Fort Dimanche, where he died from ill treatment."

Papa Doc was sad and angry: sad to be without two of his daughters, angry that he had heeded calls for mercy and spared Dominique. He formally charged Dominique with treason and ordered him to return to face trial. Dominique refused. This did not sit well with the dictator—whose word was law. He was finding it harder to rule his own family than to rule Haiti at large. Duvalier lashed out at his wife, physically, and here Jean-Claude came into play: Sixteen years old, he pulled his father off his mother, and locked him into another room.

In exile, the Dominiques had a child, Alexandre, named after his paternal grandfather, who had been done in by his maternal grandfather, the dictator. That dictator was missing his daughters more and more—especially Marie-Denise, his eldest. He pardoned Dominique. And, at Christmas 1968, Marie-Denise came home. Dominique and sister Simone stayed abroad, for a prudent period.

Duvalier had long been in bad health, and now he was in rapid decline. He needed Marie-Denise, as a trusted arm. She set about reorganizing his office, and she lost no time in firing his secretary. She herself became his secretary. She sent the secretary's brother—her brother-in-law, Nicole's husband, Foucard—into exile. Nicole herself went into exile, too. She went to Miami, but not as Madame Foucard: Nicole was living openly as a lesbian, and had a partner.

Marie-Denise was almost a dictator-by-proxy. In March 1969, a report went out over the English-language wires: "For Decisions in Haiti, 'Clear It with Denise.'" The report explained, "When tough old 'Lifetime President' François Duvalier is asked these days for decisions on ruling Haiti, he says, 'See Denise—she's in charge now.'" The 28-year-old presidential daughter was "sexy and petite," said the report. And she was enjoying her new power to the hilt. "By day she struts around the Presidential Palace in dungarees, with two guns on her shapely hips." By night she "puts on one of her $3,000 Paris gowns and swings—often at El Rancho, Port-au-Prince's best hotel." Amusingly, the report said that Marie-Denise was faithful to her husband "in her fashion."

Would Marie-Denise Duvalier Dominique, a young woman, become dictator of Haiti? The wire report posed this question. Many in Haiti were posing the same question.

There were two leading candidates to succeed Duvalier, both of them presidential offspring: Marie-Denise and Jean-Claude (who was 17 at the time of the above-quoted report). Marie-Denise had many advantages: She was the eldest child; she was ambitious; she was energetic; and she was savvy. But she was also a woman—and that tipped it to Jean-Claude. The young man himself said that the successor ought to be Marie-Denise. Ruling a country was more her bag. But their father decided otherwise.

Papa Doc informed the people of his choice in an interesting way. "Caesar Augustus was 19 when he took Rome's destiny into his hands," he said, "and his reign remains the 'Century of Augustus.'" The Haitian constitution was Duvalier's plaything, and it said that a person had to be at least 40 years old to be president. Duvalier had that revised downward to 18. One of his principal toadies, Joseph Turgot, said, "Dr. François Duvalier is the greatest genius of our race. Every president for life has the right to choose his successor." Like a good democrat, Duvalier submitted his choice to a popular referendum: Did the people approve of Jean-Claude as the next president? Yes, they did, by 2,391,916 votes to zero. A classic Duvalier election.

From the Duvalier faithful, there went up a cry, a slogan: "After Duvalier, Duvalier!" And that's what they got. Papa Doc died in April 1971; Baby Doc, age 19, became president for life. He was the youngest national leader in the world.

It would be hard to imagine less suitable material for leadership. Jean-Claude was an object of sport. First, he was fat. Then, he had a funny walk. Also, there was the question of his mental ability. Everyone said, in so many words, that Baby Doc just wasn't very bright. In the days before Papa Doc's death, a news correspondent, Terry Johnson King, wrote a report that was typical in its tone. "I met Jean-Claude a

Duvalier *père*, Duvalier *fils*

number of times when, as a youth, he attended palace receptions." Jean-Claude was "a chubby child," a "perspiring lad in a white linen suit." He was "unblinking" during pre-reception rituals, but "always the first at the caviar when the Green Room doors were opened for the buffet."

Jean-Claude had virtually no intellectual interests. He had never liked school or applied himself. Everyone said he was lazy—unusually, thoroughly lazy. But he pursued pleasure with some vigor. He liked to go hunting, ride motorcycles, and have parties. Mainly, he liked girls, in great quantities. Incongruously, he played the viola. And he was president—president for life.

In the early years, there were regents: people who really ran the country. Chiefly, these were three: the president's sister Marie-Denise; his mother, Simone, who retained the title "First Lady," and was also called "Mama Doc," though not warmly; and Luckner Cambronne, an erstwhile lieutenant to Papa Doc. Cambronne had a couple of further distinctions: He was Mama Doc's lover, and he became infamous as the "Vampire of the Caribbean." That was because he made a fortune selling Haitian blood and cadavers to interested parties abroad. Cambronne once said, "A good Duvalierist is prepared to kill his children [for the dictator] and expects his children to kill their parents for him."

Jean-Claude's declaration of independence from the regents came in 1980, when he was 28. He married someone, and what a someone she was: Michèle Bennett. She was unsuitable and objectionable in every way. She could not have come more unsuitable or objectionable. Let me recount the ways.

Michèle was a mulatto, and therefore an affront to the Duvalierist ideology of *noirisme*. (Jean-Claude, by the way, was light-skinned. These things mattered, and matter, intensely in Haiti.) She was the daughter of Ernest Bennett, a very shady businessman. She was a divorcee. Her first husband was Alix Pasquet Jr., son of a famous fighter pilot and anti-Duvalierist—who was killed in 1958 when he participated in a coup against Papa Doc. Michèle had two children by Alix Jr.: The first was Alix III. She was mentally unstable, a woman who had tried to kill herself many times. And she was more than a "good-time girl," more than loose, more than normally promiscuous: She had simply slept with everyone.

But the dictator of Haiti was absolutely smitten with her. By all accounts, he was addicted to her sexually. His mother and the other senior Duvalierists were appalled, and did everything they could to stop the marriage. Mama Doc moved to have Michèle exiled, but Jean-Claude blocked his mother. He married Michèle on May 27, 1980. At a cost of $3 million, it was one of the most expensive weddings ever staged, and in one of the poorest countries on earth.

The ensuing power struggle between Mama Doc and Michèle Bennett Duvalier was epic. In a little less than a year, Michèle got the upper hand. She forced Mama Doc out of the palace, and wrested her title away from her. From now on, no one would be called "First Lady" but Michèle. The widow was demoted to "Guardian of the Duvalierist Revolution." In a further display of triumphant and vindictive power, Michèle had all of her mother-in-law's relatives exiled, nearly 100 of them. Simone Duvalier was lonely and defeated.

Michèle assumed great governmental, or dictatorial, powers—more than Jiang Qing or Nexhmije Hoxha, and probably more than Elena Ceauşescu. Only a short time before, she had been a reviled and cast-off "slut"; now she was a virtual co-dictator. She spent money—the national wealth—in staggering sums, buying up jewels and furs and the like (yes, furs, in the Caribbean). Her family, the Bennetts, prospered, including in the drug trade. Haiti's government was not only one of the cruelest but also one of the most corrupt in the world.

The young Duvaliers had two children: first, a son, Nicolas, born in January 1983. His full name is François Nicolas Jean-Claude Duvalier. Jean-Claude, the dictator, made it clear that Nicolas would be the next president for life. He and Michèle had a daughter, Anya, in December 1984 (though the girl's paternity was questioned—Michèle had begun taking lovers).

In 1985, Haitians began to revolt. By April 1986, the Duvaliers could hold on no longer. They were forced out—literally, out of the country. They went out in style, as they would have seen it. They had a final champagne party at midnight. Then, in the wee hours, they flew off on a U.S. cargo plane into exile in France. They had plenty of loot with them, on that roomy plane. And they had many millions stashed in banks abroad.

They lived high in a town called Mougins in the hills above Cannes. They also had a chateau outside Paris and two apartments in the city. Typical of their possessions was a Ferrari Testarossa. Investigators into the Duvaliers' finances found some amazing expenditures, including $9,752 for two children's horse saddles, bought at Hermès.

Early in their exile, the Duvaliers were interviewed by Barbara Walters, the famous newswoman from American television. "I think that whatever one may say," Jean-Claude told her, "I did the best that I could to try to improve the material conditions of my people, and I have absolutely no sense of guilt, no reproach whatsoever to myself." In a 1988 interview with *Paris Match*, he said, "I never saw myself as a dictator. I believe I was a well-loved president." He then made a statement that bordered on filial impiety: "It's crazy how Baby Doc has to pay for his father Papa Doc's reputation." Haitian authorities wanted Baby Doc extradited to stand trial for human-rights violations, but France refused.

The Duvaliers, who had been married in that $3 million wedding, grew apart. Michèle had lovers, he had lovers. (Some of his were procured by Michèle's own brothers.) In 1990, they divorced. Neither was a natural parent, but Michèle got custody of Nicolas and Anya. Jean-Claude Duvalier, who had been endlessly rich, went broke. He never tried to work, in his years of exile. The ex-dictator did not even dictate a book. When the money ran out, he lived off the kindness of sympathizers.

One person who sympathized was his girlfriend, Véronique Roy. They lived together. Véronique's grandfather was Paul Magloire, who was president of Haiti from 1950 to 1956. He was a military dictator.

During the Duvalier years, he was an exile in America. Only when the second Duvalier was forced out in 1986 did he return home. And now his granddaughter was paired with this second Duvalier.

Speaking of interesting pairings: Max Dominique was no longer married to Marie-Denise; he was living as the common-law husband of her sister Simone. Marie-Denise married someone else. Like her brother, she went broke, and she was then taken in by a couple in Miami: Luckner Cambronne, the Vampire of the Caribbean, and his wife.

September 2007 saw the 50th anniversary of François Duvalier's rise to power, and, in France, his son and successor made a major statement: "If, during my presidential mandate, the government caused any physical, moral, or economic wrongs to others, I solemnly take the historical responsibility." Hedged as this was, it was a rare apology in the annals of dictators. Duvalier said he had been "broken by 20 years of exile." Touching as this may have been, Baby Doc was angling for something: a return to power. He said that his father's old political party, the National Unity Party, was stirring. "The watchword is already launched, the instruction is given. Militants and militant sympathizers of the National Unity Party, be ready. We live in waiting for the revival."

In January 2010, Haiti suffered a catastrophe of a non-political kind: an earthquake, which killed more than 100,000 people. A year later, Jean-Claude went home—home to Haiti. He kissed the ground on his arrival and said, "I know the people are suffering. I wanted to show them my solidarity." He also said he was "determined to participate in the rebirth of Haiti." Forthwith, he was charged with corruption and other abuses. He would plead not guilty, and give a modicum of testimony. In this testimony, he was utterly defiant, denialist.

The legal proceedings were lackadaisical, and Jean-Claude was hardly bothered by them. He lived well in a villa overlooking Port-au-Prince. As in France, he lived off the kindness of sympathizers—also of people who were making an investment, just in case Baby Doc returned to power. He never did. Nor was he ever convicted or acquitted in court. He died in 2014, age 63.

His son, though, is in government—the Haitian government. As of this writing, Nicolas is an adviser to the president, Michel Martelly. There are some—this will not surprise the reader—who want him to run for president. Will Papa Doc and Baby Doc be succeeded by the man we might call "Grandbaby Doc"? "After Duvalier, Duvalier—and Duvalier"? The Duvaliers of Haiti seem unlikely to equal the record of the Kims in North Korea, but stranger things have happened. In any event, Haiti has known little but suffering, ruled by a Duvalier or not.

11

CASTRO

Castro has ten children—or fifteen or more. No one knows for sure, except for the dictator himself, probably. In 1993, Ann Louise Bardach, interviewing Castro for *Vanity Fair* magazine, asked him how many children he had. At first, he declined to answer. Then he said, "Almost a tribe"—which must be one of the few charming or true things he has ever said. His state media are forbidden to mention his family. People outside Cuba know more about his family than people inside. And even the most knowledgeable outsiders run into limits. In 2000, the *Miami Herald* published an article headed "Castro's Family." The subheading was, "Fidel's private life with his wife and sons is so secret that even the CIA is left to wonder." It's not entirely clear, by the way, that Castro has a wife.

Ten children are known about for sure. Or is it nine? Or eleven? In any case, two of the children—daughters—live in Miami. In other words, they are in the heart of the Cuban exile community. One of them is a full-blown and noted critic of her father's regime. She is a Svetlana Stalin, we might say. Castro has a sister in Miami—also a full-blown and noted critic—and one or two granddaughters. "People vote with their feet," goes an old saying. Some of Castro's family have done this, along with more than a million other Cubans. Many have died trying. Castro and his supporters call people who leave the island, or want to, *gusanos*—worms.

He has always had a great many supporters in free countries, Castro has. His Caribbean colleagues, the Duvaliers, should have been so lucky. In 2002, Carole King, the American singer-songwriter, crooned to him one of her hit songs: "You've Got a Friend." He does, yes, those great many. They see him as a champion of social justice and a fearless foe of *yanqui* imperialism. And if he has had to break a few eggs along the way in order to make an omelet out of Cuba, so be it.

Fidel Castro was born in 1926. From 1953 to 1959—when he was in his late twenties and early thirties—he led the Cuban revolution. The target was Fulgencio Batista, a military dictator. Castro triumphed on New Year's Day 1959—and quickly set up his Communist dictatorship, complete with gulag. Almost 50 years later, in 2008, he formally handed power to his younger brother, Raúl. At this writing, Castro lives on, in his late eighties, penning articles and receiving admirers.

In 1948, age 22, he got married. His bride was a beauty named Mirta Díaz-Balart, the sister of a friend of his, Rafael. The Díaz-Balarts were a prominent political family in Cuba. Later, they would achieve prominence in the United States. Two of Rafael's sons would serve in Congress. They were, and are, strong democrats, anti-Communists, and advocates of human rights. Castro liked to have some fun with visiting congressmen: "Say hello to my nephews, would you?" A year after their marriage, Castro and Mirta had a son, Fidel Jr., known as "Fidelito" ("Little Fidel"). Castro was not the husbandly or fatherly type, however. He had girlfriends, one-night stands, and mothers of other children.

There was a beauty named Natalia Revuelta Clews, called "Naty." Not just any beauty, she was a society beauty, like Mirta. Naty was married to Dr. Orlando Fernández, a cardiologist. And she fell in love with Castro and his cause. She sold her jewels to buy him weapons. She distributed pamphlets on the streets of Havana. (In Castro's Cuba, a totalitarian state, there would be no distribution of pamphlets—not opposition ones.) In 1956, she gave birth to a daughter, Castro's daughter: Alina. Naty derived the name from a salutation. Once, she sent a letter to Castro's mother, Lina. She began it, "A Lina"—"To Lina." And when her daughter came, she was "Alina."

Castro wanted verification of paternity. How could he get that? He sent his sister, Lidia, to check for birthmarks. She inspected the baby's left arm. "Well, at least she has the beauty-spots triangle." Then she inspected the backs of the baby's legs, from the knees down. "And here is the other birthmark. This baby girl is definitely a Castro." (Naty would tell Alina all this, and Alina would put it in a memoir, written in exile.)

Until she was ten, Alina would not know of her paternity. She was Alina Fernández—Dr. Fernández had "chivalrously" lent her his name. That was her word for it, later on: Fernández had acted "chivalrously," to protect this girl. He knew all about his wife's relationship with Castro. But he was apparently unwilling to see the child suffer for it, to the extent he had any say in the matter.

Fernández and Naty had had a daughter of their own, Natalie. When Castro came to power, things got sticky for the family, as for so many others. And one day, Fernández and Natalie were simply gone. They had fled the country. Little Alina was horrified. Beyond the shock of an absent sister and father, or father figure, there was this: The dictator of the country had said over and over, on radio and television, that anyone who left the country was a worm. A lowly, loathsome worm. Now Alina was convinced that her "doctor daddy" and Natalie would turn into worms, right on the plane that was bearing them away.

Sometime before Alina was born, and about four years before Castro seized power, Mirta and Castro were divorced. Mirta had custody of their son, Fidelito. And she was soon engaged to be married again. Her husband-to-be was Emilio Núñez Blanco, who, like Mirta, belonged to a prominent political family. His father, for example, was the Cuban ambassador to the United Nations. Castro hated the Núñez family, as a revolutionary would. And the thought of Fidelito in these arms burned him.

In the summer of 1956, Castro was exiled in Mexico, conducting the revolution from abroad. Mirta and Emilio were about to be married. And Castro made a request of his ex-wife: Could he have Fidelito for two weeks? Mirta agreed, but had a condition: Castro would have to give his word of honor that he would return Fidelito after two weeks. He gave it. He promised he would send Fidelito back via Lidia (Castro's sister, who had checked Alina for birthmarks). Off Fidelito went to Mexico. And, immediately, Castro began a new life for him. He placed Fidelito with a married couple who were supporters of the revolution: They would serve as foster parents. The boy even got a new name, though not the name of either of his foster parents, curiously. He was called "Juan Ramírez." Essentially, Castro kidnapped his son. He announced that he would not return him to his mother, surrounded as she was by enemies of the revolution. Almost three months later, Mirta and those enemies, with the help of the Mexican authorities, "rekidnapped" him. Fidelito was back home.

And where was home? Mirta and her husband lived in both Havana and New York. They had Fidelito go to school in New York. A report in the *Chicago Daily News* later said that Mirta had feared for Fidelito's life in Cuba. He was the son of the guerrilla leader, after all. And there were rumors that the son was the target of assassination by anti-revolutionary forces.

Fidelito was in the United States when his father's revolution triumphed on the first day of 1959. Mirta had him fly home to join his father, who would have custody of Fidelito forever. Why did she do this? She was probably unaware of what was coming. She also thought that Castro had certain rights over their son. Furthermore, we might ask a question that lies deep in psychological territory: Did Mirta ever truly break with Castro? Did she ever really fall out of love with him? Did she hang on to him, at some level, through all his many offenses, personal, national, and international? Some people think she did. It was not unknown for women to remain in love with Castro—Naty did. In any case, I will depart from the psychological and speculative to record a fact: In those first, heady days, Castro had Fidelito, age nine, at his side. They paraded together atop a Sherman tank.

Definitely not in love with Castro was his sister Juanita. She fully supported the revolution—but she revolted at what her brother made with power. Namely, a totalitarian dictatorship. She actually went to work for the CIA, as she revealed in memoirs published years later (2009). She helped dissidents, hounded by state security, escape capture, imprisonment, and execution. She later wrote that she felt no remorse about turning against her brother, and working against him. "I didn't betray him. He betrayed me. He betrayed the thousands of us who suffered and fought for the revolution that he had offered, one that was generous and just and would bring peace and democracy to

Cuba, and which, as he himself had promised, would be 'as Cuban as palm trees.'"

In the sixth year of the dictatorship, 1964, Juanita fled to the United States. She was about 30. She said she could not "remain indifferent to what is happening in my country. My brothers Fidel and Raúl have made it an enormous prison surrounded by water." In Miami, she would open a pharmacy (Mini Price).

But we should now return to Fidelito—and an episode in May 1959, just a few months into the dictatorship. The boy was in a terrible car accident, which necessitated an operation to remove his spleen. He was in danger of dying. His father was scheduled to go on television that night, to speak at length. He would give speeches, or long statements, in response to journalists' questions. Cuba was far more open in May 1959 than it would be. The noose was still tightening. Journalists could still question the leader, after a fashion.

Studio personnel wanted to cancel the program, but Castro said no. He explained that a doctor was going to operate on Fidelito later that night. The doctor would let him know when he was about to begin. At that point, he would leave the studio and go to the hospital. Meanwhile, the program would proceed. And, indeed, it began at its scheduled hour of 9.

There are various accounts of this unusual night, but I will quote Georgie Anne Geyer, who in her 1991 biography of Castro, *Guerrilla Prince*, writes,

> The first question from the panel of journalists came, and Castro talked for about half an hour; the second question came, and again a long answer. It was during this second question that Castro received a note that the doctor was waiting for him. Still he did nothing. At that point, the moderator, the famous writer Jorge Mañach, turned to Castro, on the air, telling him that they knew his son was badly hurt and publicly inviting him to leave the panel and go immediately to his son. Still, he hesitated.
>
> By now, the audience of forty to fifty was itself restive and even increasingly angry, for this was a country where "family" had always been the most hallowed of concepts. A woman in the audience finally yelled out to the *líder máximo*, "Comandante Castro, who is it who rules in Cuba?"

"The people," Castro shouted back, triumphally.

"Then," the woman persisted stubbornly, "the people want you to go and see your son."

At this, but only at this, Castro jumped up, threw back his chair theatrically with sudden determination, and left the TV station.

Fidelito survived. He had experienced more than his fair share of turbulence before he was ten, and he would experience more. Jorge Mañach, by the way, was soon in exile. He was forced out in 1960 after criticizing the regime.

As the dictator's only child—only publicly known child—Fidelito was a celebrity in Cuba. He evidently did not enjoy this status. An American news report said that his face would turn red when he was approached by autograph-seekers. At the Rex Cinema in downtown Havana, he would use a side door to avoid them. Eventually, Castro placed his son out of view altogether. It is not exactly clear why he did this. Sensitivity to the boy's feelings? Sensitivity has never been outstanding among Castro's qualities, as a father or a ruler.

When it came to education, Castro had very clear ideas about Fidelito: He would study nuclear physics, and he would go to the Soviet Union to do it. The USSR was Castro's great patron. Fidelito went to Lomonosov University in Moscow. He had an assumed name—another one. Some say it was José Raúl Fernández, some say it was Raúl Martínez. Maybe it was both, at different times. At any rate, he studied at Lomonosov, then went to work at the I. V. Kurchatov Institute of Atomic Energy, also in Moscow. He married a Russian woman, with whom he would have several children.

In 1980, when Fidelito was about 30, Castro gave him a job—a substantial job, and one for which he should have been well equipped: executive secretary of nuclear affairs at Cuba's Atomic Energy Commission. Fidelito had been out of the public eye for years, and now he was back in it. He looked much like the old man, with a bushy beard and all. He was huskier than his father, but otherwise the spitting image, almost. Some in Cuba say that Fidelito has always lived in awe of his father, and of course in the shadow of his father, and has consciously imitated him (to the extent he can).

He worked at the Atomic Energy Commission until 1992. Then, his father fired him. There was some break, some rift. Why? This is another mystery, often addressed, never to complete satisfaction. Castro accused his son of mismanagement and incompetence. It may have been true. Some analysts believe that Fidelito traded on his father's name too freely. That may have been true, too. After his fall from grace, Fidelito spent some years in the wilderness. Then, in 2000, his father rehabilitated him (we might say): giving him a position at the Cuban Academy of Sciences. Today, Fidelito lives very comfortably, and travels around the world as a scientific adviser to the regime.

Castro has other sons—a slew of others, including five by one woman. She is Dalia Soto del Valle, who met Castro in 1961 or thereabouts. She was yet another beauty, from a wealthy family, who fell for the "guerrilla prince" (who was king at this point). Over ten or fifteen years, they had their quintet of sons: Alexis, Alex, Alejandro, Antonio, and Ángel. How to account for all those A's? And all those Alexanders (or variations upon)? "Alejandro" (the Spanish form of "Alexander") is Castro's middle name. Also, he idolized Alexander the Great. Moreover, "Alejandro" was Castro's nom de guerre during the revolution. As for "Ángel," it was Castro's father's name.

It is widely said and written that Dalia and Castro are married. It's probably true. They are supposed to have married in 1980, after the death of Castro's longtime companion and aide-de-camp, Celia Sánchez. (Another way of describing Sánchez is "consort." That was the word frequently used in the English-language press. Castro and Sánchez had no children together.) The dictator himself, for what it's worth, has denied that he and Dalia are married. He did so in an interview with an admirer, Oliver Stone, the filmmaker, in 2003. Married or not, Castro and Dalia are something like a married couple, and she and those five sons constitute something like a regular family for Castro.

Most of the sons went to Lenin High School in Havana. At least one of them then studied in the Soviet Union, like Fidelito. They entered the computer and medical fields. The truth of the matter, however, seems to be this: They mainly make money in business—insider business, rigged business, the kind typically available to dictators' sons. Be that as it may,

Antonio Castro

Alex Castro does some honest work. He is a photographer, who snaps pictures of his father performing official functions. These have been published in media around the world.

The best-known of the sons, by far, is Antonio—an orthopedic surgeon. And one of those "businessmen." And a handsome playboy. He is photographed in swanky clubs, smoking rich cigars, in the company of beautiful young women—a Cuban James Bond. Less glamorously, he has served as physician to the Cuban national baseball team. He has had an unofficial position with the team as well: preventer of defections. Cuban baseball players, like Cuban ballet dancers and others, jump at the chance to defect. Antonio has a broader role to play in baseball, too: vice president of the International Baseball Federation.

One curiosity about Antonio's profile is that he is a golfer. If you believe some reports, he is no mere duffer but a champion golfer, a tournament-winner. There are famous and goofy pictures of a young Fidel Castro playing golf with his comrade Che Guevara. They are wearing military fatigues and combat boots. But Castro effectively banned golf in Communist Cuba, condemning it as a "bourgeois" pursuit. It could be that Castro has indulged Antonio in golf. Antonio is said to be the dictator's favorite son.

Adding to his profile, Antonio is acclaimed a champion fisherman. But reports of sporting prowess out of totalitarian countries ought to be taken with grains of salt. The North Korean dictatorship swore that Kim Jong-il had eleven holes-in-one in his very first round of golf. His score overall, said state media, was 38, for the 18 holes. This is something that Hogan, Nicklaus, and Woods never dreamed of.

In 2008 and 2009, Antonio was the target of a hoax, or a prank—a prank with a point. The prankster was Luis Domínguez, a Cuban-born democracy activist in Miami. Online, Domínguez pretended to be a beautiful young Colombian woman, smitten with Antonio. Domínguez called this fictional character "Claudia Valencia." Later, to the world at large, he explained the origin of his prank. Antonio accompanied the Cuban baseball team to a tournament in Cartagena, Colombia. He was like a rock star there. Fans asked to have pictures taken with him, and plenty of those fans were beautiful young women. That gave Domínguez the idea: He could get close to Antonio, and the closed world of the Castros, by posing as one of those women.

For eight months, "Claudia" chatted with Antonio, her "Tony," online. "Guess where I am?" said the young Castro in early 2009. The answer was Russia, where he was on an official visit with his uncle Raúl. "I will make love to you nonstop," he continued. And so on.

When the ruse was all over, Domínguez said that he had had various motivations. He wanted to penetrate that closed world of the Castros. He wanted to show that the Cuban security system was not foolproof. And he wanted to illustrate the great gulf between the way ordinary Cubans live and the way elites live. For instance, the regime makes it impossible for most Cubans to have access to the Internet. The likes of Antonio have ample access and every gadget. Fidel Castro has always preached "revolutionary morality," which involves great material sacrifice. Such morality is not for his sons.

All of the sons with Dalia Soto del Valle have names beginning with A, as you know, and I will tell you something vulgar but perhaps amusing: Certain Cuban-American democracy activists refer to the boys as "the five A-holes." But, for dictator's sons, they are pretty well behaved. They have privileges, of course—their own, non-revolutionary morality—but they are not lords of the island. By most accounts, they carry themselves fairly modestly, not making nuisances of themselves, not swaggering or strutting, and certainly not raping and pillaging, like a Vasily or a Nicu.

We might credit Castro with not glorifying or even promoting his sons, much. Generally speaking, he is not family-minded. He is cold to family and the world alike. His interest is himself, his favorite person. Raúl, by contrast, is family-minded. Even Fidel's kids have gone to him when they have had problems, not to their own father.

Among Castro's other children is a man named Jorge Ángel Castro. He was probably born in 1949, just before Fidelito, the official son. He may have been conceived on a train. A daughter, Francisca Pupo, was conceived in the backseat of a car. She was born in 1953. And for many years she has lived in Miami—like another Castro daughter, Alina Fernández. Francisca and her husband, quite simply, won a visa in a lottery run by the U.S. interests section in Havana. They arrived in Miami sometime around 1999. Francisca went to work at a daycare center. She does not care to speak about herself, Castro, or Cuba at all. But as her half-sister Alina has pointed out, she lives in Miami: Francisca voted with her feet, which says a great deal.

There are other Castro children, or alleged children, we could mention, including another Alejandro. Also a son named Abel, whose mother was Castro's translator. But let's turn to the life of Alina Fernández— who wrote a book, *Castro's Daughter: An Exile's Memoir of Cuba*. It is an honest and painful book, the kind that reviewers like to describe as "searing."

Alina, as you recall, is the daughter of Castro and a mistress, Naty Revuelta. As you may also recall, she was born in 1956, three years before the revolution's triumph. Shortly after that triumph, Castro dropped by Naty's home and gave Alina a doll. The doll had a beard, and a military cap, and stars on the shoulders, and combat boots. It was a guerrilla, a kind of mini-Fidel. Alina was a little skeptical of the real Fidel. She writes, "I did not want to give the man a kiss. His face was too hairy. I had never seen anything like it at such close range."

When Alina was ten, Naty told her that the hairy man, the dictator, was actually her father. "Mommy, Mommy, call him!" the girl said

Alina Fernández

excitedly. "Tell him to come here right away! I have so many things I want to tell him!" She certainly did. In her memoir, Alina writes, "I wanted him to find a solution to all the shortages: of clothes and things like that; of meat, so it could be distributed again through the ration books. I also wanted to ask him to give our Christmas back. And to come live with us." (Naty had suspended Christmas in her household, in solidarity with the revolution and the revolutionary regime. In 1969, Castro would in fact ban Christmas. He allowed its public observance again in 1998.)

Obviously, Castro did not live with Naty and Alina. Both mother and daughter sent him a great many letters, which he generally ignored. He visited now and then—sometimes years would pass. Once, Castro gave Alina a piece of advice: "Your mom has a problem. She is much too good. Don't be that good to any man."

It was not easy to be the dictator's daughter, at least not for Alina. People gave her letters to give to her father—letters detailing their woes. Their loved ones had been shot by Raúl or Guevara. Their loved ones were being beaten up in prison, owing to some horrible misunderstanding. They themselves had been dispossessed of their homes or businesses. They could not get visas to join their spouses in exile. Etc. Alina managed to give Castro some of these letters, but he put them politely aside, and her mother made her stop. Svetlana, too, had delivered letters to her father—who ordered her not to serve as a "post-office box."

Naturally, there was some prestige that went with being the dictator's daughter, but there were taunts, too: "Hey, listen, if it's true that Fidel's your father, why don't you tell him to distribute some food, eh?" Alina also had to endure insults to her mother, who had had that illicit relationship. And, like Svetlana, Alina sometimes felt guilt, albeit unreasonable guilt: over her father's expropriations, executions, and other crimes.

One day, Castro told Alina that she was welcome to have his name: She could be Alina Castro. She told him, "I think I'm going to keep the name Fernández. It's been my name for a long time, and I don't like having to explain things to people." Castro replied that he didn't mind one way or the other. Alina's real reason for turning down the offer was this: When people asked her to intervene with Castro or his dictatorship, she could say, "I don't know what you're talking about. I have no relationship to him. Don't listen to gossip." If she became Alina Castro, that dodge would be impossible.

Castro attended her first wedding. As he was leaving, he pulled her aside and said, "Don't let me know when you get your divorce." She said, "Don't worry. I still don't have your phone number." She did indeed get divorced and married several more times. She had a child, a daughter. And she had a host of problems, Alina did, including anorexia. About life under Communism, she suffered disillusionment after disillusionment. Like many people, she was appalled by the privation, the lies, and the violence against innocents. Unlike many people—unlike almost everyone—she had protection. She could speak her mind. She writes, "I was the only person in the country with freedom of expression. I could speak freely about the lack of freedom, without having a police squad get me out of bed, beat me up, and take me to jail."

The next sentence in her book is one of her most interesting: "To assume that strange responsibility cost me a lot of anxiety."

Alina did not like the surveillance that was sometimes inflicted on her. And she did not want her daughter to grow up in a police state, no matter who was running it. In 1993, at age 37, Alina defected. She did so with the aid of a wig and a false passport. She sought asylum in the United States and received it. Days later, she was joined by her daughter (whom the regime simply let go). Alina's mother, Naty, stayed, ever the loyalist to Castro. In 1997, Alina published her fascinating and highly valuable book. Like her Russian predecessor, Svetlana, she chose to live not by lies. She would speak the truth, whether people wanted to hear it or not. Incidentally, she is as unsparing about herself as she is about Fidel Castro.

In Miami, she hosted a radio program, *Simplemente Alina* ("Simply Alina"). In a city full of anti-Castro and pro-freedom voices, hers was one of the most distinctive. In a 2002 interview, she said, "Fidel has ruined Cuba. He has slaughtered its people and bankrupted the country. And for what? I don't think even he really knows." In August 2014, something unusual happened: She went home—home to Cuba, just for a visit, to see her mother, who was elderly and ill.

Fidel Castro, too, is elderly, and frail, if not ill. Other dictators have had their sons succeed them. Castro has had his brother succeed him. And after Raúl, if Cuban Communism persists? Guillermo Fariñas, a prominent Cuban dissident, has made a prediction: Either Raúl's son Alejandro—another Alejandro, another Alexander!—or Fidel's son Antonio, the doctor-businessman-sportsman-playboy, will rise to the top. The former is already close to the top, a heavy in state security. When the dictatorship falls, if it falls, we will know more about the Castro family, and about more important matters, too.

12

QADDAFI

Q addafi had eight children. They came of two wives. He may have
had an adopted child or two as well, but their existence is in dispute. What Ion Mihai Pacepa says of his old bosses the Ceauşescus is
true of the Qaddafi regime and many other dictatorships: "One never
knew what was truth and what was lie." In a culture that especially
prizes sons—namely, the Arab culture—Qaddafi was rich in them: He
had seven. They were a gruesome crew, in the image of their father. A
few of them vied to succeed him. One of the sons tried to go straight,
which is to say, tried to be a good Western-style liberal or at least an Arab
reformer. He made great strides in this direction. In the end, however, he
returned to the fold, defending his father and the dictatorship with arms.
Three of the brothers died in that war—the Libyan Civil War, which was
fought in 2011—along with their father. Two of the brothers are today
imprisoned in Libya. The other two live freely, in the Persian Gulf.

Moammar al-Qaddafi ruled Libya from 1969 until the end in 2011.
They murdered him grotesquely. They did the same to his son Mutassim.
Father and son were put on display in the city of Misrata. Their corpses
were laid out in a commercial freezer at a market. For four days, Libyans
filed by.

In 1969, the year he seized power, Qaddafi married Fatiha al-Nuri, the daughter of a general. They divorced the next year. While in the hospital for appendicitis, Qaddafi had met a nurse named Safia Farkash. He promptly married her instead. But he had fathered a son with Fatiha—Muhammad, born in 1970. With Safia, he would have six more boys and a girl, born between 1972 and 1983.

Muhammad was one of the less gruesome Qaddafi children (and still is). He had little to do with the machinery of oppression. Apparently, he was not one of the sons who wished to succeed their father. Muhammad studied engineering in his native country, then earned a degree in Britain: a Ph.D. in engineering and management from the University of Liverpool. At home, he was not idle. He had a couple of plush jobs. He was chairman of the General Posts and Telecommunications Company—therefore boss of the mail, cell phones, satellites, and the Internet. He was also head of the Libyan Olympic Committee. Sports and dictators' sons seem inseparable.

In 2006, Muhammad made a notable public comment. He was speaking at an awards ceremony for an international competition to memorize the Koran. In preceding days, the pope, Benedict XVI, had made remarks construed as unfriendly to Islam (misconstrued, actually). He subsequently apologized. But Muhammad Qaddafi was having none of it: "If this person were really someone reasonable, he would not agree to remain at his post one minute, but would convert to Islam immediately." The pope remained a Catholic—but he did resign his post seven years later.

The Qaddafi son after Muhammad was Saif. He was the rebel, so to speak, the one who tried to go straight. We will save him for last, because he is so interesting and comparatively complicated.

After Saif came Saadi, who was as sports-mad as any dictator's son—specifically, soccer-mad. He was head of the Libyan Football (or Soccer) Federation. But he was also a player: the captain of his home club in Tripoli and the captain of the Libyan national team. Did he occupy those spots on merit? No, not remotely. To say that Saadi Qaddafi had special privileges in Libyan soccer would be an understatement. What he wanted, he got. Referees did not dare cross him. Broadcasters were not permitted to mention anyone else's name. What I mean is this: They called Saadi by name, but every other player by the number on his jersey.

Once, Tripoli's rivals in Benghazi angered Saadi greatly. The story goes, Benghazi fans dressed an ass in a Tripoli jersey—Saadi's jersey. Not one to take a joke or an insult, Saadi had the Benghazi stadium demolished and the city's team banned.

Saadi tried to make it as a player on the European circuit, and he succeeded, to a degree. He signed with teams in Italy. He hired one of the greatest soccer players in history as his personal coach: Diego Maradona, the Argentinean. He hired one of the greatest tracksters in history as his personal trainer: Ben Johnson, the Jamaican-born Canadian sprinter. Johnson had his Olympic gold medal revoked when he was found to have used illegal substances. Saadi was found guilty of doping, too—but he played little for the Italian teams in any case. He was sadly below a professional level. In reality, the teams wanted him around for the money he spent, and the business deals in Libya he could open up.

His countrymen told a joke: Other professional footballers are paid to play; Saadi pays to play.

In a 2011 interview, a former teammate, Jay Bothroyd, was kinder than those jokesters. Reminiscing about Saadi to the *Telegraph*, he said, "He wasn't the best, but he did it as a hobby" (play the game, that is). "He's a billionaire, but it was something he wanted to do. He wanted to play football, to come in every day and train. And he did it, to be fair. He never expected any special treatment."

All the Qaddafi children were rich, filthy rich, thanks to the oil revenue that the dictator funneled their way. Saadi was a shareholder in the renowned Turin team, Juventus. (This was not one of the clubs that signed the hapless player, however.) He spent money on drugs, booze, women, men—the "high life" that many very rich and spoiled kids would spend on, especially dictators' children. For some reason, he did not always pay his bills: In 2010, an Italian court ordered him to pay the half a million dollars he owed the Grand Excelsior Hotel in Rapallo, on the Italian Riviera. He had stayed there for more than a month with his posse, then skipped town.

In 2006, the dictator gave Saadi something to do—something besides play at soccer and live the high life: Saadi would spearhead the Zuwara Free Trade Zone, a stretch of Libya that was supposed to be the country's Hong Kong. It would welcome Western-style businesses, and abide by Western-style rules. Saadi himself said, "We are talking about two systems and one country" (adapting the slogan used for the relationship between Hong Kong and Communist China). He promised an environment where even Jews and Christians could operate freely. Pressed on whether he could go so far as to envision the building of synagogues and churches, he said, "Yes, there's no problem. There won't be any limitations."

Thanks to spillage from WikiLeaks, the computer-hacking organization, we have a memo from a U.S. ambassador to Libya, Gene A. Cretz. In 2009, the ambassador wrote,

> Although the Zuwara Free Trade Zone is an ambitious and expensive project, Muammar al-Qadhafi likely views it as a relatively small price to pay if it helps occupy the notoriously ill-behaved Saadi and lend a patina of useful engagement to his otherwise less than sterling reputation. Saadi has a troubled past, including scuffles with police in Europe (especially Italy), abuse of drugs and alcohol, excessive partying, travel abroad in contravention of his father's wishes and profligate affairs with men and women. His bisexuality is reportedly a point of extreme contention with his father and partly prompted the decision to arrange his marriage to al-Khweildi al-Hmeidi's daughter. [Hmeidi was a top Qaddafi official.] Creating the appearance of useful employment for al-Qadhafi's offspring has been an important objective for the regime.

An Arab dictator's son who has homosexual affairs, as well as other affairs, must be under exceptional pressure. (Never mind Moammar Qaddafi's own sexual tastes, and the sadism that went with them.) When Saadi's house was ransacked at the end of the civil war, the ransackers found gay porn, according to the Associated Press—in particular, a video called "Boyz Tracks."

The next son, Mutassim, was a playboy himself, although he evidently stuck to one side of the fence. We know a fair amount about him from one of his girlfriends, Talitha van Zon, a Dutchwoman who was a *Playboy* centerfold. Mutassim lived a life embodying a typical Qaddafi combination: luxury and glamour, brutality and power. In appearance, he was what you might call goonishly handsome, like most of the Qaddafi sons. Every Christmas, he would fly himself and an entourage to Saint Barts, the ritzy and enchanting island in the Caribbean. They partied raucously, through New Year's. To entertain himself and his guests, Mutassim would hire the biggest pop stars of the day, including ones who went by just one name, such as Beyoncé and Usher. Among the two-named stars who performed was Mariah Carey.

The Dutch pin-up, Talitha, once asked Mutassim how much money he spent, not at Christmas, but in his life in general. He did some calculating in his head—and came up with the figure of $2 million a month.

In the 1990s, when Mutassim was in his twenties, something very curious happened. Little is known about it, but the suspicion is that Mutassim participated in, or even led, a coup attempt against his father. For this shocking act of political and filial betrayal, he was exiled to Egypt—and brought home in 2006, when Qaddafi forgave him. In fact, he gave Mutassim the title of "national security adviser." In this capacity, Mutassim met with two consecutive U.S. secretaries of state: Condoleezza Rice and Hillary Clinton.

Mutassim had a sense of being in competition to be the next Qaddafi dictator. His chief competition was his older brother Saif, thought to be the frontrunner. He also had a younger brother or two to worry about. Mutassim was apparently the favorite of the "old guard" or "conservatives," who were keen on dictatorial strength and less keen on reform. Talitha van Zon reported the following about Mutassim: "He worshipped his father. He talked a lot about Hitler, Fidel Castro, Hugo Chávez [the strongman who ruled Venezuela from 1999 till his death in 2013]. He liked leaders who had a lot of power. He always said, 'I want to do better than my father.'"

Possibly the most thuggish of the Qaddafi sons was Hannibal. He left a trail of wreckage, as most of them did, really. Hannibal was the sort of fellow who hits women. Whether he is less thuggish in his present exile, few of us can say. He does not make headlines as he once did.

He was the sailor in the family, trained in the maritime arts. Eventually, he controlled Libya's shipping and seaports for his father. The young man went to business school: the Copenhagen Business School. No Qaddafi child was what you would call a normal student. As John A. Byrne, a business writer, has explained in an article, Hannibal was tutored by a Copenhagen professor who sometimes traveled to Tripoli, "where he was met by chauffeured cars, put up in a five-star hotel, and summoned for private sessions to Hannibal's home, where gazelles and antelopes strolled around a garden."

During and after the civil war, there were amazing reports from the homes that the Qaddafis had fled (more amazing than the one about Saadi's pad). One such report was filed by Portia Walker for the *Independent*: "The former home of Hannibal Gaddafi lay ransacked, a bullet-proofed BMW abandoned in the garage and a dead gazelle rotting on the overgrown lawn." (You have seen, as we always see, various spellings of the family's last name.)

Hannibal's encounters with the law were numerous and notorious— the law in Europe, I mean, for in Libya the name Qaddafi *was* the law. In 2001, Hannibal attacked police at the Hilton Hotel in Rome. This was at 3 in the morning, when he was presumably in a fighting mood. The officers had been guarding Hannibal's own room. He struck them with bottles, and emptied a fire extinguisher on them for good measure. He then pleaded diplomatic immunity, as he would habitually do.

In 2004, Hannibal led French police on a high-speed chase through the center of Paris. He was drunk in his black Porsche, doing 90 miles an hour down the Champs-Elysées. He ran red lights. At one point, he went the wrong way. When the police finally stopped him, six of his bodyguards arrived in other cars—and attacked the police. The Libyan embassy stepped in to smooth things over.

The next year, once again in Paris, Hannibal beat his girlfriend, who was eight months pregnant. She was Aline Skaf, a Lebanese lingerie model. In the Grand Hotel, he beat her so severely that she had to be hospitalized. Hannibal then waved a gun at security guards. He moved to a different hotel, the Royal Monceau, and smashed up a room, rock star–style. A French court convicted him in absentia—and gave him a four-month sentence (suspended) and a small fine.

By 2008, Hannibal had married Aline, and she was again pregnant. They went to Geneva, where Aline was to give birth. At the Hôtel Président Wilson, they brutally beat two of their servants. Back home in Libya, they could beat or torture their servants to their hearts' content. In Geneva, they were arrested. So were their bodyguards, after they attacked the arresting officers. Aline, feeling faint, was taken to a hospital; Hannibal was taken into custody, then released on bail. Back home, the dictator and his family were furious—not at Hannibal and his wife, but at the Swiss. It was Switzerland that had brought shame on the family, not Hannibal and Aline's behavior.

Interestingly, Qaddafi's daughter, Aisha, cited the Hebrew Bible. The Swiss would face "an eye for an eye, and a tooth for a tooth," she said. The dictatorship undertook a number of retaliatory measures. They forced the Libyan branches of Swiss companies, such as Nestlé, to close. They also imprisoned two Swiss businessmen, who were perfectly innocent, having done nothing like assault servants.

At Christmas 2009, Hannibal, Aline, and their children were in London, ensconced in a suite at Claridge's, the storied hotel. At 1:30 on Christmas morning, staff heard a woman screaming. Police were called, and they went to the Qaddafis' suite. The bodyguards would not let them in. More police were called, and they broke through. Inside, they found Aline beaten to a pulp. A witness said, "She was bleeding heavily from her nose and face. Her nose was clearly broken and it looked like she would need surgery." In the aftermath, Hannibal slipped away in an embassy car.

The Qaddafi women circled the wagons: Sister Aisha, though great with child, flew in from Tripoli and urged Aline to say that she had injured herself in a fall. Safia, the mother of Aisha and Hannibal, urged the same over the phone. Aline obeyed.

She herself was a torturer. At the end of the civil war, a reporter for CNN, Dan Rivers, found an Ethiopian woman at one of the Qaddafis' villas. Was it the one with the dead gazelle? Could have been. The woman's name was Shweyga Mullah, and she had served as nanny for Hannibal and Aline's children. The woman was in terrible shape, as the photos printed in newspapers documented: They were unbearable to look at. The nanny forthrightly explained what happened.

Aline had the habit of burning her with boiling water. She did this as punishment. Once, there was a very serious attack. It came when the Qaddafis' daughter would not stop crying. Aline lost her temper, and ordered the nanny to beat the child. The nanny demurred. So, Aline took the nanny into a bathroom, tied her hands behind her back, tied up her feet, and taped her mouth shut. Then she started pouring boiling water over her head.

The nanny's body became covered with open, oozing sores. "There were maggots coming out of my head," she told the reporter, "because she had hidden me and no one had seen me."

Eventually, a guard found her and took her to a hospital. When Aline found out about this act of mercy, she told the guard she would imprison him if he dared to do it again. The nanny said, "When she did all this to me, for three days she wouldn't let me sleep. I stood outside in the cold, with no food. She would say to staff, 'If anyone gives her food, I'll do the same to you.' I had no water—nothing."

The nanny Shweyga Mullah became a bit of a cause célèbre. Money from around the world was contributed for her care. She recovered in Malta, to which she had been removed.

I will say one more thing about Hannibal, then proceed to the next Qaddafi son. Perhaps this final item will provide a little comic relief—though comic relief of a ghoulish variety. After the war, it emerged that Hannibal had ordered the building of a cruise liner. It was to be built to his specifications, of course. The ship would be called the "Phoenicia," and it would be 1,100 feet long. We are talking about a vessel roomy enough for 3,500 passengers. Hannibal's most striking specification was a shark tank: a 120-ton chamber meant to hold two sand tiger sharks, two white sharks, and two blacktip reef sharks. When the Qaddafi regime went bust, Hannibal discontinued payments. The ship was completed, but de-Hannibalized. There would certainly be no shark tank. The *Phoenicia*, renamed the *Preziosa*, was bought by an Italian-Swiss cruise line.

The company's CEO remarked that he had no idea why Hannibal had specified a shark tank. Some speculated darkly that Hannibal might have fed people into it, in the manner of a James Bond villain. He was probably not beyond it.

The son who followed Hannibal in the family line was Saif—a second Saif, the first Saif being the dictator's second child (and Mother Safia's first). That son is Saif al-Islam, meaning "Sword of Islam." The younger Saif was Saif al-Arab, or "Sword of the Arabs."

It is said that he was injured in the U.S. bombing attacks of 1986, when he was three or four years old. But reports of this kind are difficult to trust: To say it once more, regimes such as Qaddafi's are not models of honesty and transparency. In April 1986, Libyan agents bombed a discotheque called "La Belle" in West Berlin. This was an establishment frequented by American servicemen. Three people were killed in the attack, including two U.S. soldiers. More than 200 were injured. In response, the U.S. president, Ronald Reagan, ordered strikes on Tripoli and Benghazi. The Americans hoped to degrade the Libyans' capacity to commit terror.

When it came time for higher education, Saif al-Arab attended the Technical University of Munich, known as TUM. He upheld the Qaddafi children's tradition of scandal and violence. In November 2006, Saif visited a Munich nightclub called "4004" with a female companion. 'Round midnight, she performed a striptease for him, right on the dance floor. A bouncer threw her out, which incensed Saif. He and the bouncer exchanged blows. Later, Saif planned an acid attack on the bouncer, which the authorities caught wind of. Saif made himself scarce.

In due course, he resurfaced, only to have another incident in 2008: He was caught trying to smuggle arms from Munich to Paris in a car bearing diplomatic plates. The arms included an assault rifle. Prosecutors dropped the case against Saif, causing the police and others to say that higher authorities in Germany feared Libyan retaliation against German interests. The prosecutors denied this, but it seemed clear that Germany had learned a lesson from Switzerland's problems. Qaddafi struck back at Switzerland after the arrest of Hannibal and Aline. The message to other countries was, perhaps: Go very easy on the Qaddafi boys.

The seventh and youngest of them was Khamis, born in 1983. Like Saif al-Arab, he is said to have been injured in the 1986 American raids. He would receive a very good military education, attending the academy in Tripoli and then going for further training to Russia. He graduated from Moscow's famed Frunze Academy. Back home, he was given a brigade to command, the most important brigade in the country, protecting the core of the regime. In this youngest son's honor, it was renamed the "Khamis Brigade."

Like big brother Hannibal, he attended business school, though not in Copenhagen: He went to Madrid to study at the IE Business School. His education included an internship with an American technology corporation, AECOM. In the course of his internship, he was touring important U.S. military sites, including West Point. (That must have been interesting for a young man who was bombed by the Americans as a child.) The tour took place in early 2011. He had to scurry home, however, when the Libyan Civil War broke out. He commanded the Khamis Brigade, futilely.

Aisha, the Qaddafis' sister, was born in 1976, between Hannibal and Saif al-Arab. Her father adored her. She must have been his favorite child, along with the first Saif (al-Islam). In her young womanhood, Aisha cut a relatively glamorous figure. She dyed her hair blond, prompting the Arab press to dub her "the Claudia Schiffer of North Africa." (Schiffer was a German supermodel.) According to some reports, Aisha obtained a prestigious degree in Paris: a Ph.D. in law from the Sorbonne. Whether this is true or not, a point can be made about Qaddafi: He may have bombed and terrorized Europe quite a bit, but he liked to send his children there to study. When Saddam Hussein, the Iraqi dictator, was captured by American forces and put on trial, Aisha joined his defense team. "I feel duty-bound to defend anyone wrongly accused," she said. Furthermore, she made clear that she admired Saddam a great deal.

Her Claudia Schiffer days came to an end when she donned the veil. In 2006, she was married to a cousin of her father's, Ahmed Qaddafi, an army officer. They were to have four children together. And if Nicu Ceaușescu could have an honorary U.N. position, Aisha Qaddafi certainly could: In 2009, she was made a goodwill ambassador. A biography was written of her, *Princess of Peace*.

In October 2010, not long before the end, the princess gave an interview to Colin Freeman of the *Telegraph*. In it, she praised Qaddafi as both a father and a grandfather. "We are very close as a family," she said, "and while he is always very busy, every day I insist that we have a gathering with him. My boys love being in his tent, and they enjoy drinking his camel's milk." Freeman asked her what she thought of the late Reagan, who ordered the bombings of 1986. "That is the route of Allah," she said. Reagan "went crazy and got Alzheimer's. That is his punishment, I think."

At the beginning of this chapter, I noted that there were Qaddafi children, or alleged children, whose existence is in dispute. Here is the problem: In the wake of the 1986 bombings, Qaddafi said that the Americans had killed his adopted daughter, a four-year-old named Hanna. The public had never known about this girl. Throughout the world, including in America, this killing was used against Reagan: who was so belligerent (went the line), he even killed the little girls of leaders with whom he was at odds. In 2006, Qaddafi organized a Hanna

Festival of Freedom and Peace, in honor of the twentieth anniversary of the girl's death.

Five years later, when the Qaddafi regime fell apart, reporters and others made a perplexing discovery: There was a Hanna Qaddafi, apparently a daughter of the dictator, alive and well. She was a doctor. She had spent some of her teenage years in London. She was now married with children. According to her passport and other legal documents, she was born in November 1985—meaning she would have been an infant at the time of the American strikes, not a four-year-old.

What gave? There have been several theories put forth. One is that, after the American strikes, Qaddafi adopted a girl named Hanna posthumously, in order to score a propaganda point. Another is that he indeed had a daughter named Hanna, who did not die in the strikes. Another is that he adopted a second daughter, naming her Hanna in memory of the prior daughter. The truth is, no one knows, outside the Qaddafi family and its circle.

There is another adopted child, possibly: a boy (now a man, if he is still alive) named Milad, Qaddafi's nephew, who, according to lore, led the dictator to safety during the American raids. In gratitude, goes the story, the dictator adopted his nephew as his very son.

There is no question about Saif—Saif al-Islam, the dictator's second son, and first with his wife Safia. He was the one who tried to go straight: who tried to rise above dictatorship, embrace liberal values, and perhaps redeem the Qaddafi name. He was a playboy, like some of his brothers. But he was not a brute, and he had a sense that dictatorial rule, whether by his father or anyone else, was not right.

He had plenty of education, Saif did. He took a bachelor's degree in engineering in Tripoli; an MBA in Vienna; and a doctorate at the London School of Economics. His Ph.D. came from the school's department of philosophy. The thesis he wrote had a flurry of buzzwords in its title: "The Role of Civil Society in the Democratisation of Global Governance Institutions: From 'Soft Power' to Collective Decision-Making?" I have said "he wrote"—but did he write the thesis himself? There were charges he did not. Whatever the case, Saif gave the school 1.5 million pounds.

He was a man of wide interests, a man of parts. He had four pet tigers, including two extremely rare ones: white Bengals. He loved to play with his big cats. He also enjoyed falconry. In addition to being an

Saif al-Islam Qaddafi

engineer, a business expert, and a philosopher, he was an architect and a painter. In London, he had an art exhibition: *The Desert Is Not Silent.* When people hooted at the very idea of his having an exhibition, he said, "We have to be realistic: I am the leader's son, and that gives me an advantage. But you also have to give people evidence of your talent." Not many dictatorial children concede their advantages.

By the way, did Saif give evidence of artistic talent? Put it this way: He was not as good a painter as Zoia Ceauşescu was a mathematician, but a better painter than Elena Ceauşescu was a chemist.

In his happiest days, Saif was a toast of society, hobnobbing with Rothschilds and royalty in places such as Saint-Tropez and Corfu. (The royalty included at least two princes: Andrew of Britain and Albert of Monaco.) He touted friendships with Tony Blair, the British prime minister, and other democratic leaders. He surrounded himself with gurus and retainers, including three eminent political scientists from America: Benjamin Barber, Robert Putnam, and Joseph Nye. PR firms on both sides of the Atlantic were paid to burnish Saif's image.

He did not have a post in his father's dictatorship, officially. He said that he would not accept a post until Libya had a constitution and a "more democratic and transparent" environment. One thing he did for his father was serve as a troubleshooter and negotiator. Qaddafi would dispatch his respectable son around the world in pursuit of Libya's interests, or at least the dictatorship's.

Saif ran the Qaddafi Foundation, sometimes described as a "charity," sometimes described as a "human-rights organization." These terms had little meaning in Libya. Also, Saif had two newspapers, a TV station, and a radio station. Those entities did not operate in freedom, but they operated with fewer restrictions than other Libyan outlets. They vented some of the frustration felt by Libyans in general. Saif was testing the limits, and pushing them.

Remarkably, he could talk back to his father—challenge his father, even rebuke him, and largely get away with it. Why did Qaddafi stand for it? Perhaps he admired Saif's nerve, or saw in this son a respectability or legitimacy that he himself could never obtain. In 2007, it was reported that Qaddafi and Saif had an angry exchange of letters. The reason: Saif had admitted to al-Jazeera, the Qatari-based television network, that Libya tortured prisoners in order to gain confessions from them. The next year, on CNN, he made a point about Libya's relations with other countries: "We tried to terrorize our enemies, yes." He claimed, however, that Libya had abandoned its bad old ways.

The West was enamored with this son, understandably. He was a man you could do business with. *Newsweek* had an article about him titled "Our Man in Libya?" The *New York Times* called him "the un-Qaddafi." *Esquire* magazine listed him as one of "The 75 Most Influential People of the 21st Century." Westerners wanted him to succeed his father in power, and so did reform-minded people in Libya, especially the young. Saif would scoff at the idea of succession. "To me, dynastic rule is like going backwards in history," he said, "something from the period of the monarchy, when really we need to advance." One of his standard lines, when the question of succession came up, was, "Libya is not a farm to inherit."

Always, in any number of forums, he talked about democracy, and the crying need for democracy in Libya and throughout the Arab world. One night, at dinner, an American congressional aide asked him, "What does Libya most need?" Saif said, "Democracy." The aide said, "You mean more democracy?" Saif said, "No! 'More democracy' would imply that we had some."

I myself encountered Saif once, in 2005. It was at the annual meeting of the World Economic Forum in Davos, Switzerland. Qaddafi's son was the guest at a "media coffee." With about ten of us sitting around a table, he discoursed on a range of issues, including his pet theme, democracy. He said—and here I paraphrase, but closely—"Do you know why we Arabs have lost all our wars against Israel? Because Israel is democratic, and we are undemocratic. So, in one of our states, the worst general becomes army chief of staff, because he is no threat to carry out a coup d'état. Loyalty to the strongman is all that matters. Democracy, on the other hand, is a competitive mechanism—and that's why Israel wins."

An Israeli at the table said, humorously but nervously, "Please don't ever have a democracy."

Something else interesting happened at that session. Toward the end of it, someone asked Saif about the Holocaust, and the widespread Arab denial of the same. Saif began his answer hesitantly: "I am not a historian. I don't know all the facts." He then trotted out the familiar line that Arabs cannot be anti-Semitic, being Semites themselves. The Jews and Arabs were cousins, he said. Being an astute fellow, he sensed that his answer was not working in this room. A person should not deny the Holocaust, or give the appearance of doing so, in a room full of international media. So he said, "It is incorrect to deny the Holocaust." And why was that? Because it was the Red Army that liberated Auschwitz. "We learned about it from the Russians, not from the Zionists, not from the *New York Times*. So, if Arabs deny this, it is incorrect."

The World Economic Forum official who was running the session said, "On that conciliatory note, we must adjourn." You and I may not regard an admission that the Holocaust occurred, because the Soviet Union said so, as conciliatory, but in some atmospheres it evidently is.

Like many people, in the Arab world and elsewhere, Saif always maintained that he was not anti-Jewish, merely anti-Israel. "I have Jewish friends," he said. "What I do stand for is opposition to Zionism and the state of Israel." He did indeed have Jewish friends—including at least one Israeli. She was Orly Weinerman, a model and actress, with whom he had a romantic relationship for six years: from 2005 until the war in 2011, when he was captured and imprisoned. In 2006, *Der Spiegel* magazine reported this relationship. Weinerman denied it, as surely she had to: How could the son of an Arab dictator get away with dating an Israeli? Think how the anti-Saif forces in Libya would have used that information against him! If Saif hoped to succeed his father—as he almost certainly did, no matter what he said publicly—this detail could sink him. When Saif was captured, Weinerman admitted their relationship, appealing to Saif's friends, especially Tony Blair, to try to save him. "The fact that Saif was prepared to involve himself in a loving relationship with a Jew," she said, "is a measure of how open and civilized he is."

In 2008, Saif gave a daring, bridge-burning speech in Libya, decrying decades of "stagnation" and the curse of dictatorship. He said that he was giving up politics, and in fact left Libya. But three years later came the war: and he returned home, throwing in his lot with the family and the dictatorship.

The revolt against Qaddafi began in February 2011, in the first months of what was called the "Arab Spring." This was a period of protest and war that started in Tunisia, with the overthrow of longtime dictator Zine al-Abidine Ben Ali. The spring turned wintry in just a couple of years. But it was encouraging, even thrilling, while it lasted. In Libya, NATO joined the rebels, sealing Qaddafi's fate.

Among the Qaddafi children, Saif was second to none in defending the dictatorship. He even changed his appearance: No longer was he the smooth-skinned Renaissance man who held art exhibitions in London and clinked glasses with the prince of Monaco. He grew a beard, in the style of fundamentalist Muslims. He gave wild-eyed rants on television. He vowed, "We will fight until the last man, until the last woman, until the last bullet." Saif was now his father's prime minister, in all but name. Because the regime was firing freely on civilian protesters, the International Criminal Court issued a warrant for the dictator's arrest. It issued one for Saif, too. He was charged with crimes against humanity: specifically, "murder" and "persecution." He answered, "This court is a Mickey Mouse court."

He mocked NATO forces, questioning their staying power. "They want to finish as soon as possible, because they are hungry, they are tired. For them, Libya is like fast food, like McDonald's. Because everything should be fast: fast war, fast airplanes, fast bullets, fast victory. But we are very patient." (NATO proved patient too, in this instance.)

Saif was angry that Westerners who had been pleased to be in his company, and take his money, were now against him. They were "cowards turning on us," he said. The London School of Economics renounced his donation. People were saying that the school had granted Saif a Ph.D. only to get the loot. Saif said, "I am proud of my work at the LSE, and of being an alumni." (He had picked up the modern habit of using "alumni" in the singular.) "This is the reason I became a benefactor. The way these people are now disowning me is disgusting."

The man had a point. His father had a point, too, and in fact the same point. About his erstwhile friends in the West, he said, "These people saw Libya as a huge money-making opportunity but have all but abandoned us after taking our money for years."

The Qaddafi children, all of them, were now in bad odor. The United Nations dropped Aisha as a goodwill ambassador. The IE Business School in Madrid expelled Khamis, given "his links to attacks against the Libyan population." The young man was probably not thinking about school regardless. He was commanding the Khamis Brigade. His brother Saadi, the soccer player, was commanding special forces. Another brother, Saif al-Arab, was commanding other forces.

Three of the brothers would fall: Saif al-Arab, Khamis, and Mutassim. The third of these was killed with his father, and, as you remember, laid out in that commercial freezer in Misrata.

His pin-up friend from Holland, Talitha van Zon, had a scare in the war. She had gone to Tripoli, to be with Mutassim. In a hotel, she was surrounded by a group of rebels and feared for her life. She thought they were going to burn her alive. She leapt from a balcony. She broke an arm and injured her back. Hotel staff took her to a hospital, and she was soon evacuated to Malta. Before she left, she told the press, "Coming to Libya in the middle of a war was the biggest mistake of my life."

What about the other Qaddafi children? Three of them, Muhammad, Hannibal, and Aisha, fled to Algeria, Libya's neighbor to the west. Qaddafi's wife, Safia, was with them. The escape was dangerous and dramatic. Hours after crossing the border, Aisha gave birth to a girl, her fourth child. Saadi, meanwhile, escaped to another neighboring country, Niger. The next year, in 2012, the Qaddafis in Algeria were given asylum in Oman, the Persian Gulf state. Saadi had less luck: In March 2014, Niger extradited him to Libya to stand trial.

The last Qaddafi child standing in Libya, after the others had fled or been killed, was Saif—Saif al-Islam, the child who had tried to break away from the dictatorship and go straight. As late as October 22, two days after his father was killed, he said, "I am alive and free and willing to fight to the end and take revenge." He was finally captured on November 19, trying to flee to Niger, as Saadi had. He has been held by the Zintan Brigades, in northwest Libya, all this time. The International Criminal Court insists that the Libyans hand over Saif for trial in The Hague, but the Libyans insist on trying him themselves. The wheels of justice, if that's what they are, are turning slowly.

I should be careful about playing psychologist in this book—but perhaps I could put Saif on the couch for just a moment. It seems clear that he wanted to be something that, in the end, circumstances would not allow him to be. Or, to be slightly stricter about it: He could not find it within himself to surmount those circumstances, to be what he wished to be.

I believe that he had genuine Western leanings—that he was serious about liberalization and modernization. I don't believe it was all an act. I think he knew dictatorship was wrong. I think he was embarrassed about it, for some years (while enjoying the wealth the regime generated for him). But when the crunch came, he could not cut his ties to his family and to his father in particular, and became just another despot, or despot's helper. When the crunch came, he was not much different from Nicu or Saddam's boys or Bashar Assad—or from Hannibal and Saadi and the rest of the Qaddafis, for that matter. During the civil war, James Verini, a veteran reporter in Africa, had an article in *New York* magazine. He reported that a Western associate of Saif's had sent him a text message—sent it to Saif, that is. The text said, "You're better than this."

Was he? Is he? Maybe, but the pull of blood and power proved very strong. You might contend that all of these dictators' children are tragedies, but Saif is more tragic than most.

13

ASSAD

Assad had six children—two daughters, followed by a string of boys. One of them was groomed to succeed him. He died in a car crash. So, another son was called home from his studies abroad to be groomed. A son much less inclined to leadership, even to politics. That son has wound up killing many more than his father did, which is extraordinary.

Hafez Assad (the father) became dictator of Syria in 1970. He was an air-force officer, an Alawite, and a Baathist. The Alawites are a small religious minority within Syria. The Baath Party is a socialist party, with aspects of national socialism. It has ruled Syria since 1963. Assad was styled the "eternal leader." While he did not prove exactly that, Syria has been ruled by just two men in the last 45 years, and counting: Assad and his second son.

Born in 1930, Assad married sometime in his middle or late twenties. His wife was a distant relative, Aniseh Makhlouf. They had a daughter, Bushra. She died in infancy. They then had a second daughter, born in 1960. They named *her* Bushra, too. (We see that a custom is at work here. Moammar Qaddafi may have had one Hanna, who died, and then another, named in the previous daughter's honor.) In the next seven years, the Assads had their string of boys: Bassel, Bashar, Majd, and Maher.

It will not surprise the reader that Bushra was Assad's favorite child, by most accounts. She was his eldest child and only daughter. She was tall, attractive, lively, and smart. Later in life, she could be impossibly imperious. Always, she has been keenly interested in politics and the dictatorship. She went to Damascus University, as all her brothers would. She studied pharmacy. After graduation, she had a role in the development of Syria's pharmaceutical industry.

In his 1988 biography of Assad, Patrick Seale gives us a taste of the family's domestic life. Actually, this taste comes from the eldest son, Bassel, who told Seale, "We saw our father at home, but he was so busy that three days might pass without our talking to him. We never had breakfast together, or dinner, and I can't remember our ever lunching together as a family, or only once or twice, on formal occasions." Even when the family was on summer holiday together, the children rarely saw their father, who was a workaholic: who did everything he could to keep himself on the throne and the country stable (so long as that stability was on Assad and Baathist terms).

Nonetheless, Bushra and her father enjoyed a warm relationship. Especially in his later years, he brought her into the councils of government. He also had her accompany him on foreign trips. Was Bushra like Papa Doc Duvalier's daughter Marie-Denise, or Kim Jong-il's daughter Sol-song? Might she have been the successor had she been of the other sex? Yes.

As it was, it had to be Bassel. Actually, before Bassel, it was Assad's younger brother Rifaat, born in 1937. He helped his brother seize power in 1970. He was an army officer, and, once the dictatorship was established, he was its enforcer—its much-feared fist. When the Muslim Brotherhood rebelled in the city of Hama, the Assads put this rebellion down. They killed 20,000, maybe more. Rifaat was known as "the Butcher of Hama." But responsibility rested, of course, with the top brother.

The Hama massacre was carried out in February 1982. Late the next year, in November, the dictator suffered a medical crisis: a heart attack and other problems. Rifaat, itching for the throne, thought it would be a good time to stage a coup. He almost succeeded. Rifaat had his factions,

Bassel Assad

Hafez had his. But Hafez rose from his sickbed in time to block this rebellion.

By some reports, he wanted the disloyal younger brother tried before one and all, on television. By these same reports, Bushra intervened to counsel her father against such a move: Retaliation of this kind would be more trouble than it was worth. Assad sent Rifaat into exile. For the last 30 years and more, Rifaat has lived on some of the most fashionable avenues in Europe.

In many eyes, Bassel looked like the ideal successor. He has long existed in the glow of legend, but the legend may be, to a considerable degree, true. I will relate it.

He was a golden boy. He was handsome, talented, and kind. He was adept at everything he tried, including sports, academics, and the military arts. An equestrian, he was dubbed "the Golden Knight" by state media. (That is undoubtedly true.) He could sail and shoot and parachute. He loved fast cars. (Also undoubtedly true.) One of his great academic interests was computers. He had moral qualities, including honesty. He was a natural leader, exciting the admiration of all types of people. He had the common touch, being able to walk into a souk and mingle with perfect ease.

Again, this is the legend. And, whatever the facts, Bassel was a glamorous figure. He provided a contrast with his father, who was severe-looking and remote. An adjective frequently applied to Hafez, in the English-language press, was "dour." We can safely say that many Syrians looked forward to Bassel's assumption of power.

He was afforded an extensive military training, and rose quickly through the ranks. He was the dictator's son, sure. But he had some ability as well. Before long, he was the head of presidential security. He also conducted anti-drug and anti-corruption campaigns. These campaigns were in keeping with Bassel's image as a man of rectitude.

Assad prepared the country for Bassel's succession in the usual fashion of dictators. Father and son started to appear on posters together. The dictator began to be styled "Abu Bassel," or "Father of Bassel." He introduced his son to various foreign leaders. The grooming was virtually seamless.

But on the morning of January 21, 1994, Bassel died. He was rushing to the airport in his new Mercedes coupe. It was a foggy morning, and he was trying to make a flight—a Lufthansa flight to Germany. The flight was fogged in regardless. The airline tried to get word to the dictator's son that he need not rush. Bassel was going at a very great speed when he entered a traffic circle outside the airport. He struck a barricade and flipped several times. He died instantly. He was 31 years old.

There is a story told about how his father was informed, a story impossible to verify. I will go ahead and tell it, because it is plausible. None of the leading generals was willing by himself to inform Assad that his son had died. So they all trooped in together—safety in numbers. Assad looked at them, thought, and said, "Which one of you has led this coup against me?"

As may be needless to say, Assad was shaken by Bassel's death. The body was flown to the Assads' home village, Qardaha, for burial. Assad flew with the body. He insisted that the coffin be placed in the plane's cabin next to him. At the funeral, he was seen to collapse. A headline in a state newspaper read, "Goodbye, Our Golden Knight."

There was a cult of Bassel before, and now, in death, it exploded. Schools, parks, and all manner of things were named for him. In August 1994, more than seven months after the accident, the *Miami Herald* ran an article headed "Basilmania." ("Basil" is another transliteration of the Arabic name.) The article began, "James Dean was never mourned like this." The late Bassel was often compared to Dean, the young American actor who died in 1955 when he crashed his Porsche.

The *Herald*'s correspondent, John Donnelly, wrote, "Basil's picture is omnipresent. Taped to car windows. Gracing apartment complex entrances. And filling any spare space in shops. There's Basil on horseback. Basil praying. And most common of all, Basil behind dark glasses"—meaning the aviator glasses that were almost his trademark. The tragic death of a famous young man had a lot to do with this mourning and mania, of course. But there was something more, as Donnelly pointed out: Syrians had expected Bassel to be their next leader; they "perceived him as a humane version of his father"; and now they were worried about who would be next.

Books were written about Bassel, with such titles as "The Light of the Generations." Reporting from Damascus in 1996, the *Philadelphia Inquirer*'s Alan Sipress wrote, "The conventional wisdom is that police won't stop a car for running a red light if there's a Basil sign in the window. In the same vein, families of political prisoners have hung Basil posters on their homes to ward off harassment from security services."

Basselmania lasted for years. The regime called him "the martyr of the nation." Amid the ubiquitous pictures of the martyr were slogans: "We are all Bassel." "Bassel is our model." "Be like Bassel."

The dictator was rocked by his eldest son's death, true, but not so rocked that he failed to act immediately: That morning—January 21, 1994—he called his second son, Bashar, home. Bashar was an ophthalmologist. Age 28, he was doing a residency in London, at the Western Eye Hospital. He would practice ophthalmology no more. He would be groomed.

A new slogan was formulated: "Hafez is our symbol. Bassel is our model. Bashar is our hope." Posters showed three men: Assad, Bassel, and Bashar. Foreign diplomats in Damascus cracked, "The Father, the Son, and the Holy Ghost."

Bashar Assad

Everyone says that Bashar was very different from his late brother, and everyone is right. Bashar was quiet, shy, and nerdy. Awkward in personality, he was awkward in looks, too: tall and skinny and long-necked. He did not glide through the world confidently and glamorously—that was Bassel. And he had no interest whatsoever in politics or power. He wanted to practice medicine and enjoy his hobbies, such as photography.

He saw his father in his office exactly once: when he was seven years old and had had his first French lesson. Excited, he wanted to tell his dad. He next entered that office after Assad's funeral, when he himself was dictator.

This information comes from Don Belt, writing for *National Geographic* in 2009. Bashar told him, "My father never talked to me about politics. He was a very warm and caring father, but even after I came home in 1994, everything I learned about his decision-making came from reading the notes he made during meetings, or by talking to his colleagues."

After that call in January 1994, Bashar's life was turned upside down. He was put on speed-grooming. Whether he was inclined to military leadership or not, he would have to become such a leader. He was enrolled in the Homs Military Academy. A short while before, he had been in the ambience of the London ophthalmological community. Now he was in Syria, immersed in tank tactics. The change must have been jarring. But Bashar adapted. He had little choice—his father or fate or some combination had determined his destiny.

Here is a logical question: Why could not Bashar's younger brother Maher have been designated? The question is logical because Maher was a military guy, and he relished it. Reading the mind of Assad, the father and dictator, we might say there were two reasons to prefer Bashar over Maher. First, Bashar was the older, the next in line, after Bassel. Second, Maher may have relished the military and power and violence all too much. He was a hothead—unstable. Maher was a dictator's son in the mold of Vasily Stalin, Nicu Ceauşescu, several Qaddafis, and so on.

In any event, he would come to dominate the military, presiding as the No. 2 man in Syria under Bashar. Know this, too, just for the record: The Assads' mother, Aniseh, is rumored to have favored Maher as her husband's successor. Her youngest boy was not too violent or unreliable for *her*.

We need to return to the couple's only daughter, Bushra—whose marriage is interesting and important. Her beau was Assef Shawkat, an army officer: not a bigshot, just a middling fellow. Bushra was probably the most eligible woman in all of Syria, the biggest catch in the country. Shawkat would have seemed an unlikely beau on many grounds.

He was ten years older than Bushra, and had five children. Was he married when he started going with Bushra, or divorced? Reports vary. Married or divorced, he had a reputation for womanizing. He was from an average family, not an elite family. The dictator had a host of reasons to oppose a liaison between his daughter and Shawkat. And he did.

So did his then–heir apparent, Bassel. In fact, Bassel had Shawkat jailed several times to keep him from seeing his sister. But Bushra persisted. Why? I call on Pascal: "The heart has its reasons that reason knoweth not."

Bassel, as we have said, died in 1994. A year later, Bushra and Shawkat eloped. Think of what chutzpah this took, on Shawkat's part:

You do not up and elope with the sole daughter of an absolute dictator who hates you. Ten years later, in 2005, a Syrian newscaster talked about Shawkat to the *New York Times*. He was trying to illustrate Shawkat's boldness. He was also trying to explain Shawkat's position in Syria. He said, "Anyone who could go into the home of Hafez Assad and take his daughter away without his permission has the power to do anything." Later, the poor Syrian had second thoughts about what he had said. The *Times* reported, "The newscaster, who originally spoke on the record, called back later agitated and asked not to be identified for fear of retribution."

Shawkat's protection lay in the fact that Assad was so fond of Bushra. Ultimately, he accepted Shawkat, or at least tolerated him, and gave him jobs suitable to his new standing (as dictatorial son-in-law). Bushra worked hard to ensure her husband's prominence. Along with his brothers-in-law, Shawkat would be at the top of the Syrian military and intelligence chain.

Above, I compared Bushra to Marie-Denise Duvalier. I will again. Marie-Denise wanted a married man with children. Papa Doc strongly opposed him. She was probably the only person in the country who could defy her father. He loved her. She got away with it. And so did Bushra Assad.

Between Shawkat and his youngest brother-in-law, Maher, the hothead, there were tensions. In fact, Maher whipped out a gun and shot him. He did so in interesting circumstances. Shawkat was criticizing Rifaat Assad, the exiled uncle who had attempted a coup in 1983. Rifaat was now mounting a propaganda campaign against the regime. Maher did not like to hear criticism from Shawkat. Uncle Rifaat was an enemy, true, but he was family, and Shawkat was not (in Maher's view). Angry words were exchanged—and Maher drew his revolver and shot the offender. The offender, Shawkat, recovered. And the brothers-in-law reached some sort of modus vivendi.

Bushra and Shawkat would have five children (same as Shawkat had had with his previous wife). All of these were named after members of the Assad family. Three of them were called Bushra, Bassel, and Maher.

I have not yet discussed the third of the dictator's four sons, Majd. Very little is known about him. He apparently had mental problems that made it impossible for him to function. We know that he studied electrical engineering and that he married. He died in 2009 after what state media described as a "long illness." He was 43. Syrians whispered that, unable to go on, he committed suicide. It is impossible to know this.

Hafez Assad could not exactly name his successor and leave it at that. He was the dictator and Baath leader, yes, but there was intrigue, or potential intrigue, underneath him. He had to maneuver a bit. He had to get Bashar groomed, fast, and clear away any potential resistance to the young man's succession. This involved some demoting and promoting. In his 2012 book on the Assads, David W. Lesch uses an apt phrase: "race against time." Assad was not in robust health. And he had only so many years to "build Bashar's legitimacy and power base within the Baath Party, the government and, especially, the military." Could he hang on long enough? He did. Assad died in June 2000, age 69. Bashar was 34. His father was buried in the mausoleum next to Bassel. Bashar, the second son, took over.

One onlooker in Spain was unhappy. That was Uncle Rifaat. He acted the stickler for democratic propriety, saying, "What is happening in Syria is a real farce and an unconstitutional piece of theater." He vowed, or threatened, to return home at "the appropriate moment." He would then "fulfill the will of the people." Authorities in Damascus made it plain that, if he came back, he would be killed. Rifaat stayed away.

Bashar enjoyed a honeymoon, certainly in the world press. People on several continents were understandably pleased at the prospect of rule by this quiet, polite, diligent young man who had practiced eye surgery in London. He should be a refreshing change from 30 years of his father's autocracy. The press reported that Bashar liked Phil Collins, the British rock star, and the Electric Light Orchestra, a British group. Cynical types were reminded of the initial word about Yuri Andropov, the Soviet chief who took over from Leonid Brezhnev in 1982: He was supposed to enjoy Glenn Miller and Scotch whisky. That made him rather liberal or at least human, some thought, or hoped.

Adding to Bashar's political honeymoon, he got married. The bride was Asma Akhras, born in London to Syrian parents: the father a cardiologist, the mother a retired diplomat. Growing up in England, Asma was known as Emma. She went to King's College London, majoring in computer science. She then went to work in investment banking:

Deutsche Bank and J.P. Morgan. On top of these credentials, Asma was a beauty, a beauty on the *Vogue* level (literally, as we will see). Bashar met her when she was a teen. He was doing his residency in London. When he took power, she was 24, and moved to her ancestral land to marry him.

It was storybook, really, except for one thing—one fly in the ointment. Bashar's mother Aniseh objected that Asma was a Sunni, not an Alawite. Or so the reports say. Bashar brushed aside this objection (if it was an objection). He and Asma would have three children—the first of them a son, named after Grandpa Hafez.

Before there was an Arab Spring, there was a Damascus Spring. This refers to the first year or two of Bashar's rule. In his opening speech as leader, he said, "We must have our own democratic experience, which will result in strong democratic institutions that will resist all instability." He allowed citizens more room to breathe, and speak. Ali Ferzat, a Syrian cartoonist and one of the most famous cultural figures in the Arab world, started a satirical magazine: *Al-Domari*, or "The Lamplighter." It was the first independent magazine in Syria since the Baathists took power in 1963. "There was joy on the streets," Ferzat told me in a 2013 interview. "After 40 years of forced silence, the people had a voice. There was a magazine that expressed their concerns. I remember we sold out even before we went to press."

The fun soon came to an end. Sensing a threat to his power, Bashar stopped liberalization and cracked down. In this, he was encouraged by his younger brother Maher. He was Bashar's enforcer. As Rifaat was to Hafez—before his coup attempt, that is—Maher was to Bashar (and still is). The difference is that Maher is crueler and crazier than Rifaat, "Butcher of Hama" though the uncle may have been.

The Arab Spring began in Tunisia, then spread to Egypt, Libya, and Yemen. It came to Syria on March 15, 2011. Protesters massed in the streets and squares, demanding the right to breathe. They were tired of dictatorship. If other Arabs could speak up and talk back, why couldn't they?

For *Vogue* magazine, the timing was awkward. They had just published an issue featuring Asma Assad, "A Rose in the Desert." That's what the piece was called, and that's what she was. The piece gushed about her as "glamorous, young, and very chic—the freshest and most magnetic of first ladies." (This gushing was hard to deny.) "She's a rare combination: a thin, long-limbed beauty with a trained analytic mind who dresses with cunning understatement." There was more, a lot more. I will quote just a few more sentences: "She's breezy, conspiratorial, and fun. Her accent is English but not plummy. Despite what must be a killer IQ, she sometimes uses urban shorthand: 'I was, like...'"

Embarrassed, *Vogue* scrubbed the piece from the Internet. Why so keen an embarrassment? Again, the timing was awkward. The protesters in Syria were unarmed, and Bashar, Maher, and their gang were firing on them, wantonly. They were murdering them en masse.

Yet the protests mounted. By August, it seemed that Bashar would have to flee, as Qaddafi in Libya was fleeing. Ali Ferzat drew a cartoon. It showed a desperate Bashar trying to hitch a ride with Qaddafi. The regime did not care for this cartoon. Goons came and broke both of Ferzat's hands. They warned that, next time, it would be worse. The regime certainly knew how to send a message. Earlier, a singer named Ibrahim Kashush had excited crowds with democratic songs. Bashar's men slit his throat, ripped out his vocal cords, and threw his corpse into a river. There would be no more singing.

Maher was visibly, openly monstrous. He fired on unarmed protesters personally. He seemed to revel in the bloodletting. He was seen taking photos of corpses (his handiwork). The European Union described him as "the principal overseer of violence against demonstrators." He was widely known as Syria's "thug-in-chief." Even Recep Tayyip Erdogan, the boss in Turkey, and no violet, was critical: "I say this clearly and openly, from a humanitarian point of view: He [Maher] is not behaving in a humane manner. And he is chasing after savagery."

Bushra's husband, Assef Shawkat, was doing his part, too. Once rivals, he and Maher were cracking down together, under Bashar's leadership. The family was going all out to save the family dictatorship. The fighting in Syria grew into a civil war (though some Syrians object to this term, saying that the fighting is a matter of the regime's aggression against the people, plain and simple). In July 2012, rebels attacked the National Security Bureau in Damascus. Shawkat was killed, and Maher was badly injured. Apparently, he lost one leg and the use of an arm. He was not seen until a photo appeared in June 2014. Maher was shown with George Wassouf, a Syrian singer very different from the murdered Ibrahim Kashush: Wassouf is a supporter of the dictatorship.

Bushra, now widowed, fled with her children to the Persian Gulf—Dubai. Her mother fled a few months later, to the same place. The Assad women—Bushra, Aniseh, Asma, and Maher's wife Manal—had been sanctioned by the EU. Their financial assets were frozen and the women barred from traveling to Europe. They were regarded as accessories to the Assad regime's crimes.

At this writing, the Syrian war is in its fifth year. Some 200,000 people have been killed, and 3 million have been made refugees. Bashar may not have wanted to become dictator, or planned on it, and he surely did not want to become a national butcher, or plan on it. But he did not let his father down: He has done whatever is necessary to hang on to power and keep the family business going. Saif al-Islam Qaddafi, the humane, Westernized son, proved loyal when his father's dictatorship was under threat. Bashar, in power, proved no less.

By the way, would Bassel have been any different? Would the golden boy have made a better, more humane, more democratic ruler than Bashar? Educated guesses say no.

As early as 2010, before the Syrian war began, little Hafez—Bashar and Asma's firstborn—was being talked about as the next dictator of Syria. He was only eight. At age eleven, in August 2013, he actually made world news. A Facebook post was circulated, said to have been written by the boy. It appeared to be authentic. He ranted about the United States in the manner of the regime's leaders and mouthpieces. At the time, the Americans seemed ready to intervene in Syria.

Wrote Hafez II (assuming that the post was indeed by him), "They may have the best army in the world, maybe the best airplanes, ships, tanks than ours, but soldiers? No one has soldiers like the ones we do in Syria. America doesn't have soldiers, what it has is some cowards with new technology who claim themselves liberators."

The boy continued (if it was he), "I just want them to attack sooo much, because I want them to make this huge mistake of beginning something that they don't know the end of it." The Americans "don't know our land like we do, no one does, victory is ours in the end no matter how much time it takes."

One commenter, evidently a loyalist of the regime, said, "Like father like son! Well said, future President!"

14

SADDAM

Saddam Hussein had five children—two boys, then three girls. He may have had an "extra" or two, but this cannot be confirmed. Some say that the two boys grew up to be even worse than their father. Really? How could this be? None of our dictators surpasses Saddam Hussein in evil. But here is the testimony of Georges Sada, a former Iraqi general, writing in his 2006 memoir, *Saddam's Secrets*: "They were worse than Saddam, a hundred times over." Such hyperbole can be forgiven once you know the sons—especially the elder.

I should pause for a word about nomenclature: In this sketch, I will often refer to the dictator as "Saddam," not because I think he should be known by his first name, like a rock star or athlete, but because "Hussein" was not really his last name. It was his father's name (first name). There is no last name on the order of "Smith." I will have another word about nomenclature, of necessity, later.

As Hafez Assad was the boss of the Syrian Baath Party, Saddam Hussein was the boss of Iraq's. Assad was able to pass on his dictatorship to a son; Saddam and his family did not get that opportunity. And although the two Baath parties were branches of the same tree, or leaves on the same branch, they had no use for each other. They were determined enemies.

Saddam Hussein ruled Iraq from 1979 until the Americans toppled him, in the Iraq War, in April 2003. Saddam's rule was absolute—a personal and all-pervading tyranny. General Sada has a striking sentence in his book: "During the dictator's thirty-five-year reign of terror, he transformed Iraq into a very small country—from twenty-seven million hard-working men and women to just one man." Iraq was more or less a one-man show, certainly a one-clan show. Saddam was a great admirer of Stalin, his model. He liked to quote one of Stalin's maxims: "No man, no problem." In other words, if you eliminate a man—kill him—you have no problem. This was not merely a theoretical concept for Saddam. General Sada writes, "He was truly a genius at doing evil." The Americans captured Saddam in December 2003, and the Iraqis hanged him three years later: on December 30, 2006.

He was born on April 28, 1937. Coming from a troubled home, he was raised by a maternal uncle, Khairallah Talfah. This man was his mentor, a father figure. He was also a great admirer of Hitler. In 1940, Khairallah penned a little book called "Three Whom God Should Not Have Created: Persians, Jews, and Flies." He later became mayor of Baghdad. Among the children in his home was a daughter, Sajida, the same age as Saddam. There was also a son, Adnan (who will play a part later in this story). When Saddam and Sajida were quite small, a marriage was arranged between the two cousins.

They married in 1958, by most accounts. Sajida was an elementary-school teacher; Saddam was just beginning his career of political thuggery. The two would have their five children together, from 1964 to 1972. Saddam told a women's magazine something remarkable in 1978: "The most important thing about marriage is that the man must not let the woman feel downtrodden simply because she is a woman and he is a man." No matter what he said, do not mistake Saddam for a progressive.

His dictatorship, as I have mentioned, was a clan-centered one. Important positions were filled with blood relatives. Saddam did not like to keep a happy family, either. He enjoyed playing people off one another, letting no one get too comfortable. He liked to maintain a constant state of turmoil, anxiety, and fear. If an individual or faction was up one day, he or it would be down the next. "Saddam Hussein constantly played political chess," writes Joseph Sassoon, in his 2012 study of the regime (*Saddam Hussein's Ba'th Party*). The dictator made clear that he would be crossed by no one, not even his nearest and dearest. "Look, Georges," he said to General Sada, "if my sons Uday and Qusay step one millimeter over the line and don't behave exactly as I want them to, I won't hesitate to chop off their heads."

Uday was the first son, the first child, born in 1964. He was educated in a cursory kind of way: waved through the University of Baghdad with a degree in engineering. Any teacher who did not give him the highest score was subject to dismissal, following torture. Later, Uday was given a Ph.D. in political science. A thesis was evidently written for him, "The World after the Cold War." It was published as a high-quality book—an expensively produced book—whose cover showed Saddam Hussein as an Arab version of Saint George slaying the dragon.

In some respects, Uday was like other dictator's sons—for example, in the jobs he was given. He was the head of the youth ministry, and the soccer federation, and the Olympic committee. He was on the governing board of Saddam University. He headed the Saddam Fedayeen, who were a militia, sort of an Iraqi Tonton Macoute. Their uniforms were based on the movie *Star Wars*—the dark forces in that movie. The helmets were stamped with Saddam Hussein's face in profile, accompanied by the words "Allah, the Homeland, and the Leader."

Uday owned several media outlets, including a newspaper, *Babel*, and a television station, Youth TV. He had a food-processing company, Super Chicken, and an ice-cream company, The Wave. His biggest millions came from smuggling, during the days of U.N. sanctions on his father's regime.

Uday was like other dictator's sons in his personal tastes and hobbies, too. He had a private zoo, stocked with lions, cheetahs, and other such specimens. He also enjoyed hunting animals from helicopters over the desert. He liked cars—fast cars, luxury cars. He owned over a thousand of them. To the polls one day, he drove a pink Rolls-Royce. To the *polls*? Yes. On a couple of occasions, Saddam staged a referendum on his rule. On this particular day—when Uday drove the pink Rolls—Saddam won by a vote of 100 percent to zero. And there was a 100 percent turnout. Papa Doc could not have done better.

The following will seem very familiar to you: Uday would cause any number of car accidents, and face no consequences at all. So it has been with many dictator's sons. He had thousands of bottles of very expensive wine and liquor, and "mountains of pornography," as one news account had it after the fall of the regime. Moreover, he engaged in rape, torture, and murder. This is all business as usual, or at least recognizable business, where dictator's sons are concerned.

But Uday was worse—probably much worse—than the others. Looking on, Vasily Stalin might have shuddered. Hannibal Qaddafi might have blanched. About Nicu Ceaușescu, I wrote, "I could fill pages with appalling details." One could fill more with details about Uday. One obituary described him as "Caligula-like"—which may be unfair to Caligula. Uday had a name for himself, "Abu Sarhan," The Wolf.

He raped anyone and everyone. He raped constantly. His goons would kidnap girls and women for him. He would simply point them out. He kidnapped and raped the daughters of ordinary men, of course. But he kidnapped and raped the daughters—including the underage daughters—of powerful men, too. For example, the governors of provinces. No one in Iraq could stop Uday, except for one man: the dictator. Uday would crash weddings, abducting the bride. One groom killed himself on the spot. Another time, Uday kidnapped and raped a newly-wed on her honeymoon. Afterward, she threw herself off a balcony, in shame. One time, a girl had the audacity to complain about being raped and beaten. Uday "had her covered with honey and torn apart by hungry dogs," in the words of one news report.

I mention these things—which maybe I should not—not because they are extraordinary or sensational, but because they were routine.

Uday had a passion for torture, and he may have had an addiction to it. Not content with pumping a bullet through a man's head, he would have to drill holes through that head. He took special pleasure in mutilation. He cut off body parts whenever he could. Torture, for him, had to become ever more imaginative. He grew bored with routine torture. He dropped people into acid baths. He even owned an iron maiden, the medieval torture device. It was no *objet d'art*. After the fall of the regime, a news report said that the iron maiden "was clearly worn from use, its nails having lost some of their sharpness."

Uday was well known for torturing athletes when he thought they had underperformed. Vasily was not nice to athletes: He jailed them, for example. Uday was more likely to throw them off a bridge. He had athletes dragged through gravel and then immersed in sewage. He had them beaten to death. One time, he made soccer players kick around a concrete ball. If that was the worst that happened to them, they were lucky.

Of course, Uday simply killed whomever he wanted killed, in ways gruesome or straightforward. He had that sort of license. Sometimes he would order his men to do the killing, but often he did it himself. One aspect of his terror was the sheer randomness of it. (Same with his father, from whom he learned.) You never quite knew what would set him off, or ignite his passion. He was psychotic (like his father). Even his entourage had to be nervous, always. No one was spared his caprice, or psychosis.

He had a huge collection of videotapes featuring himself. These were singular, often shocking home movies. When his palaces were ransacked, the movies were found and watched. I wish to quote at length from a *Newsweek* report, because it describes the atmosphere in which Uday moved, or that he created:

One of the most memorable tapes is of a birthday celebration. When the drunken Uday becomes bored with sullen dancing girls, he pulls out a machine gun and starts shooting in the air in time with the beat from the band. When that palls, he fires at champagne bottles with his pistol and orders one of his flunkies to throw beer bottles in the air for him to shoot at with an assault rifle. For fun, he aims a few rounds over the heads of his guests, some of whom throw themselves on the ground in terror, only to arise laughing and clapping at the prank, and, no doubt, in relief at still being alive. Uday then finishes off the party by shooting directly over the heads of the band members, who, amazingly, keep playing. The keyboard player crouches behind his instrument, still pounding the keys, as Uday shoots up the HAPPY BIRTHDAY sign hung at head level across the stage. When he runs out of bullets, Uday shakes hands with the frightened singer, and just to show he's a good sport, tells the keyboard player: "See all those holes? All those bullets could be in your belly." Then he laughs.

We will turn now to the dictator's second son, Qusay. He was "more low-key" than his brother, as people say. Less flamboyant. The critic Harry Haun, reviewing a movie based on Uday's life, called Qusay "a relative Goody-Two-Shoes." That may be, but the word "relative" should be stressed. Qusay was Saddam Hussein's son, and he did plenty of torturing and murdering (though rape was evidently not a predilection or practice).

Qusay was born two years after Uday, in 1966. He, too, went to the University of Baghdad, studying law. Thereafter he rose in his father's regime. He idolized his father, mimicking him in dress, speech, and everything else. He became head of the top intelligence service—the Special Security Organization—and the Republican Guard. He was instrumental in the crushing of rebellion after the Gulf War in 1991. He oversaw the destruction of the famous southern marshlands—and with them the Marsh Arabs and their way of life.

Qusay married a girl named Sahar, with whom he had three sons. Uday married either once or twice. The marriage or marriages were brief, in any case. He was a wife-beater, unsurprisingly. There were apparently no children. Uday is said to have hated Qusay, the more respectable of the two boys. But they lived, killed, and died together, as we will see.

October 18, 1988, was an important day in Uday's life. It was an important day in Kamel Hana Gegeo's, too. Gegeo was the valet of Saddam Hussein. He was possibly Saddam's favorite servant. Gegeo was the son of a cook and a governess in the dictator's service. On the day in question, the vice president of Iraq, Taha Muhie-eldin Marouf, held a party in honor of the first lady of Egypt, Suzanne Mubarak (wife of Hosni). Gegeo was a guest at the party. But Uday was not. He crashed the party and killed Gegeo, in front of one and all. He clubbed him to death, or carved him up with an electric carving knife, or kicked him to death, or carved him up with an electric rose pruner. There are many accounts. What is known for sure is that he killed him. Why?

Gegeo apparently introduced Saddam Hussein to a woman named Samira Shahbandar, who became the dictator's mistress, and then his wife. Saddam wed Samira without ever divorcing his original wife, Sajida. Gegeo was thought to have facilitated trysts between his boss and Samira (as a good valet would). Uday resented this. He was loyal to his mother, yes, and his mother may well have put him up to the killing.

The dictator and his boys:
Uday on the left, Qusay on the right

But he was also worried about his own position: How would this new relationship, this new marriage, affect his chances of succeeding the old man as dictator? Would his father and Samira have children? And was Gegeo, so close to his father, a threat to him—to Uday, that is?

Saddam Hussein was absolutely furious at his son's murder of Gegeo. Indeed, he had a murderous fury. Some thought that he might kill Uday. To the people of Iraq, Saddam told an interesting story. It's interesting that he felt the need to address them at all. Dictators seldom air dirty laundry.

He told them that Uday had killed Gegeo when trying to get the valet to quiet down. Gegeo was firing his gun at a villa near the presidential palace, you see. Uday ordered him to stop. The valet defied him—whereupon the dictator's son killed him. Saddam said that Uday was in jail (which was true), pending a judicial investigation. He said that Uday, distraught, had tried to kill himself three times. (His ineptitude would have been odd. He rarely failed to kill others.) Saddam said, "It is my constitutional responsibility to enforce justice in the society ... and that does not exempt anyone."

Immediately, there was a campaign to spare the young man. The victim's parents—the cook and the governess—pleaded for clemency.

That was big of them. In a letter published in all the state newspapers, the father—or someone writing in the father's name—asked for the judicial investigation to be called off. The murder of his son, he said, was "an act of fate and the will of God that could not have been avoided." Also weighing in was King Hussein, from neighboring Jordan. He urged the Iraqi dictator to go easy on Uday. There had to be a cooling-off period, he said.

As near as can be determined, Saddam kept his son in jail for 40 days. Then he exiled him to Switzerland, where Uday was to serve as an assistant to the Iraqi ambassador. Predictably, Uday spent his days drinking and brawling. The Swiss tired of his presence, and expelled him in 1990. His father welcomed him back into the bosom of the regime.

A word about the femme fatale, Saddam's mistress and second wife: Samira. She was from an old and distinguished Baghdad family, unlike Saddam, who was a ruffian from the sticks. He may have admired her respectability. When the two met, she was married, to an official at Iraqi Airways. According to one account, Saddam had the husband kidnapped and refused to release him until he agreed to divorce his wife. The man, with a laudable instinct for survival, did so. In compensation, Saddam made him the director of the airline. He also offered him his choice of former mistresses—the dictator's former mistresses.

Some speculate that Saddam and Samira had a son, Ali. They also speculate that Saddam took two more wives, making four altogether. Neither of these things can be confirmed.

Back to the murder of Gegeo: Saddam Hussein was so enraged by this, as you know, that some wondered whether he would kill Uday. Uday's mother was one of them. Sajida apparently asked her brother, Adnan, to intervene with Saddam. Adnan was a cousin whom Saddam was raised with. They had long been brothers-in-law, as well as cousins. Adnan was a general, and Iraq's defense minister. He and the dictator were so close, some regarded him as a likely successor.

Adnan talked to Saddam about Uday and the murder of Gegeo. He also, evidently, expressed his displeasure at the marriage to Samira—which had humiliated his sister. Saddam was not one to take criticism, no matter how gently expressed or well intended. In May 1989, Adnan died in a mysterious helicopter crash. The crash was no mystery, really:

Saddam had him killed, almost certainly. This was a blow to Sajida, among other people.

Saddam and Sajida had three daughters: Raghad, Rana, and Hala. They were born in 1968, 1969, and 1972, respectively. Hala seems to have had two husbands—the second of whom was a general named Kamel Mustafa. Raghad and Rana were married to two brothers. These brothers, their husbands, were cousins of their father's. They were Hussein Kamel and Saddam Kamel.

Let's not be tripped up by names, if we can help it: The dictator was Saddam Hussein; the first son-in-law was Hussein Kamel; and the second son-in-law was Saddam Kamel. I will occasionally refer to the sons-in-law as "the Kamels" (as I will refer to Uday and Qusay as "the Husseins").

If the dictator was capable of love, he loved Hussein Kamel, his cousin and son-in-law. Some people say that Hussein Kamel was like a son to him. You even hear that Hussein Kamel, early in Saddam's reign, saved the dictator's life. This cannot be confirmed. But the dictator gave Hussein Kamel his firstborn daughter, Raghad, to marry. That couple went on to have five children—three sons and two daughters. The other couple, Rana and Saddam (Saddam Kamel), had four children—three sons and a daughter.

The dictator promoted Hussein Kamel speedily. The young man was a general, and in charge of Iraq's WMD program. That is, he presided over the dictator's chemical, biological, and nuclear weapons. Hussein Kamel was obviously a candidate to be the next dictator. His brother, Saddam Kamel, did pretty well himself. He was a colonel and the head of special forces protecting the dictatorship.

As you can well imagine, the Hussein brothers, Uday and Qusay, hated the Kamel brothers, their brothers-in-law. They especially hated Hussein Kamel, the senior brother. And the primary hater was Uday. He must have hated Hussein Kamel more than Maher Assad hated *his* brother-in-law, Assef Shawkat. You recall that Maher shot Shawkat. Uday did not go so far as that, but a ferocious fistfight broke out between him and Hussein Kamel in 1992, at an official ceremony. Those who had attended talked about it for a long time after.

Over the years, the Hussein brothers and the Kamel brothers competed for power. The dictator, the master manipulator, must have enjoyed this competition, to a degree. Eventually, the Husseins gained the upper hand. More and more, the dictator trusted his own sons. The sons-in-law lost favor with him. Uday could smell victory.

It all came to a head in August 1995. There was a party and there was Uday—so, naturally, there was violence. A news report put it this way: "Believing he had been insulted, [Uday] opened fire with a submachine gun, accidentally killing several Gypsy dancers and wounding his uncle Watban, a former interior minister, in the leg." Forget the dead dancers, who were nothing to the clan-centered regime: Uday shot his uncle in the leg so many times, it had to be amputated. The Kamel brothers now thought that the Hussein brothers could kill them. Kill them with impunity. They particularly thought that Uday could, and would, kill them. So they made a run for it.

They ran to Jordan. Later, Rana would say that the husbands informed the wives—the dictator's daughters—only the night before. The wives duly followed the husbands. The pretext was, everyone was going to take a flight to Bulgaria, leaving from the Jordanian capital, Amman. The Kamel brothers formed a convoy including Mercedes sedans, GM pickup trucks, and military vehicles. There were about 30 in the party: the Kamels, their wives, their children, and assorted army officers. They went through the desert unimpeded. General Kamel would later explain, "I am a known personality, and I don't think that a checkpoint of a few soldiers would dare to stop me."

Arriving in Jordan, the Kamels and their wives went straight to the royal palace, asking King Hussein for asylum. He granted it. King Hussein knew all about Iraq's first family, especially the firstborn son, Uday. The king told an Israeli journalist, understatedly, "I think it might have been a family crisis."

Saddam Hussein dispatched Uday to Amman, to meet with King Hussein. The meeting was brief. Uday demanded that the defectors and traitors be returned. The king said no. Saddam also dispatched agents to kill the Kamel brothers. Their plan was thwarted. In Washington, President Bill Clinton vowed to protect Jordan from any retaliation by Saddam Hussein. He said that the king's decision to shelter the fleeing Iraqis was "an act of real courage."

At a press conference, General Kamel said there would be repercussions back in Iraq, following his group's defection. "It is natural that a lot of people, not within the ruling family, will be randomly apprehended.

Also, there are going to be executions." He would have known. And he was undoubtedly correct. Furthermore, General Kamel vowed to overthrow his father-in-law's regime. "We will work inside Iraq and the whole Arab world to topple the regime of Saddam."

The family was sheltered at a fortified farm in Naour, about 20 miles from Amman. The general sang to Western powers, including the United States. In other words, he told them what he knew about Iraq's WMD program. That should have been everything.

If we can credit Saddam Hussein with having feelings, the dictator was shaken by this defection—not just by the defection of his daughters and grandchildren, but by the defection of Hussein Kamel. "The sudden departure of his son-in-law," writes Joseph Sassoon, "was a severe blow to Saddam Hussein, who always had a soft spot for him, had relied on him, and had trusted his judgment." Elsewhere in his book, Sassoon writes that the dictator was "deeply hurt" when Kamel defected, "and many who knew him or worked with him detected changes in his personality: he became more paranoid and less trusting, more inclined to solitude and less interested in detail."

Over in Jordan, things were not going well for General Kamel. He had expected to be a hero in the world at large, for his daring stance against Saddam Hussein. He at least expected to be appreciated and thanked. But he was soon isolated, and in a corner.

Some doubted that his defection was authentic. Maybe it was a ruse instead. Could this son-in-law of Saddam's, who was so close to him, really have abandoned the regime and turned against it? Plus, the brothers had taken their wives and children with them. That was suspicious. You don't just wrest the dictator's family from him. Also, Iraqi exiles in opposition were reluctant to work with General Kamel. He had so much blood on his hands. He had been a major cog in the killing machine, after all.

With King Hussein, he had a falling-out. Criticism of the king by Hussein Kamel had reached the royal ears. The general was wearing out his welcome in Jordan. By Western countries, he was denied asylum. Maybe worse, the wives and children were restless. The wives were bored; the children were homesick. One and all wanted to go home, except, surely, the Kamel brothers. General Kamel was sick with worry, experiencing a breakdown. The pressure must have been tremendous.

And relief was offered in the form of a pardon. Saddam Hussein promised that the brothers could come home, with no penalty. Evidently, Sajida traveled to Jordan to issue a personal guarantee. It was now February 1996, six months after the group's defection. On behalf of everyone, General Kamel made the fateful decision to return home. In a final gesture, King Hussein provided a fleet of limousines.

The regime in Baghdad announced that a pardon had been granted. It said that the brothers would be treated like "ordinary Iraqi citizens." In a sense, they were. They had defied and betrayed Saddam Hussein, and they were killed.

Not immediately, though. It took three days. The limousines arrived at the Jordanian-Iraqi border shortly after midnight on February 21. Uday was there to meet the family. He separated the wives from their husbands.

In Baghdad, the men were ushered in to see the dictator. He forced them to sign papers divorcing their wives. He ripped the epaulets from their uniforms. And he told them to go to their father's villa. The women, for their part, went to their father, the dictator, to ask his forgiveness. He said he would give it—to them, but not to their husbands, or ex-husbands. Them, he could not forgive.

Drunk with revenge—literally drunk, and mad for revenge—Saddam sicced a small army on the villa where the Kamels were ensconced. A battle raged for hours. Two of Saddam's men were killed (and later given state honors). But everyone in the villa was killed, most certainly including the onetime defectors. Watching from a car were Uday and Qusay. Uday is reported to have spat on Hussein Kamel's corpse.

Two and a half months later, Saddam Hussein spoke about these killings. He said he had not wished them. He had forgiven his former sons-in-law. But the men's own clan—their extended family—could not keep from killing them, to wipe the stain from the common honor. They had not consulted him, said Saddam. If they had, he would have forbidden the killings. All of this was a lie. But another statement was not. Speaking about Hussein Kamel, the dictator said, "The hurt caused by this particular person is much larger than the hurt caused by many others who have betrayed us before, and those who will betray us after."

Some eight years later, the two daughters, Raghad and Rana, gave a remarkable interview to Hala Jaber, a correspondent for the (London)

Sunday Times. They recalled the events of 1995 and '96. Rana said that, when the news of the revenge killings came, the daughters' mother, Sajida, was stricken. "I recall seeing my mother suddenly bend over as if a huge weight had just landed on her shoulders, as she tried to hold our hands and control us. 'My daughters' catastrophe has broken my back,' she repeated over and over again. My mother never looked the same from that day on."

Rana herself collapsed on a sofa. "I stayed like that for the next seven days," she told Jaber, "unable to talk, eat, or drink. All I did was breathe and cry." Her former self had died. Gone forever was "the spoiled daughter" without responsibilities, and "the loved wife" whose every wish had been her husband's command.

Raghad, the older daughter, chose her words very carefully. She made herself clear enough, though. "If I told you that what happened was correct or acceptable, I would not be accurate. Our leaving the country in that manner [i.e., the defection] was wrong regardless of the reasons. Running away from a problem was not the correct way." But: "The outcome of the return was 100 percent wrong." The family's problems could have been resolved "in a different manner," by which Raghad meant: other than by killing.

She defended her father while saying she was not defending him. Saddam's decision to kill his daughters' husbands, she said, was "influenced by many hateful people who carried no love for the family.... This is not to defend or justify my father and the decision he made, or felt forced to make, at the time. But this is the truth."

Was Raghad upset with her father, for the murder of her husband (and her sister's)? Or was her devotion to her father too great to allow for that? Her reaction, she said, was "a normal one, which left me angry for several years." But the passage of time dissipated that anger, and she saw the killings in a bigger picture. She said that she sympathized with the difficulties faced by her father. Raghad sounded a lot like Edda Mussolini Ciano, who needed to come to terms with her own husband's death at the hands of her own father.

On February 25, 1996, two days after the killing of the Kamel boys, an Associated Press report went around the world. Referring to the dictator, the headline in one paper was "Hussein Proves He's in Charge; Killings May Lead to Iraqi Dynasty." The last line of the article was,

"Now that [Hussein Kamel] has been eliminated, Uday Hussein's path to power is apparently clear."

Yet something happened later that year—in December 1996: Uday, the scourge of Iraq, was shot. He was shot eight times, in an assassination attempt. While driving his Porsche, he was set upon by two gunmen. They disappeared, never to be found. And many people—hundreds of people—were killed by the regime in an effort to find them. Thousands more were arrested.

Any number of people could have taken a shot at Uday. Any number of people had a motive. These people included the uncle, Watban Ibrahim, who lost a leg to Uday, at the party before the Kamels' defection. They included the family of Uday's former wife, or the families of his former wives, whom he abused. They included the families of the countless girls and women he raped, tortured, or killed. They also included whatever associates of the Kamels remained. Uday placed his sisters Raghad and Rana under house arrest for a while.

He was partially paralyzed by the bullets. One remained lodged in his spine. He recovered sufficiently to walk with a cane. After the fall of the regime, investigators found 193 canes among his possessions, half of those canes sliding open to become swords or guns. It should be said, even for the monster Uday, that he endured great physical pain, in the final years of his life. Not as great as the pain he inflicted, however.

There was no question of his succeeding his father now. He was more unstable, more psychotic, than ever. Even Saddam saw this. Ceauşescu knew that Nicu was too crazy (or too drunk) to succeed him; Hafez Assad probably knew that Maher was out of the question. Saddam recognized that Uday was too damaged. So people assumed that the heir was Qusay, the No. 2 son. Qusay took over some of Uday's jobs, such as the leadership of the Saddam Fedayeen.

And yet Saddam made a fascinating statement about succession. He made it to American interrogators, after his capture. He said that he had not drawn up a plan for succession. He made no promises to Qusay or anyone else. For one thing, he saw what happened in Oman in 1970: The prince, Qaboos, became sultan after staging a coup against his own father. Saddam did not want his sons, either of them, to grow too powerful. He did not want to leave himself vulnerable. He was no dummy, and trusted no one.

He survived the first big war against him: the Gulf War. He had invaded and occupied Kuwait, and the Americans and their allies expelled him from Kuwait. But they left him on the throne in Baghdad. The second big war, the Iraq War, came in March 2003. The Americans and their allies toppled the regime in about three weeks. The dictator and his men scattered, going on the lam.

The Americans drew up a Most Wanted list. No. 1 on it was Saddam Hussein. Nos. 2 and 3 were Qusay and Uday. If Uday knew that he was listed behind his brother, it must have bothered him. No. 10 was Saddam's only surviving son-in-law: General Kamel Mustafa Abdullah Sultan al-Tikriti, the husband of Saddam and Sajida's third daughter, Hala. He turned himself over to enemy forces in May.

It took these forces a few months to catch up with Uday and Qusay—who had commandeered a home in the northern city of Mosul. In all probability, the owner of the home tipped off the Americans. After a four-hour battle, the brothers were dead. So were one of their bodyguards and Qusay's eldest son, Mustafa (age about 14). The Americans displayed the corpses of Uday and Qusay, which rubbed many in the West the wrong way: They thought that this act was ghoulishly exhibitionistic and triumphalist. American authorities thought it was necessary for Iraqi peace of mind: People could know that these scourges were at last well and truly dead. Some thought it was too good to be true anyway.

Most believed it, however—and the celebration across the nation was deafening. Many people died in this wave of relief and jubilation, because Iraqis fired their guns in the air, as Arabs have long done when celebrating. Bullets that go up, come down, and sometimes kill people. Writing in the *Telegraph* eight years later, Colin Freeman remembered the night that news of the boys' death came: "The Iraqi capital erupted with so much gunfire that I thought a full-scale insurrection had broken out; by contrast, the celebrations when Saddam was caught five months later were more muted." Saddam's Iraq was called, in the title of a famous book by Kanan Makiya, the "Republic of Fear." A significant part of that fear was instilled by Uday and Qusay.

Where were their sisters? Hala was thought to have fled to the Gulf—Qatar—hours before the war began. Mother Sajida was thought to have fled with her. As for Raghad and Rana, they stayed in Iraq until late July, when their brothers were dead. They did not live in their usual style or places, however. They had to lie low. In June, Raghad talked on the phone to the *Sunday Times*: "I spend my days cooking typical Iraqi food, washing dishes, doing housework, laundry. I do things I never did in the past because since I was a child we always had maids, housekeepers, and lived in big houses with swimming pools." She said she did not venture out much. "I don't like the situation, the American troops everywhere, seeing the statues of my father broken, his pictures torn down. You can imagine how I feel."

Yes, we can. In this period, Raghad and Rana were working out where to run to, when the time came to do it. Raghad said, "All I want is to be able to live peacefully, with no fear and nobody asking us any awkward questions." How many other Iraqis must have felt that way, in the 35 years of Saddam's rule?

When Raghad and Rana ran, they ran to Jordan—again. They had been defectors there seven years before. At that time, King Hussein granted them asylum. Now he was dead and one of his sons was on the throne as Abdullah II. He, too, granted the girls asylum. His spokesman said, "They are Arab women who have run out of all options." The women were in a talkative mood. Asked by CNN whether she had a message for her father, Raghad said, "I love you and I miss you." Rana praised her dad in the following fashion: "He had so many feelings and he was very tender with all of us. Usually the daughter is close to her mother, but we would usually go to him. He was our friend."

At the end of the year—December 13, 2003—Saddam was captured. The tyrant was "dragged from his spider hole," as world media said. Hala Jaber asked Raghad what she had always loved most about her father. Raghad answered, "I mostly loved his humanity and endless care, but, in order for me not to sound critical of those opposed to his politics, I should add that at least that was how he was towards us."

She was now the oldest surviving child. And, from Jordan, she led a campaign in her father's behalf. She pleaded for his release. She organized his legal team (on which Moammar Qaddafi's daughter Aisha served, as you recall). Raghad was seen as a loyal daughter and an Arab Pasionaria. She told an Arab newspaper that, in court, her father was acting like "a lion." She herself was a lioness, from the point of view of Saddam partisans.

In April 2006, she sat for an interview with al-Arabiya, the Saudi-owned TV network. The interviewer asked an extraordinarily difficult question: "Are you prepared for another tragedy?" In other words, was Raghad prepared to see her father put to death? She answered, "This is the toughest question a daughter could be asked about her father. This is the toughest question I could be asked. My father is dear to me, even more than my children. I can tell you that he is definitely more dear to me than my children.... All I can say is that it is Allah's decision."

Before the year was out, on December 30, Saddam Hussein swung.

Nine days later, the second-oldest daughter, Rana, poured out her heart to Hala Jaber. "No mother will ever produce a hero like him for a long, long time. My loss is enormous and nothing will substitute for it. It is bigger than the loss of my two brothers, for he was my only hope and it was from him that I gained my strength."

Not much has been heard from Rana since that time (and Hala, the third sister, was always an unknown quantity in the family). Raghad, however, has been a semi-public figure. She lives the high life in Amman, the life of a filthy-rich exile. She is the ex-princess of a dictatorship, or the princess of an ex-dictatorship. She is a rather chic lady, a fashion-plate. She looks like her father, especially in the eyes, which flash and glower. She has a penchant for designer shoes and handbags and other luxury items. One of her favorite shops in her adoptive city is Boutique de France. By all reports, she is none too polite with staff. She is still the dictator's daughter.

And while I am in the mode of gossip, I should say about Raghad what I said, chapters ago, about Carmen Franco: She is a frequent customer of the plastic surgeons.

She also took up jewelry design. In 2015, she came out with a ten-piece collection, described by a newspaper as "nostalgic." A bracelet was inspired by a gift from her father. A pair of earrings was inspired by a gift from her husband, Hussein Kamel. Edda-style, she carries both of these men in her heart.

Most important, she has taken on a political role, emerging as the defender of the Saddam Hussein legacy. She is the keeper of her father's flame. Indeed, Raghad is called "Little Saddam," and she has earned the name. After her father's execution, she was an enthusiast for the insurgents against the Iraqi government. She was also, allegedly, a funder of them. The same charge was made against her mother, Sajida, in Qatar. Both of them were wanted by the Iraqi government as fugitive criminals. The government requested their extradition. Neither Jordan nor Qatar coughed up its guest.

When the Islamic State—also known as ISIS or ISIL—seized swaths of territory in 2014, Raghad was exultant. "I am happy to see all these victories," she said. Interpol issued a warrant for her arrest, on the grounds of "inciting terrorism in Iraq." *Der Spiegel* dubbed her "Terrorpatin," or "Terror Godmother." There is no question that Saddam would be proud, and that his daughter would be proud of that pride.

In the days after Saddam's hanging, David Jones of the *Daily Mail* talked with Raghad's personal assistant, Rasha Oudeh, who made a comment about Saddam's family—"perhaps recklessly," as Jones noted. The assistant said, "They are strange people, so strange. They can murder each other, and other people, and they can be extraordinarily gentle with one another."

At the same point in time, Hala Jaber asked Raghad herself whether she might have wished for a different life. Yes, said Raghad. She could imagine a life in which her mother had remained an elementary-school teacher and her father had become "a simple lawyer." (He attended law school for a while.) Then she could have grown up "in a normal way, far from all the greediness and problems that power and leadership bring." The seven of them, five children and two parents, "would then have been the happiest family, enduring only what others endure." Svetlana Stalin, you remember, often said that she wished her mother had married a carpenter.

Raghad said that she hoped none of her children—five of Saddam Hussein's grandchildren—would ever get near politics or power. So far, no grandchild of Saddam's has loomed on the horizon.

15

KHOMEINI

Before there was the Iraq War or Gulf War, there was the Iran–Iraq War. It was fought from 1980 until 1988. Even now, it's hard to say who won. Definitely not winning were the million or so dead. Saddam Hussein commanded Iraq; his counterpart in Iran was the ayatollah Khomeini—who had seven children, five of whom survived infancy. That is the consensus of biographers and other students of Iran. As so often with dictators and their families, the facts are a little muddy. In any event, there were five Khomeini children beyond doubt.

The first and last of them were boys. Each of those served as primary aide to his father. Each of the two died relatively young, under circumstances deemed suspicious. From his five children, Khomeini had many grandchildren, some of whom became critics of the regime he established, one of whom became an outright champion of freedom and democracy. That man lives in Iran, and he is not in prison, apparently. But he is under close surveillance, and muzzled.

Ruhollah Khomeini led the Iranian revolution—a revolution of fundamentalist Shiite Islam—which overthrew the shah in 1979. The shah had ruled Iran since 1941, styling himself the "king of kings." Khomeini was the "supreme leader," and for life. "Life" turned out to be ten years: Khomeini died in 1989, a decade after his revolution. He set up a regime that far surpassed the shah's in brutality. For these several decades, Iran has been a horrifying example of totalitarianism, theocratic branch.

There is some doubt about Khomeini's birth year, but he seems to have been born in 1902. He was the son and grandson of mullahs (i.e., scholars and expounders of the sacred law). Khomeini himself became a mullah—and an ayatollah, and a grand ayatollah. Ultimately, he was known simply as "the Imam." In 1929, he married Khadijeh Saqafi, the daughter of a prominent cleric. The bride was 16, her groom 27. By all accounts, they had a solid and happy marriage. Their children, particularly their daughters, would always say how kindly their father treated their mother. One daughter said that she never heard her father so much as ask his wife to bring him a glass of water. He performed such tasks himself.

The first child, Mostafa, was born in 1930. (He was named after Khomeini's father.) The fifth and last child, Ahmad, was born in 1945. (He was named after one of Khomeini's grandfathers.) In between came the three girls: Zahra, Sadiqeh, and Farideh. The daughters describe a gentle and tolerant father, though stern and inflexible when it came to religion. In 2009, Zahra said that Khomeini often played hide-and-seek with his kids, "taking care to protect the younger children more, hiding them under covers." Zahra remembers just one argument between her parents: over a rubber ball that Khadijeh had bought for Ahmad. Khomeini did not think that the boy should have something so frivolous and distracting.

In July 1989, a month after Khomeini died, Zahra did some reminiscing for the *Sunday Times*. Her father was a dad, yes, but he was also the ayatollah. An illustration: "If I wanted to play at a house, and he knew there was a boy there, he would say, 'Don't go there, play at home.' You couldn't say, 'Come on, Dad, let me go,' because what he said was based on Islam, not on his own opinion." A very interesting bit of testimony came from Ahmad's wife, Fatemeh. Khomeini once told Ahmad, "I love you because you are obedient toward God. If you stand against God, I will stand against you. And if it is necessary according to the law, I will even send for your executioner." This might be interpreted as mere parental hyperbole. But chances are, Khomeini meant every word.

At the beginning of 1963, the shah embarked on his "white revolution," a series of reforms including the emancipation of women and the opening of certain governmental posts to non-Muslims. This program, Khomeini could not abide. He launched a campaign against the shah. The shah abided this for several months, then had Khomeini arrested. The arrest occurred in the first week of June, in the holy city of Qom, Khomeini's base. The shah's agents came in the middle of the night, as such agents so often do. Khomeini's elder son, Mostafa, then in his early thirties, was at his side.

The story of the dark-of-night arrest of Khomeini is interesting and dramatic. There are several versions. In his 1985 biography of Khomeini, Amir Taheri says that, as Khomeini was trundled off, Mostafa ran from rooftop to rooftop, shouting, "Oh, people of Islam, wake up!" He then threatened to jump unless the agents released his father. Khomeini told him to calm down and return home. Baqer Moin, in his 1999 biography, writes,

> From the roof top Mostafa saw his father being taken away, and his first instinct was to jump on the car to prevent it from moving off. But his father chided him with a movement of his hand as one of the commandos took out his revolver and aimed it at Mostafa, shouting: "If you move I will fire." The helpless Mostafa could only cry out to the sleeping city: "Oh people, they have taken Khomeini away," but by this time the car was already on its way to Tehran.

The car, by the way, was a Volkswagen Beetle.

In Tehran, Khomeini was briefly imprisoned, then confined to house arrest. In April 1964, he was allowed to return to Qom. There, he resumed his campaign against the government. In November, the shah had him arrested for a final time, and exiled him.

He went to Turkey. On arrival, he wrote to Mostafa, giving several instructions and telling him to be nice to his mother, brother, and sisters. Mostafa needed the admonition; he was a bit of a hothead. Khomeini did not want Mostafa to join him in exile. He wanted him to stay in Iran and represent the cause, so to speak. Mostafa, like his father, was a mullah, and a revolutionary.

Mostafa soon showed up in Turkey, though, and was greeted by a stern question from his father: "Did you come or did they bring you?"

Have you come of your own free will or were you forced out? Mostafa explained that he had been arrested and exiled, just like his father. The father was relieved. He told his son, "If you had come voluntarily, I would have told you to go back."

The son was quite different from the father. They were mullahs and revolutionaries, of course. Both wanted to impose theocracy on Iran. But the father was disciplined to the point of fanaticism—in his diet, exercise, and so on. He kept the strictest of schedules. Probably the word most applied to Khomeini, in English, is "austere." Mostafa was volatile and self-indulgent. He liked to eat. In fact, one of the Khomeinis' hosts in Turkey called him a "glutton." And yet, Mostafa was dear to Khomeini. The son was his father's "inseparable companion," as Amir Taheri writes. Khomeini called Mostafa "the light of my eyes."

In October 1965, the Khomeinis went from Turkey to Iraq, which would be the main country of their exile. They lived in Najaf—like Qom, a holy city to Shiite Muslims. In due course, Khomeini summoned other family members, including Ahmad, his younger son. Now he had both boys at his side.

Ahmad was another mullah. And he and his brother of course had things in common. But they had distinct personalities. Mostafa was filled with religious fervor and political zeal (which, in the revolutionary cause, amounted to the same thing). Ahmad was more relaxed, the kind to enjoy sports and novels. (His mother had done well to choose a ball for him.) But Ahmad was not a live-and-let-live liberal. He was a full and apparently eager participant in the family business. He underwent military training with the Palestine Liberation Organization in Lebanon.

Some 13 years into the Khomeini exile—on October 23, 1977, specifically—something curious happened: Mostafa died. He was 46. Immediately, the revolutionaries said that SAVAK killed him. SAVAK was the shah's secret police. But Khomeini never said that SAVAK killed his son. He never called his son a martyr. Nor did he permit an autopsy. Similarly, Ahmad never said that his brother had been the victim of foul play. Probably, Mostafa died of a heart attack. Some say that he drank too much or ate too much. Some say that he had a drug problem. What is certain is that the revolution made great use of his death. Khomeini said that his son's death was nothing less than a gift of God.

Memorial services were held all over Iran. The biggest one, in Tehran, drew more than 3,000 people. These events were as much political rallies as memorial services. Khomeini's followers seized the occasion to renew their denunciations of the government. In Iraq, Khomeini received photos showing the crowds. He studied them with keen interest. They showed the strength of his movement. In death, Mostafa Khomeini was dubbed the "Morning Star of the Revolution," alternatively the "Dawn of the Revolution."

It was now Ahmad, the remaining son, who became Khomeini's top aide and inseparable companion. He had always been in Mostafa's shadow—a typical little brother. Now he was all Khomeini had (given that the father could not countenance his daughters' participation in politics). A year after Mostafa's death, in October 1978, they went to a third country of exile: France. They had worn out their welcome in Iraq. The man who gave Khomeini the boot was Saddam Hussein, who was not yet formally boss of Baathist Iraq, but informally, yes.

The Khomeinis flew to Paris, settling in the suburb of Neauphle-le-Château. Paris was not exactly a holy city for the ayatollah, and neither was little Neauphle-le-Château. But he was not there to soak up French culture. He was there to bide his time. And, in January 1979, a mere three months after his arrival in France, his time came.

Rocked by revolution, the shah left on January 16. Khomeini returned to Tehran in triumph on February 1. As supreme leader for life, he imposed his will on Iran, although he interpreted his will as God's will. Khomeini achieved the status of a demi-god. He enjoys that status still, among Iran's revolutionary believers.

On assuming power, Khomeini and his men imprisoned, tortured, and killed more people than the shah and SAVAK ever dreamed of doing. The shah had built Evin Prison, the notorious facility in northwestern Tehran. But it took Khomeini and his gang to make full and terrifying use of it. Evin was a seat of brutality. Rape was a constant tool. According to Marina Nemat, 90 percent of Evin's prisoners in the early 1980s were under the age of 20. "It was the high school from hell," she jokes, darkly. She herself is a survivor of Evin. The prison is still operating, and in the same way—"Evin" is a byword for terror in Iran.

Ahmad's role in his father's regime was the same as his role in exile: top aide, right hand. He was the chief of staff, the gatekeeper,

Ahmad Khomeini

the screener—all of those words have been used to describe his role. If you wanted to see Khomeini, you had to go through Ahmad. Also, he was his father's eyes and ears, his contact with the world beyond his quarters.

In November 1979, approximately eleven months after the original, came the "second revolution," as Khomeini called it: the seizing of the American embassy by Khomeini-supporting students. The imam himself quickly blessed this act, and his regime held American personnel hostage for 444 days—until January 20, 1981, when Ronald Reagan was inaugurated in Washington, replacing President Jimmy Carter.

Ahmad was, naturally, Khomeini's liaison to the hostage-taking students. At first, the Americans expected Khomeini to set the situation straight. Maybe the embassy had been taken over by hotheads, whom the imam would cool down. Gary Sick, a national-security aide to Carter, would recollect the following: "It was with relief that we learned that Ahmad was on his way to the embassy. What we had not expected was that Ahmad would clamber excitedly over the embassy wall, losing his turban in the process, and congratulate the students for their action. As that fact became known, the deadly seriousness of the situation became apparent for the first time."

One of the hostages, Robert O. Blucker, also had a recollection of Ahmad. "He was fingering his worry beads and smiling and talking to them," meaning the captors. "He didn't want to look at any of us."

In that first month—November 1979—Khomeini decided to release two groups of hostages: women and blacks. There were 13 in these groups all together. (Fifty-three other hostages remained; the next summer, one of them would be released, for medical reasons.) Khomeini explained that Islam had a special respect for women. (Never mind that his people were raping, torturing, and killing them in Evin Prison and elsewhere.) He further explained that his regime regarded the black hostages as victims of America. The releasees were accompanied to the airport by Ahmad.

Across the Western media, Ahmad was usually portrayed as a "moderate," at least in the context of the Iranian revolution. In June 1980, *Newsweek* magazine published an article about him with a punny, and almost inevitable, headline: "The Son Also Rises." "Although he wears the robes and turban of a mullah," said the magazine, "he is believed to be one of the few voices of moderation among the Islamic fundamentalists who control Iran today." The magazine also used the phrase "comparatively enlightened."

When Khomeini became frail and sick, his son became more important to him than ever. The father leaned on the son for everything. With his eyesight failing, Khomeini had Ahmad read to him. Also reading to him were daughter Zahra and daughter-in-law Fatemeh (Ahmad's wife). Baqer Moin, in his biography, gives us a glimpse into the final days: "Fatemeh and Ahmad lived with Khomeini and he often took their children with him on his daily walks in the high-walled garden of his house in Jamaran," a community in the north of Tehran. "It was his only distraction from a heavy schedule."

Not content with being the imam's son—or merely the imam's son—Ahmad had great political ambition. Some thought he would succeed his father as supreme leader. He very much wanted to be prime minister (a less exalted position, to be sure). But he was blocked by no less a figure than his father—who made it clear to Ahmad that a high official position was not in the offing. Khomeini himself did not want to be involved in the day-to-day administration of Iran. He wanted to be the religious head, above the fray. He did not want any of his family involved, either. As Ali Alfoneh, a scholar of Iran, put it to me, "Khomeini instinctively knew that direct executive responsibility would make him and the family vulnerable to public criticism." Khomeini had a remarkable "sense of strategic management," as Alfoneh says.

In that 1980 *Newsweek* article, about the rising son, a Western diplomat in Tehran was quoted anonymously. "If the old man died tomorrow, Ahmad would become a quite insignificant mullah with a famous name."

That is exactly what happened. Ruhollah Khomeini died in June 1989, at the age of 86 (or thereabouts). His son was eased out of power, as a man with a similar name, Khamenei, became supreme leader. Ahmad was relegated to overseeing his father's mausoleum in the Paradise of Zahra, a cemetery of Tehran. He had some ceremonial posts in government as well. He served on advisory councils. But, again, these posts were ceremonial. Ahmad had fallen, and he resented this loss of status. He became a bitter critic of the regime's leaders. It is possible—many believe this—that he became a plotter against them, too.

He regularly issued statements, often of a strident nature. In 1991, after the Soviet empire had essentially collapsed, he spoke of the long-term battle against America, the Great Satan (as his father had characterized the country): "We should realize that the world is hostile to us only because of Islam. After the fall of Marxism, Islam replaced it, and as long as Islam exists, U.S. hostility exists, and as long as U.S. hostility exists, the struggle exists." Two years later, the PLO and Israel signed a peace agreement—which Ahmad condemned as "treachery to the aspirations of the Palestinian nation and the world of Islam." In February 1995, he gave a fiery speech marking the 16th anniversary of the Iranian revolution. Addressing America directly, he said, "Death to you!" The next month, on March 17, he himself died—and went into the mausoleum that he had overseen.

Why did he die, age 49? Officially, he died of a heart attack. He may have. He may also have been killed by the revolution's leaders, tired of his complaints and, possibly, plotting. The suspicions about Ahmad's death are far more credible than the suspicions about Mostafa's, which are scarcely credible at all. Put it this way: There are very well-informed and reasonable people who believe that Ahmad was murdered by his father's political heirs. In any case, his son Hassan became overseer of the mausoleum.

The ayatollah Khomeini had three daughters, as you know. The most prominent of them has been Zahra. Born in 1940, she is an academic, a professor of philosophy at the University of Tehran. She is also a political and civic leader. Zahra is the secretary-general of the Women's Society of the Islamic Republic of Iran. In addition, she leads two groups dedicated to Palestinian rights, or, more frankly, the destruction of Israel.

Her views are a mixture of the "liberal" and the "conservative," to use convenient though inadequate shorthand. She believes that women have a part to play in various aspects of Iranian society, including politics. "As with men," she has said, "their talents must be allowed to flourish." At the same time, she does not believe that women should be allowed to go without the hijab. Nor does she approve of any debate on the subject. "These are divine laws for men and women and should be observed. The hijab or covering of women immunizes them from abuse and protects families. If men know there is no question of anything outside the family, they will be more loyal to their wives." (Make of that what you will.)

In Iranian politics, she has supported candidates and other figures judged moderate or reformist. On Israel, she is irreconcilable. I will illustrate what I mean.

In 2002, she gave a speech to the women's auxiliary of Hezbollah, the Lebanese guerrillas, who are backed by the Iranian government. She said that "the late imam Khomeini" recognized no legitimacy in Israel at all, "presenting the only remedy to the Middle East crisis as the total and unquestionable annihilation of Israel." In 2006, after Hezbollah triggered a war against Israel, Zahra sent a letter to the group's leader, Hassan Nasrallah, saying, "The jihad you have commenced at present is not to defend a land alone but also Islam, the Koran, and all Muslims." She added, "The only bitter and heartrending side of the holy jihad is the martyrdom of the Lebanese and Palestinian hero children"—she meant suicide bombers, primarily. These were children forced by their elders to kill themselves, and others along with them. Their "martyrdom," said Zahra, "is moving for every free man."

Giving interviews, especially to the Western press, she usually presents her father as a kind of liberal, who would bless liberalizing efforts in Iran today. For example, she has portrayed Khomeini as a free-speech advocate: His view was that "Islam is freedom to express oneself." She has also portrayed him as a women's-rights advocate: "He wanted women to play a full part in society, not just as typists or nurses." She has even claimed that "music was a big part of his life." One should be careful about contradicting a daughter on the subject of her father—Zahra knew him intimately—but this is surprising, at a minimum.

The year he took power, Khomeini banned music—the broadcast of. "Like opium," he said, "music stupefies persons listening to it and makes their brains inactive and frivolous." He said that the shah's regime had "corrupted and degraded" Iranian youth through the broadcast of music.

Speaking of Iranian youth, let's now turn to Khomeini's grandchildren. He had 15 of them. And, as I indicated at the top of this chapter, they are an interesting, sometimes startling bunch. In 2013, a headline appeared at *Asia Times Online*: "Khomeini's Rebel Grandchildren." "Rebel" may be going too far, except in one case, but the Khomeini grandchildren have shown some boldness. The article under the headline said, "Seven of the 15 grandchildren have openly criticized the laws and the leadership since the mid-1990s."

These children—middle-aged men and women, all of them—have indeed criticized the Iranian regime, but they tend to do so in a special way: They say that the current leaders, whoever they may be, have departed from the path of their grandfather. "The Imam would not have wanted it this way," they contend. He is not here to contradict them. Ali Eshraghi, the son of Khomeini's middle daughter, Sadiqeh, has said, "If today we are targeting certain political forces and certain politicians, it is really because people consider us faithful custodians of the thoughts of the imam Khomeini, and so we get upset with whoever wants to move our country and our revolution away from the path outlined by the founder of the Islamic Republic."

In 2008, Ali's sister Zahra—named after her aunt, we can assume—said that the regime was keeping the Khomeini family off radio and television. "They are threatening our family in very different ways," she said. "Their purpose is to eliminate Khomeini's name, his family, and his true friends."

Zahra Eshraghi was born in 1964. Like her aunt, she studied philosophy. Unlike her aunt, she opposes the obligatory wearing of the hijab. She follows the law of her country, of course, but she chafes against it. In 2003, a *New York Times* interviewer asked her whether she ever felt like throwing off her headscarf in public. Zahra replied, "Do you want to issue me my death sentence?"

Two years later, she was interviewed by the *Daily Telegraph*, which described her as "a leading light in Iran's reformist movement." Zahra made some remarkable statements—such as, "Our constitution still says that the man is the boss and the woman is a loyal wife who sacrifices herself for her family. But society here has changed, especially in the last ten years." (Zahra was speaking from Tehran.) Then she added the usual touch of a Khomeini grandchild: "If my grandfather were here now, I am sure he would have very different ideas." She further said, "As a woman, if I want to get a passport to leave the country, have surgery—even breathe, almost—I must have permission from my husband."

Zahra is part of a royal marriage, so to speak, her husband being Mohammad-Reza Khatami, a leading reformist politician, and the younger brother of Mohammad Khatami, who was Iran's president from 1997 to 2005. Zahra's husband may be a moderate or even a liberal now (in the Iranian context), but at the beginning of the revolution, he was a hostage-taker.

The Khomeini children and grandchildren enjoy protection, certainly to a degree, but they are not quite untouchable. Consider an episode in 2009. There was a presidential election, widely deemed fraudulent. The fraud led to mass democratic protest across Iran (ruthlessly put down by the regime). Zahra and her husband were on the side of the losing candidate, Mir-Hossein Mousavi, who became the symbol of the opposition, which is to say, of the protest. The day after the election, Zahra and her husband were arrested and briefly detained.

Zahra and Ali have a sister, Naeimeh Eshraghi, who is a petrochemical engineer. She is a proponent of openness in Iran. She does what she can to circumvent state censorship and rally supporters online. In 2012, she made clear to the *Daily Telegraph* that her name is no guarantee against official retaliation. "Not only am I concerned that the security forces may one day knock on my door, but also in fact think that it is quite possible that this may happen and then I would not be different from many other prominent free thinkers of our country who have ended up being in jail."

Bold as the Eshraghi kids and other Khomeini grandchildren may sometimes be, the one who takes the cake is Hussein Khomeini. He is unrivaled. The son of Mostafa, he was born in 1958 or '59. That means he was about 20 when the Iranian revolution triumphed. Not entirely separate from the family business, he is a cleric or mullah, defining himself as a "liberal religious person." He has been a critic of the regime, and a thorn in its side, from the beginning.

In 1981, two years in, he was arrested. That was after he addressed a May Day rally, saying that totalitarianism had been established "in the color of religion." He also said that "the new dictatorship"—i.e., his grandfather's—was worse than that of the shah or the Mongols (centuries before).

Years later, he explained that he had been appalled by the killing that the religious revolutionaries undertook. Not only were they killing people involved in the shah's regime, they were killing people who had the most tenuous links to that regime. It was a mass bloodletting. For some years, Hussein believed in an Islamic republic, humanely governed. But he eventually turned against the concept altogether. He was a democrat, pure and simple.

When the United States and its allies overthrew Saddam Hussein in early 2003, Hussein Khomeini moved to Iraq—back to Iraq, we could say, for he had lived there with his family in exile. The media marveled at this development. In London, the *Observer* said, "It is difficult not to get a sense that perhaps history is repeating itself." Would another man named Khomeini plot a revolution for Iran while in Iraq? This one a democratic revolution? Hussein said he hoped that momentum from Saddam's overthrow would lead to the overthrow of his own country's dictatorship.

Hussein was an unabashed supporter of the American invasion and occupation of Iraq. In fact, he chafed when a reporter for the *New York Times* used the word "occupation." It was a "liberation," he said. In another interview, he said, "The destruction of this regime was one of the great blessings of our time." He meant Saddam's regime, of course. In still another interview, he described the American invasion as "the arrival of goodness."

His father and grandfather—and his uncle Ahmad, to boot—had hated America, the Great Satan. Hussein held the opposite view. "American liberty and freedom is the best freedom in the world," he said. "The freedom for the individual that is written into the American constitution, you do not see in such concentration in any other constitution in the world." On another occasion, he said, "Freedom is an essential element and foundation of all religion, and the United States of America stands for freedom."

What Iran needed, he insisted, was "a democratic regime that does not make use of religion as a means of oppressing the people and strangling society." He said, "Any regime that represses is bad. But a dictatorship that combines state and religion is especially unacceptable. There is nothing Islamic about this." Over and over again, he called for the separation of mosque and state.

What's more, he called for the American invasion of Iran, or at least invited it. The regime in Tehran was "the world's worst dictatorship," he said. "Freedom is more important than bread." And "if there's no way for freedom in Iran other than American intervention, I think the people would accept that. I would accept it, too, because it's in accord with my faith."

In September 2003, he traveled to the belly of the beast, as the Iranian revolution sees it: Washington, D.C. Not to the White House, but, perhaps even worse, to the American Enterprise Institute, known as a hotbed of "neoconservatives," embarked on a democracy project. In a talk at AEI, Hussein lamented what he viewed as U.S. indifference to the Iranian situation. "Iran is intervening in Iraqi affairs extensively. Maybe this will cause the United States to pay attention to events in Iran." He also reflected on the meaning of the religious life. Freedom of religion is important, he said, but so is freedom of nonreligion—"since religion must be freely embraced to be meaningful."

While in America, Hussein had a secret meeting. It was with none other than Reza Pahlavi, the shah's son. These were two Iranian princes, engaged in a tête-à-tête. It would have been nice to be a fly on the wall (a Farsi-speaking fly). But Hussein later described the experience as "an ordinary meeting with a man who shares my suffering." He continued, "The cause of our suffering is one and the same, namely tyranny, though each of us has his own political orientation."

The public statements made by Hussein Khomeini during the year 2003 were extraordinary, given his lineage. And that is putting it too mildly. Neil MacFarquhar of the *New York Times* had an admirable sense of history when he reported an interview with Hussein. He said that Khomeini's grandson "grinned at the idea that he was following in the footsteps of other famous revolutionary offspring, like the daughters of Stalin and later Castro, who split with their families" and, of course, went to America.

In the first days of 2004, something strange happened: Hussein went home—to Iran. He went home to the country ruled by the government he had been calling for the overthrow of, even by means of foreign intervention. Why? Michael Ledeen, the scholar who sponsored him at AEI, gave the best explanation he could. "His grandmother sent him a message a few days ago," he wrote. This message did several things. It stressed the importance "for the family"—the grandmother's words—of Hussein's return to Iran. It warned of danger to his children. And it conveyed a promise from the regime that no harm would come to him. "Thus, according to family sources," wrote Ledeen, "Mr. Khomeini was blackmailed into returning." From everything we know, that rings true. Perhaps Hussein will be in a position to tell us what happened, one day.

He had about nine months outside of Iran, speaking freely. In the years since, the regime has had him under close watch, and his public statements have been few. For some reason, he gave, or was allowed to give, an interview in 2006. The occasion was the 27th anniversary of the revolution, and the venue was al-Arabiya. Hussein was his familiar, rebellious self. He stated the simple truth that Iran's was "a dictatorship of clerics who control every aspect of life." He said, "My grandfather's revolution has devoured its children and has strayed from its course." And he once again called for help from outside: "Freedom must come to Iran in any possible way, whether through internal or external developments. If you were a prisoner, what would you do? I want someone to break the prison"—in other words, to force the doors open, and the chains off.

Hussein's grandmother, Khadijeh Saqafi, the imam's widow, surely had a role in protecting her grandson while she was alive. She died in 2009, at age 96. Thousands attended her funeral. She was buried in the mausoleum next to her husband.

The Khomeini children and grandchildren, the rebel Hussein quite aside, are in an odd position in Iran. They are the offspring of the hero and guide of the revolution. But they are not quite untouchable, as we have seen, and they are individuals. Naeimeh Eshraghi once observed, "We have always kept a balance between belonging to a certain family and having an independent identity of ourselves as well."

Above, I quoted Ali Alfoneh, an Iranian-born expatriate scholar. I will end with a wise word from him—wise and blunt: "The descendants of Ruhollah Khomeini live in golden cages. The regime provides for them, corrupts them, and controls them."

16

MOBUTU

Mobutu had 17 children—perhaps more, but 17 is the consensus. He had his children by two wives and assorted other women, including the identical twin of one of the wives. His first son, he groomed to succeed him. That son predeceased him. Another son was a brute and enforcer—nicknamed "Saddam Hussein." Another son has run for president of the country, twice, without success.

Mobutu Sese Seko was born Joseph-Désiré Mobutu in the Belgian Congo. The year was 1930. He rose in the army and in 1965 staged a coup: becoming boss of the "Democratic Republic of the Congo." His was a typical one-party dictatorship, with a gaudy cult of personality. Mobutu was known as "Guide," "Savior," "Messiah," and "Redeemer." Many people credited him with supernatural powers, and not benign supernatural powers either: Through magic, he could make an enemy blind, people believed. Formally a Catholic, he consulted witch doctors, especially before making important decisions. A former cabinet member reported having seen him drink human blood.

In 1971, Mobutu changed the name of the country to "Zaire." He also changed people's names. That is, he forbade them to have European names. This was part of his policy of *authenticité*, a bid for African pride, and the rejection of Western influence. His own name had been Joseph-Désiré. Now he would call himself Mobutu Sese Seko Koko Ngbendu Wa Za Banga. This is a mouthful, and none too humble: It means "The all-powerful warrior who, because of his endurance and inflexible will to win, will go from conquest to conquest, leaving fire in his wake." *Authenticité* also dictated a new wardrobe. No longer could people wear Western clothes; they had to dress in a style deemed African. For men, this meant an abacost, a type of tunic, similar to a Mao suit. The word *abacost* comes from the French phrase "A bas le costume," i.e., "Down with the suit" (Western-style suit).

Mobutu himself developed a distinctive look: horn-rimmed glasses, abacost (of course), walking stick, and leopard-skin toque—a toque made in Paris. He also added a new name or title to his collection: "The Leopard," alternatively "The Great Leopard."

In the first years of his rule, he tortured and murdered, in standard dictatorial fashion. This cemented his primacy and unchallengeability. But, for the balance of his rule, he preferred to buy off any rivals or potential rivals. He had a lot of money to distribute. In fact, he was one of the original "kleptocrats," which is to say, rulers who exist to steal, and who maintain control by their theft. Mobutu stole colossal amounts—somewhere between $5 billion and $10 billion. There was no difference between the country's treasury and his personal treasury. Zaire was a tremendously wealthy country, loaded with diamonds, for example. But the mass of people were desperately poor, while Mobutu and his associates were spectacularly rich. Mobutu spread the wealth around, in the sense that he deposited it in his personal bank accounts in various parts of the world.

He was a big spender—a very big spender, on himself and his circle. We could spend several pages detailing his expenditures, and they might be entertaining. But a couple of sentences should suffice.

Mobutu was the type to fly himself and an entourage on the Concorde to Paris to shop with stacks of millions carried in Louis Vuitton briefcases. And I will now quote Declan Walsh, reporting from Mobutu territory in 2003, six years after the dictator's downfall: Mobutu "bankrupted the country, using its legendary wealth to buy political loyalties and build palaces where pink champagne flowed like water." Mobutu did indeed like his pink champagne. Anyway, the Bourbon kings would have blushed at the extravagance with which he and his favored ones lived.

Speaking of the Bourbons, Mobutu's first wife was named Marie Antoinette. Really. They married when she was 14, he about 25. She was a decent and kindly woman—also someone who could stand up to her dictator husband. She died young, age 36, in 1977. The cause was a heart condition. Mobutu was then left with his mistress, Bobi Ladawa. He took the step of marrying her in 1980, and for a particular reason: The pope, John Paul II, was coming to town. And Mobutu wanted his relationship with Bobi legitimate in the eyes of the church.

For a mistress, he took Bobi's identical twin, Kossia. They made quite a *ménage*, as you might imagine. Sometimes the twins were at war with each other; sometimes they united forces. When they were united, they were trying to privilege Bobi's children with Mobutu over his children with Marie Antoinette. The offspring of the *premier lit* (first bed) would long be at war with the offspring of the *second lit*. And, of course, Mobutu had children with his mistress, the other twin, Kossia.

Michela Wrong paints a picture of Mobutu and Zaire in her 2000 book, *In the Footsteps of Mr. Kurtz* (Mr. Kurtz being a character from *Heart of Darkness*, Joseph Conrad's tale of the Congo). She has this to say about Bobi and Kossia and their man: "Many Zaireans, spooked by the fact they could never tell which woman, wife or mistress, was perched on Mobutu's arm during official occasions, believe the arrangement represented a good luck charm for the superstitious Mobutu." Twins, the author explains, "are regarded in many parts of Africa as possessing totemic significance."

Mobutu may have wanted Kossia for another reason. Here again I turn to Michela Wrong: The dictator, or "president," may have "felt compelled to bed the sister to avoid being cuckolded, as whoever married Bobi Ladawa's twin would, in a way, be savouring intercourse with the first lady."

In a conversation with me, Brandon Grove, a U.S. ambassador to Zaire in the 1980s, provided an example of what he called Mobutu's "childlike humor." "We would be sitting and talking in his splendid marble palace," he said, "and in would walk an African woman of some proportions." (The twins grew plump with time.) "Mobutu would say to me, 'Have you met my wife?' I would duly stand up and shake her hand. Then he would turn to me and say, 'That's not my wife.'" No, she was the mistress twin. Mobutu got a kick out of this game.

And he did not confine his sex life to the twins. He slept with many others, including the wives of his cabinet members. In 1993, an ex–cabinet member explained it this way to *Time* magazine: "The president enjoys an almost feudal droit du seigneur. He uses sex as a tool to dominate the men around him. You get money or a Mercedes-Benz, and he takes your wife and you work for him." Another observer remarked to *Time*, "The complaints of those he has cuckolded only add to his mystique as a virile and powerful ruler."

According to Ambassador Grove, Mobutu was very private where his children were concerned. Only one had prominence (as we will see in a moment). In general, Mobutu did not raise his children at home, or have them raised there by others. He wanted more for them than his country could provide. He also wanted them out of range of kidnappers. And, just possibly, he wanted them out of his hair, too. The rivalries and quarrels in his family were draining on him.

As Michela Wrong details in her book, Mobutu farmed out his children to families abroad, where they could have a sound education and doses of worldliness. They went to school under assumed names. A son, Nzanga, left Zaire at the age of six to be raised by a Belgian colonel. This son eventually obtained a college degree in Canada.

It was Mobutu's first son, Niwa, who was to be the next leader. It was he who was groomed as the successor. He was the one with the prominence. Niwa—whose name is sometimes rendered "Nywa" or "Nyiwa"—was thought by one and all to be a smart cookie. Ambassador Grove certainly found him so. "He was clearly intelligent, a quiet, almost scholarly person." Grove also found him overwhelmed and intimidated by his dictator father. "I felt that he was weighed down by his father's extreme extrovert tendencies and general bossiness. Mobutu was an overwhelming kind of guy. And Niwa seemed one of those sons who are awed by their father, overwhelmed by their father, and thus retreat into a kind of isolation."

Whether Niwa preferred isolation or not, Mobutu made him a roving ambassador. In 1981, the son traveled to China, bearing a letter from his father to Zhao Ziyang, the Chinese premier. They had the usual "cordial meeting." In the words of Chinese state media, Zhao "stressed strengthening unity with Third World countries as China's basic policy and expressed appreciation for Zaire's efforts in safeguarding African unity." A banquet was laid on for Mobutu's son.

In 1988, Mobutu named Niwa to a newly created post: minister of international cooperation. Niwa died in 1994, however, of AIDS. (This disease was taking a toll on Zaire at large.)

Among Mobutu's daughters was Yakpwa, called "Yaki." In 1992, she married a Belgian businessman, Pierre Janssen. Some chapters ago, I touched on a wedding in Haiti, the one uniting Baby Doc Duvalier and Michèle Bennett: "At a cost of $3 million, it was one of the most expensive weddings ever staged, and in one of the poorest countries on earth." That applies to this Zairean wedding, too—but Mobutu spent $3 million on his daughter's jewelry alone. The cake cost $75,000. Or rather, a special plane was hired for $75,000 to bring the cake from Paris. The cake itself was a marvel or a monstrosity, depending on your point of view: It was 13 feet high.

Yaki and Janssen later divorced, and the ex-husband wrote a tell-all book, *A la cour de Mobutu* ("In Mobutu's Court"). In his telling—a telling that can be believed—Mobutu's children leeched off their father, the same as everyone else did. They angled to get ever greater sums from him. They must have thought this way of living perfectly normal, even a birthright. The Mobutu children hardly ever saw their father. But when he got older and weaker, he got more family-minded, and gathered them around.

He was vulnerable. The United States and other powers had always propped him up, for Mobutu was their ally in the Cold War. With that struggle over, however, he was less useful to them. He was just a kleptocrat, an embarrassment. "I am the latest victim of the Cold War, no longer needed by the U.S.," he said bitterly to *Time*. An armed rebellion was closing in on him. He held out as long as he could—which was till May 1997. On the 18th of that month, he took his flight.

A Russian plane, not an American, took him and an entourage to Togo, and from there to Morocco. At Lomé, the Togolese capital, Bobi Ladawa was seen descending the plane in her nightgown. Although who's to say it wasn't her twin, Kossia?

At least one Mobutu remained in Zaire: the dictator's son Kongulu, a captain in the DSP, the presidential security division. In her book,

Michela Wrong describes him as "a stocky, bearded man with a taste for fast cars, gambling and women." He was also a brute and enforcer, as I said earlier. He earned his nickname, "Saddam Hussein." On May 18, a headline in the *New York Times* read, "Mobutu's Son Lingers, Reportedly Settling Scores." Oh, yes, he was. With his comrades, he hunted down those he considered traitors to his father. Kongulu was leading a death squad, plain and simple. A bloodcurdling scene unfolded at the Hotel Intercontinental in the capital city, Kinshasa. (This was the best hotel in town.) The squad stormed in and Kongulu leveled a submachine gun at the receptionist, demanding certain room numbers. Whether in the hotel or elsewhere, Kongulu got some scalps, before fleeing the country with the rest of his clan.

Mobutu—"Papa," to his nearest and dearest—intended to live out his days in *la belle France*. Instead, he died in Rabat, Morocco, in September 1997, four months after his flight. He was just short of his 67th birthday. A year later, Kongulu died, of AIDS. The twins lived on in Rabat, which would be the family base. But the children were scattered about the world, in such capitals as Brussels, Paris, and London. They did not live in shabby districts. Daughter Ngawali, for example, lived in the 16th arrondissement of Paris. The Mobutu children are unhindered by their name, and they may well be helped by it. They live and travel freely.

In 1998, the family set up a foundation, straightforwardly named the Mobutu Family Foundation. Its purpose would be to help "young men and women of African countries" to "achieve their best." Just how much of the Mobutu fortune, or Mobutu plunder, made it out of Zaire has long been a mystery. (Please note that, after Mobutu was forced out, the country was again called the "Democratic Republic of the Congo," as it still is.)

A Mobutu son, Manda, gave an interesting interview in March 1998. He told *Jeune Afrique*, a Parisian weekly, that the Mobutu fortune was just an "average" one. It was not to be measured in the billions. He put it in this somewhat charming way: "We're not dying of hunger, it must be said. We have a decent life." At the same time, no one should believe "outlandish figures," such as four billion dollars. "In Africa," Manda went on to explain, "a leader cannot, should not, be poor, on condition of course that he be able to distribute"—i.e., spread the wealth around.

"I don't know whether that's good or bad, but that's the reality." Manda allowed that his father bore some responsibility for the country's poverty. But "it is obviously simplistic to say Zaire was ruined and Mobutu took the money. The leader doesn't know everything. His entourage often hides or distorts the reality, covers up crimes, and protects the guilty."

Manda himself was looking toward a future in politics. And he created a little distance from his dad. "If the people choose to have another Mobutu lead them, it won't be a photocopy of the last one. There's no cloning in politics." In his adopted city, Paris, Manda founded a Congolese party called the "Popular National Rally." We will hear more about Manda and politics in a moment.

In his final days, Mobutu had a new spokesman, a younger son, the aforementioned Nzanga. He is smooth and well educated, sometimes described as "urbane." In discussions about his homeland—and politics in general—he is reasonable-sounding. Nzanga is not unlike Saif al-Islam Qaddafi. (Kongulu was more like Saadi or Hannibal Qaddafi.) After his father's exile and death, Nzanga, though one of the younger sons, emerged as head of the family, the tender of the Mobutu flame.

"I'm very proud of the name that I bear," Nzanga told Michela Wrong. He venerates his father. He treasures every moment he spent with him, and every word that his father spoke to him. In this, he is like the Mussolini sons, and other dictators' children (and other men's children, to be sure). Like other Mobutu kids, he blames conniving and venal underlings for what went wrong in Zaire. In a clever phrase—even an ingenious one—he calls his father "the tree that hid the forest." According to Nzanga, Mobutu was like a traditional tribal chief, manfully accepting responsibility for everything that happens in the tribe as a whole, regardless of whether he's personally responsible.

Nzanga returned to Zaire, or rather to the DRC, in 2003. He had an eye on running for parliament. Whatever his veneration of his father, he presented himself as a new Mobutu. "I belong to a generation that needs new leaders, other personalities. It can't be a one-man system anymore. I'm thinking of teamwork." He defended his father in this fashion: "I'm not saying it was the best of regimes, but to say my father was the worst dictator is just wrong. At least then there was peace, and people could eat. Those are the facts." The reporter Declan Walsh found

Nzanga Mobutu

him wearing a shirt that bore Mobutu's portrait and the legend "We will never forget you."

A few months after Nzanga returned, so did Manda, in the company of a sister, Yanga. A crowd of 200 people greeted him at the airport, some of them wearing "knock-offs of his father's trademark leopardskin cap," as an Associated Press report had it. The 200 were not necessarily sincere in their appreciation of the returning son or his family. A police officer told Walsh (reporting for the *Independent*) that they had been bribed with $12, a T-shirt, and a beer. A spokesman for Manda's party, the Popular National Rally, said that the party intended to compete in elections to be held in 2006. Everyone expected the leader, Manda, to run for president. A year after his return, however—in 2004—he died. The cause has not been reported, so far as I'm aware.

That left Nzanga—and a party of his own, the Union of Mobutuist Democrats, or UDEMO. (A "Mobutuist democrat" is one of the great oxymorons in politics, but the "Democratic Republic of the Congo" is not far behind. Neither is the "Democratic Republic of" anything.)

UDEMO was in part a family affair. One of Nzanga's brothers, Giala, worked for it.

In 2006, Nzanga ran for president. So did 32 others. One of them was Patrice Guy Lumumba, son of Patrice Lumumba, the first prime minister of an independent Congo, executed in 1961—by forces allied to Mobutu. Nzanga received just 4.8 percent of the vote, and Lumumba's son seems not to have shown up at all in the results. The winner, with 45 percent of the vote, was the incumbent president, Joseph Kabila, son of the previous president, Laurent—who was the rebel leader who overthrew Mobutu (and was assassinated in 2001). Sons, sons, everywhere sons.

Nzanga would serve in the government under Kabila—first as minister of agriculture, then as the "deputy prime minister for basic social needs." He and President Kabila clashed, and in March 2011 Kabila dismissed him. The next presidential election was scheduled for November of that year, and Nzanga again ran. This time, there were only ten others.

In October, Nzanga sat for an interview with the *Washington Times*. As usual, he sounded the soul of reasonableness and modernity. "Today we are a failed state," he said. He condemned the corruption of the Kabila government. He condemned the epidemic of rape by soldiers, and promised to do something about it. Concerning the past, he had this to say: "Under President Mobutu, we had problems as well, but we had security. Nobody was messing with the Congolese people." Yet he also said, "I am not here to defend the government of President Mobutu. I am my own man." And "I believe in accountability." This is not a word, *accountability*, that the leopard messiah would have recognized, at least in connection to his rule.

Nzanga garnered a paltry 1.5 percent of the vote in 2011. Joseph Kabila won again, with 49 percent. The elections were widely considered fraudulent. But at least the Mobutus and the Kabilas weren't trying to kill one another.

17

BOKASSA

Bokassa had countless children—hundreds of them. Officially, or quasi-officially, he had about 50. He had these with 17 or 18 wives. Years after Bokassa's death, one of his sons commented, "He was very affectionate. He loved children. He loved children a lot. And for that reason, he had about 50 kids." Again, that was just the official, or quasi-official, count. The son I have just quoted is named Jean-Serge. Another son was named Charlemagne—a fitting name for the son of a man who would crown himself emperor. Charlemagne Bokassa died homeless and broken in Paris at age 31.

What was Bokassa emperor of? The Central African Republic, or, in those imperial days, the Central African Empire. This is the country just north of the Democratic Republic of the Congo, or, as Mobutu had it, Zaire. Before he was emperor, Bokassa was merely president for life. Before that, he was merely president. In short, he was a dictator: dictator of the Central African land from 1966 until 1979, when he was chased out by his foreign sponsor, France. Before he died, he gave himself yet another title—the grandest of all. The aged and deposed Bokassa declared himself the 13th apostle of Christ.

The future Bokassa the First—apostleship aside—was born Jean-Bédel Bokassa, in 1921. In those days, the land was called French Equatorial Africa. He joined the French army when he was 18. He distinguished himself, especially in Indochina. Eventually, he attained the rank of captain. Bokassa was highly decorated, including with the *Croix de guerre*. He later became a grotesque and bloody dictator—but it should be remembered that he was once an able and impressive officer.

In 1960, the Central African Republic, as it was to be known, gained its independence. The country's president, David Dacko, called on Bokassa to lead the CAR's armed forces. (Dacko and Bokassa were distant cousins.) Bokassa did this till the end of 1965, when his itch to rule could be contained no longer. On New Year's Eve, an hour and a half before midnight, he staged a coup, deposing Dacko and taking power. For the next 14 years, until he was chased out, he tortured and killed repeatedly. He was mercurial, possibly crazy, a powder keg. A brooding and egomaniacal powder keg. He had many people killed on the spot, including longtime and loyal servants. He was the type to feed his victims to lions and crocodiles.

Once, he slapped the Italian ambassador in public. In Bokassa's opinion, Italy was not providing enough aid. The Italians withdrew their ambassador and left a code clerk in charge of the embassy. More often, Bokassa liked to use his cane or walking stick—a ceremonial instrument, made of ebony. It symbolized chieftainship or rule. And Bokassa beat people to a pulp with it. He beat not only his subjects but foreigners as well. He almost killed a correspondent of the Associated Press, Michael Goldsmith. Once, Bokassa threatened the U.S. ambassador, Goodwin Cooke, with his stick. Bokassa was stinking drunk at the time. He thought better of taking a swing at the American, however.

Always, there were rumors of cannibalism—credible rumors. Did he or didn't he? This cannot be known for sure, although he probably did: In Africa, it is not unknown for a warrior or strongman to feast, literally, on his enemies. Such eating is supposed to give the eater extra power. Many Central Africans believed that Bokassa had the power to change himself into animals. Through some kind of magic, he could become a monkey, say, or a rat. Bokassa had the public in the grip of fear, until the final stage of his rule, when people were so desperate and exasperated that the grip broke.

Bokassa had friends, powerful friends, abroad, and some of them we've met. Mobutu, down in Zaire, was a friend. Bokassa called him "mon frère cadet," his younger brother; Mobutu called Bokassa "mon frère aîné," his older brother. Bokassa also had a friend in the dictator we'll discuss next: Idi Amin, the boss of Uganda, to the east of the CAR. Bokassa had a quite good friend in Eastern Europe, Ceauşescu. And he had a very good friend in France: President Valéry Giscard d'Estaing. The Frenchman would come to Central Africa once a year or so to hunt with Bokassa. The Central African leader once gave him a gift of diamonds—not very good diamonds, and not many of them, but diamonds nonetheless. Giscard's acceptance of them landed him in big political trouble.

A particular friend of Bokassa's was Moammar Qaddafi, the Libyan dictator. In fact, Qaddafi converted Bokassa to Islam. Qaddafi traveled to Bangui, the Central African capital, and offered Bokassa and his chief lieutenants big money if they converted. That was all the inducement Bokassa, for one, needed. The American ambassador of the period, Anthony Quainton, told me, "He would have converted to Buddhism if you had paid him." The religion was of scant importance. Overnight, Bokassa acquired a new name: Salah Eddine Ahmed Bokassa. He also gave up the whisky he loved, Chivas Regal, in favor of orange juice (as his new religion forbade alcohol).

By the way, Qaddafi showed a new movie during his visit to Bangui. It was *The Message*, starring Anthony Quinn, about the life of the prophet Muhammad.

Bokassa's Muslim period was very brief—just a few months. Apparently, Qaddafi did not come through with the money, or enough of it. Bokassa converted back to his nominal (very nominal) Catholicism. Qaddafi's non-generosity was one reason. But there was another: Bokassa was envisioning a major event in a cathedral. A coronation, or self-coronation. We will get to that soon. First, though, we should spend some time with his wives and children.

Bokassa was a man of huge appetites, and he was in a position to act on them. He drank copiously. And he had sex copiously, if I may put it that way. He had women "by the threes and fours," as an observer put it to me. He may well have had thousands in his life. His wives, to repeat, numbered just 17 or 18. Someone would catch his eye, and he would decide that she would be his wife. This happened both at home and abroad. He explained that he always wanted the most beautiful woman, whatever the city or country. A great many men must feel this way. Unlike them, Bokassa usually got his way.

In one case, a young woman balked. She was just a girl, really, a schoolgirl—a local, a Central African. She and her family tried to flee the country. They were arrested at the border, though, and thrown into prison. For two years. They endured terrible things. Then, one night, armed guards came to take the girl away. This is it, she thought: She would be killed or "disappeared," as so many Central Africans had been. But she was taken to Bokassa. And she submitted to him, in order to save the lives of her family. She became one of the wives. Two and a half years later, she was able to escape the country.

The wives were from a variety of countries, and were in fact known by their nationalities: "the Belgian," "the Lebanese," "the Ivorian," and so on. Two of Bokassa's wives were Vietnamese, both named Nguyen. Probably the most notorious wife was the Romanian, Gabriela, who was in fact an agent of the Securitate, Ceaușescu's secret police. While ensconced in her husband's palaces, she was not exactly a loyal wife. She bedded guards and others. When Bokassa found out about it, he of course had the men killed. One day, the Romanian took the bicycle of an innocent waiter and rode around on it. Bokassa duly had the waiter beaten to death. Eventually, Gabriela became so frightened of Bokassa that she fled to Paris.

There was one wife who was *prima inter pares*, the No. 1 wife, indeed the future empress: Catherine, a girl Bokassa spotted when she was 13. She was not only beautiful, as all the wives were. She was elegant, gracious, and admired. Central Africans came to know her as "Maman Cathy."

Not a few of Bokassa's sons were named Jean, his own name; not a few of his daughters were named Marie, his mother's name. (Three or four of his wives were named Marie as well.) There was also Charlemagne, as you have heard. Bokassa could be an affectionate father, but he brooked no disobedience. If disobeyed, he did not punish lightly. He did not send his children to bed without dinner, for example. He threw them in prison—at least he did so with his sons. They stayed in prison for days, weeks, even months.

One son, Georges, rose to serve in his father's cabinet. He was defense minister for a brief time in the mid-1970s. But he ran afoul of his father, somehow—people did—and fled to France (as people did).

Go back in time a little. In 1970, the fifth year of his rule, Bokassa got it into his head that he wanted to find a daughter he had fathered with a wife in Vietnam. Bokassa had met this wife while fighting the Indochinese war. To Bangui came Martine, said to be the long-lost daughter. She was welcomed with great pomp and ceremony. But she turned out to be an imposter—not Bokassa's daughter at all. To Bangui came yet another Martine, this one Bokassa's daughter beyond doubt. Bokassa was furious at having been deceived in the first place. He was ready to deport the first Martine, the false one, but was persuaded to perform an act of magnanimity. On his 50th birthday—February 22, 1971—he adopted the false Martine as his own daughter.

So now he had two Martines: *la fausse Martine* and *la vraie Martine*, as they were known ("the false Martine" and "the true Martine"). In a public auction, he offered the hands of these daughters in marriage. The winning bidders, or suitors, were an army officer, Fidèle Obrou, and a doctor, Jean-Bruno Dedeavode. (You will find all sorts of spellings for the doctor's last name.) The officer had the false Martine and the doctor had the true. There was a double wedding: The couples were married in a grand and beautiful ceremony.

Hang on, there's more—and it gets nasty and murderous, as things did in Bokassa's realm. I will relate the events as quickly and clearly as I can. The next paragraph, a person may have to read more than once, just to absorb it.

In 1976, the army officer, Obrou, the husband of the false Martine, participated in a coup attempt against Bokassa, his father-in-law. A coup attempt and an assassination attempt. Obrou, with the others, was executed. Shortly afterward, his widow, the false Martine, gave birth to their son. The true Martine's husband, Dr. Dedeavode, killed the child, on Bokassa's orders. Bokassa did not want the babe to grow up to avenge his father's execution. On the first anniversary of Obrou's execution, his widow, the false Martine, was sent home to Vietnam. But she never made it to the airport outside Bangui. She was "disappeared"—murdered—on the way. After Bokassa's overthrow, Dr. Dedeavode confessed his guilt in the murder of the child. He was executed.

That's a heavy body count, from two marriages. Three of the spouses, plus one (newborn) child.

We are now nearing the coronation. According to the American ambassador, Quainton, the first indication that Bokassa would declare an empire came when Princess Anne was born. People wondered, "Why is this latest Bokassa child called 'princess'?" The country was a republic. Soon, though, the dictator would call himself Bokassa the First—and the country the Central African Empire. Bokassa believed himself, or declared himself, to be a descendant of the pharaohs. He also thought himself the new Napoleon, the Napoleon of Africa.

On December 4, 1977, he had his coronation. It cost somewhere between $20 million and $90 million. In any case, it cost a lot—probably as much as one year's budget for the entire country. The French paid the bill. Bokassa's crown alone was worth about $5 million. He sat upon a fantastic golden throne, which was in the shape of an imperial eagle. At the climactic moment, Bokassa placed that pricey crown on his own head, Napoleon-style. According to eyewitnesses—and as one can see in films—the coronation was at the same time garish and splendid. It was one of the strangest events of the 20th century.

An emperor needs an heir, and Bokassa chose one. Appropriately, his name was Jean-Bédel Jr. Four years old at the time of the coronation, this boy was slated to become Bokassa II. The dictator had many older sons, of course: He had been siring children for decades. But he passed them all over for this little one.

Georges, whatever his problems with Dad, might have been a natural successor. He had risen to the cabinet, after all. He was a man of politics, a man of state. But there was that father-son friction. Also, there was a question of the young man's mettle, his toughness. Brian Titley writes about this son in his 1997 study of Bokassa, *Dark Age*: "In spite of his prominence, Georges was not exactly imperial material. His speech was impaired by a serious stutter, and he spoke French with a heavy African accent. Worse still, he was a fairly decent character and often tried to mitigate his father's excesses of cruelty. Bokassa considered him weak."

Also, there was Catherine to consider: She was the leading wife, the empress herself, and she wanted one of her own sons to be the *prince héritier*. Georges was the son of a quite early wife (Marguerite Green

Jean-Bédel Bokassa Jr., the *prince héritier*,
tired at the coronation

Boyanga, who was of English and Angolan parentage). Bokassa chose
Junior, his second-youngest son with Catherine.

During the coronation, the boy sat near his father, dressed in a beautiful little white uniform. The gloves were an especially effective touch.
Being four, the prince yawned and slept a lot in the course of the long
day. But he made an adorable adornment to the occasion.

After his self-crowning, Bokassa was more pretentious and insuffer-
able than ever. He demanded to be addressed "Majesté Impériale." He
demanded that his subjects greet him "from six steps away while making a slight forward indication of the head." A new protocol was issued
to the diplomatic corps. On leaving His Majesty's presence, diplomats
were to walk backward. When he said something to you, you were supposed to respond, "Oui, Majesté." You could not say no. But if strictly
necessary, you could respond, "Oui, mais ..."—"Yes, but ..." These rules
were honored in the breach. Bokassa could actually laugh a little at his
own pretensions, at least with foreigners.

As Bokassa was living it up with wine, women, and murder, the
people of the "empire" were suffering miserably, of course. They had
nothing. Bokassa's downfall was precipitated by his response to the
protests of schoolchildren, believe it or not. In January 1979, he issued
an order: Kids were to wear a new uniform, bearing his image, manufactured by a factory owned by Empress Catherine. The uniforms were

expensive: about $25 apiece, in this woefully poor country. The children protested. This led to riots—which were quelled by a massacre.

In April, there were new protests, over the same issue. Children, audacious, threw rocks at Bokassa's Rolls-Royce as it passed. The emperor was livid. He ordered troublemakers rounded up, some 180 of them. They were between the ages of eight and twenty, roughly. They were herded into prison. And there, about a hundred of them were tortured and beaten to death. Bokassa himself almost certainly took part in the murders, cane in hand.

The French were finding it hard to defend Bokassa, and to continue to fund him. The Americans, too, were fed up. Bokassa heard that there was a negative report about him on the Voice of America. He summoned the ambassador, Goodwin Cooke. This was the occasion on which Bokassa threatened the ambassador with his cane. The ambassador said that the United States would cut off aid to the empire, regardless. Bokassa calmed down and grew reflective.

"I could resign," he said. "Yes, you could," said Cooke. "Nixon resigned, didn't he?" said Bokassa. "Yes, he did," said Cooke. (Richard Nixon resigned in August 1974, becoming the first American president to leave office in this manner.) "And he's doing all right in California?" asked Bokassa. "Yes, he's doing all right," replied Cooke. Bokassa thought for a moment—then said that his own resignation was out of the question. It was simply un-African.

In September of that year—September 1979—the French got rid of him. They acted while Bokassa was away, in Libya. They sent troops to Bangui, overthrowing the government and putting David Dacko back on the throne. He was the president whom Bokassa had overthrown some 14 years before, on New Year's Eve. Dacko was not on a throne, however: Central Africa was once more a republic.

Notwithstanding his rude dethroning by the French, Bokassa wanted to live in France. The French refused. So he went to the Ivory Coast, about 2,000 miles due west of the CAR. Bokassa's host and patron was the Ivorian president, Félix Houphouët-Boigny, a senior African politician. Bokassa called him "mon père," his father. Over in the CAR, Bokassa was tried in absentia for his crimes—and sentenced to death.

After four years in the Ivory Coast, Bokassa went to France, which was now prepared to welcome him, or at least tolerate him. He went to a chateau he had bought in the 1970s: the Château d'Hardricourt, about 25 miles northwest of Paris. The ex-emperor had in tow 15 of his children. The family had plenty of room on this capacious estate, overlooking the Seine.

Bokassa wrote his memoirs, *Ma vérité*, "My Truth"—a book bearing the same creepily relativistic title that had appeared on Edda Mussolini's memoirs. One unhappy reader was Valéry Giscard d'Estaing, now the ex-president of France. He sued, and won: A court found that 18 pages of Bokassa's book were defamatory and libelous. The court ordered the book burned. Bokassa himself watched. He rode in his Mercedes limousine to a warehouse, where he saw 8,000 copies of his testament—*Ma vérité*—go up in flames. About Giscard, he was bitter: "For twelve years we were friends. I welcomed him to my home. I gave him diamonds. He has cheated me, chased me from my country."

In this same period, the summer of 1985, Bokassa said, "I want only one thing: to return to my country. I am the emperor for life of Central Africa. My people are waiting for me." The next year, he did return. French authorities were supposed to be watching him, but they were lax. Under their noses, he drove (or was driven) to Brussels. He took a flight to Rome. There, he boarded an Air Afrique flight to Bangui.

Remember, he had been sentenced to death at home. He was ensconced in the Château d'Hardricourt. Why did he return? There were a number of reasons. For one thing, he disliked the cold winters in France. For another, he was running out of money. Mainly, however, he was bored. He missed the stage, the limelight, the action. Also, he had a messianic view of himself. He genuinely thought, or convinced himself, that his country required him.

He arrived in Bangui with a wife and five children. They were immediately sent back to Europe. The wife and children, that is: Bokassa himself was arrested as soon as he stepped off the plane. He had been tried in absentia—but now he would be tried live and in the flesh. He was charged with treason, murder, embezzlement, and other crimes, including cannibalism.

At the beginning of the trial, Bokassa was cocky, happy to be onstage again. But he turned somber as citizens testified and the evidence mounted against him. One of the testifiers was the widow of a general. She said that Bokassa had her husband killed when he refused to allow

Bokassa to have sex with her, his wife. There in court, Bokassa begged the woman's forgiveness. On other days, however, he was defiant and furious. Often, he attempted to shift blame to others—uncontrollable cabinet members, for example. Adamantly, he denied one charge. "I am not a cannibal," he said. (Nixon had said, "I am not a crook.")

That was the one charge he was found not guilty of: cannibalism (though he was probably guilty of it). All the other charges, he was convicted of. As the judge read the sentence, the defendant wept: The sentence was death. That sentence was commuted, however, to life in prison. Later, the sentence was commuted to 20 years. Finally, in 1993, after six years in prison, Bokassa was released.

He stayed in Bangui and immediately took steps to run for president. He indicated that he would run under the name Bokassa the First. He did not run, however. Mainly, he was in the grip of religious mysticism. This is when he called himself the 13th apostle. He died in November 1996, age 75.

In 2003, the CAR underwent a reconciliation process, holding a six-week forum called "the National Dialogue." The dozens of official Bokassa children sent a delegate to the forum: Jean-Serge. During the proceedings, he apologized for the "wrong" committed by his father and asked forgiveness. He said that his father should be rehabilitated, because he had built up the country. Astonishingly or not, the forum agreed. Bokassa, posthumously, was the beneficiary of a nostalgia that often sets in after a dictatorship is gone. People see that their country still has problems, and perhaps even worse ones.

Seven years after the forum, in 2010, the Central African government went even further. The country was marking the 50th anniversary of its independence. In a sweeping gesture, the government granted Bokassa a full, if posthumous, pardon. His children rejoiced at the news. They promised to set up a foundation that would compensate some victims of the old tyrant. Whether this foundation ever materialized, or payments were made, I cannot say. It seems doubtful.

There is a politician in the family, and that is Jean-Serge. The *prince héritier*, Jean-Bédel Jr., has evidently not had any kind of public life. Jean-Serge is a year older than he, born in 1972. His mother was "the Gabonese," a beautiful teen from Gabon. When his dad was overthrown, Jean-Serge was a seven-year-old at a Swiss boarding school. Back in the CAR, all grown up, he ran for parliament, and won. He even won a cabinet position: minister for youth, sports, art, and culture (a very broad portfolio).

Jean-Serge is a defender of his father, regarding him as a "patriot," as well as a "builder." But he has expressed commitment to democracy. In 2009, the BBC asked him whether he could see himself as an emperor—as Bokassa II. "I'm not nostalgic for the monarchy or empire," he answered. "It was a period in our history, and we have to accept that it's part of our history. But do I defend the monarchy? No, I don't. Actually, I think it's indefensible."

In the summer of 2014, he spoke of his father to Europe 1, a radio network. "He showed us the path of patriotism," Jean-Serge said. "I am ever more firm on the need to stop impunity, and he gave us the example. He returned to his homeland. He was tried and sent to prison." Jean-Serge also made a statement of some poignancy: "There were times in my life, when I was younger, when it was difficult to bear this name." The next month, *Jeune Afrique* ran a story about him, headed "Jean-Serge Bokassa Believes in His Political Destiny." Now, as I write, Jean-Serge is contemplating a run for president.

What of the other Bokassa children, those dozens? They are far-flung, in Africa, Europe, the United States, and elsewhere. One is in Lebanon. She is the daughter of "the Lebanese" and was born in 1975. She has lived her life in Beirut, apparently. Her name is Kiki Bokassa. Formally speaking, she is not Kiki but "Marie-Ange." And she is an artist, a painter.

In 2009, she staged an unusual event, attracting worldwide attention. She called it "72 Hours." What she did was paint for 72 hours straight. "Art for her is a way of coming to terms with her past," said Agence France-Press. Kiki herself said, "It's a kind of therapy for me. I don't think too much about it while I'm painting, but after I've finished a work I feel reconciled with my father's past." In the course of her 72 hours, she completed 40 square yards of canvas.

As we would expect from 50 or so people, the Bokassa children have experienced a variety of fates. Some of them have fallen into crime, landed in jail. "For many of them, the name Bokassa has really become a burden," wrote Peter Strandberg in 2008, reporting for *New African* (a London-based magazine). Ten years before that, a reporter for AFP,

Eric Feferberg, talked to Charlemagne in Paris. Charlemagne was 28 and living on the streets. "When you have no money, no work, then you have no friends," he said. He was estranged from his family. Like Jean-Serge, he was a son of "the Gabonese," Marie-Joëlle Aziza-Eboulia. He too went to school in Switzerland. He was 13 when his dad was overthrown.

As I mentioned at the top of this chapter, Charlemagne Bokassa died in 2001, at 31. His body was found in the Paris subway system. His mother, in the Gabonese capital of Libreville, took the news very hard. She killed herself, age about 45.

18

AMIN

Amin had 60 children. He had them with seven wives and assorted other women. "Dad had quite an appetite for women," said one of his sons, a few years after Amin's death. "It's very African, actually." One of Amin's wives was found dismembered in the trunk of a car. His Uganda was that kind of place. The 60 children have lived a variety of lives, of course. One of the sons is in the Ugandan security organization. One or two others have run for office, and will again. One has dedicated himself to reconciliation between Ugandans.

Idi Amin was dictator of that country from 1971 to 1979. He is many people's idea of a dictator: volatile, bloodthirsty, crazy, and cruel. Like Bokassa, he was widely held to engage in cannibalism. Amin was almost a cartoon of a dictator, with a massive physique, sweating in a bemedaled uniform under the hot African sun. He has often been depicted as a clown. If he was, he was a clown with teeth, a clown who killed.

He was born sometime in the mid-1920s—the date is uncertain. He served in the King's African Rifles, a regiment of the British colonial army. Like his Central African counterpart, Bokassa, he became head of the armed forces after independence. And, like Bokassa, he overthrew the president. (Milton Obote was away at the time—January 1971—attending a Commonwealth conference in Singapore.) Amin became president, field marshal, and eventually president for life. "Life" turned out to be three years: He took the title in 1976 and fled the country in 1979.

The formal and complete title he bestowed on himself was quite a mouthful: "His Excellency President for Life, Field Marshal Al Hadji Doctor Idi Amin Dada, VC, DSO, MC, Lord of All the Beasts of the Earth and Fishes of the Sea, and Conqueror of the British Empire in Africa in General and Uganda in Particular." There were several lies contained in that title, as well as grandiosity. Also, he declared himself "the uncrowned king of Scotland." He had a fascination with things Scottish. Once, he proposed that he marry Princess Anne—not Bokassa's Princess Anne, but the daughter of Queen Elizabeth II. Then, he would be king of Scotland, with Anne at his side.

Amin and Scotland may be linked for a long time. In 1998, a novel about the dictator came out, *The Last King of Scotland*. Several years later, it was made into a movie.

Amin was an extreme nationalist, or, if you like, a racist. He expelled Asians from Uganda in 1972. They had been part and parcel of the country, and in particular of its economy. After they were kicked out, the economy suffered. Amin's ultimate allies were the Soviets, the East Germans, and the ever-reliable Qaddafi. The Libyan dictator did not have to convert Amin to Islam, as he would Bokassa. Amin was born and raised a Muslim. And he had a fierce hatred of Israel. He spoke openly of destroying that country.

He destroyed a great many of his countrymen. How many? The most commonly accepted death toll is 300,000. Some say higher, some say lower. In any case, he was known as "the Butcher of Uganda." Simply giving the titles of some of the books and documentaries about him will convey what Amin and his regime were like: "A State of Blood," "Ghosts of Kampala," "Culture of the Sepulchre," "Inside Idi Amin's Terror Machine," "The Man Who Ate His Archbishop's Liver?," "Escape from Idi Amin's Slaughterhouse," "Hitler in Africa," "Death-Light in Africa"...

Amin's son Jaffar has written a book, too—one with a very different title from the ones just cited. We will discuss this later. According to Jaffar, Amin married for the first time in 1966. The next year, he married again. He married twice in 1972. He divorced the first three wives in

1974. He took his seventh and final wife in 1983, when he was in exile. The wife whose body was found dismembered in the trunk of a car was No. 2—Kay. There are several and conflicting accounts of what happened. In an interview with me, Jaffar said that Kay had bled to death from the botched abortion of an eight-month-old fetus. This is one of those murky and ghastly episodes from the Amin years.

There are 21 mothers in all, said Jaffar—21 mothers for the 60 Amin children. The first and last of those children were born almost 50 years apart: the first in 1948, probably, and the last in 1996. During his years as dictator, Amin had an excellent public-relations habit. When appearing somewhere in Uganda, he would have along with him a son or daughter whose mother hailed from the particular area.

Jaffar was born of Amin's first wife's sister, Margaret. Not until he was four was he aware that Amin was his father. At that time, he had an interesting encounter with Amin, revealing of the dictator's personality. Amin was bent over a huge, steaming plate of chicken. He commanded the child to taste it. He did, and was immediately in agony: The chicken was covered in chili sauce. Tears streamed down the boy's face; tears streamed down Amin's face, in mirth. Amin liked that kind of trick.

In a 2007 interview with the *Daily Mail*, Jaffar said, "He was a playful and mischievous man, and he was always Big Daddy to us. He loved jesting. One of his favorite jokes was to run at people with a spear. They would be shocked to see this huge figure hurtling at them. Then he would throw the spear so it landed at their feet." Jaffar went on to say, "I hated it when people called him a buffoon. I thought of him as like Muhammad Ali—he had that same sense of mischief. He was also a great fan of cartoons; he enjoyed slapstick. *Tom and Jerry* was his favorite."

Are we to believe that the dictator Amin was a jolly and lovable father to his children? We are, yes. That was definitely a side of Amin.

His downfall came when he attacked Tanzania, a neighbor to Uganda's south. Tanzania, under President Julius Nyerere, attacked back, in combination with Ugandan exile forces. They ran Amin out in April 1979. He went to Libya, where his friend Qaddafi sheltered him. Approximately 35 of Amin's children had been ferried there the month before. Amin and his family spent a year in Libya. Then they moved on to Saudi Arabia.

They lived in the city of Jeddah, in a 15-room house. The Saudis paid Amin $30,000 a month (and demanded that he stay well clear of politics). He would tell his brood, "You have to liberate Uganda with the fedayeen," meaning Islamic guerrillas. He was quite serious about this—to the point of enrolling his boys in the commando training program at the local PLO facility.

Amin enjoyed family outings, taking the wheel of his Chevy Caprice Classic station wagon. He and the family loved to grocery-shop at Safeway. But Amin's favorite food was not found at a grocery store. According to Jaffar, it was an American classic (like the Caprice): Kentucky Fried Chicken.

The exiled dictator died in 2003, in his late seventies. One of his daughters, Khadija, was 20. Seven years later, she spoke to a Ugandan government newspaper, *New Vision*, about her father's death. "It was only then, watching news footage of people celebrating in the streets, that I finally accepted who my dad really was." She read articles about him, written in the wake of his passing. She was shocked by what she was learning: the murder, the depravity. In Saudi Arabia, she explained to the newspaper, her father was treated like a hero. "I felt proud to be with him." But there had always been clues about the past. "I was too young to understand them, or perhaps I just didn't want to believe."

In 2006 came that movie: *The Last King of Scotland*. Amin was onstage again. By the way, Jaffar writes the following, in his book: "When we lived in exile, Dad continued to love and play Scottish music. He spent a lot of time playing the accordion. He played mainly Scottish military music as he was in a Highlanders band in the Fifties."

Many of the Amin children were not pleased at all with the movie. Taban, who had joined the Ugandan government earlier that year, was particularly outspoken. "It degrades our father," he said of the movie, "and it abuses the reputation of a former head of state of Uganda." On behalf of the family at large, he threatened to sue. "We will be taking action in the U.S. because that is where the companies and the actors come from. So we will take it to them in their homeland."

The suit never came. But we see a kind of loyalty, manifesting itself in litigiousness. Three years later, remember, Valentin Ceaușescu would sue over a play, in order to protect his father's name, and that of the family.

The 60 Amin children lived throughout the world, with the greatest concentration of them in Britain. When it comes to their father, they are of mixed views. Some of the children are fiercely or blindly loyal. Others of them are more skeptical about their father, or more realistic, let's say. Some keep their head down, not using the name "Amin," preferring to let it all slip away. We will look in on a few of the children—grown men and women, of course—beginning with Taban.

He was born in 1958, making him about 21 when his father fell from power. He went to Mobutu's Zaire. Eventually, he became leader of the West Nile Bank Front, a militia opposed to Yoweri Museveni, who became president of Uganda in 1986 (and is still in power today). In addition to leading a militia, Taban led a jazz band: He played many instruments, specializing in the guitar. He learned his music, his brother Jaffar told me, while being trained as an officer in Soviet Ukraine.

In time, President Museveni offered him an amnesty—and a job. The ex-militiaman became the deputy director general of the Internal Security Organisation.

"For many Ugandans," began a report in the *Sunday Telegraph*, "his booming laugh alone is enough to bring back memories of the bad old days. Taban Amin ... is every inch the larger-than-life character that his father was—a boisterous giant of a man whose personality is as big as his physical presence." It's true: Taban is practically the spitting image of his father. But he put some distance between himself and the old man when he went into the ISO. "Amin ruled in the 1970s," he said. "Now it is 2006. It is a different time. Amin's name is so tough in Uganda that some people are scared." (That's an interesting word, "tough.") "But what Amin did is not what I will do: I'm his son, but I am not his heart."

Six months after he started the job, a headline read, "Taban Amin Dragged to UHRC on Torture Charges." (The UHRC is the Uganda Human Rights Commission.) Taban is known by many as a tough or rough character, but it may also be said that he moves in a tough or rough country.

A different son, Faisal Wangita, participated in a gang murder. Born and raised in Saudi Arabia, he moved to England at 18. He committed many crimes, large and small. He fell in with a Somalian gang—which was warring with another Somalian gang. One day in 2006, Faisal and his mates attacked an 18-year-old, apparently of the other gang, and made quick work of him. That is, they murdered him, viciously. Faisal was 25 at the time. He went to prison for five years.

Britain deported him to Uganda, but hit a snag: When Faisal arrived at Entebbe Airport, the main airport in Uganda, the authorities refused to accept him—on grounds that he was not a Ugandan. This son of Amin had never set foot on Ugandan soil. Back he went to London.

His mother, Sarah, was also in London, and deeply worried about Faisal. "His life is in danger if he were to be returned to Uganda," she told the press. "There are so many people who would want to do him harm because of who his father was. I am his mother and I live here. He has no father and I am his only parent. Why should he be punished because of what his father may have or not have done?" She also said that a Jew in the British Home Office—a certain Cohen—had it in for Faisal. Why? It relates to the raid on Entebbe.

This was the Israeli operation carried out on July 4, 1976 (America's bicentennial day, as it happened). A French airliner traveling from Tel Aviv to Paris had been hijacked by Palestinian and German terrorists. They were fully welcomed and supported by Idi Amin in Uganda. Israeli commandos swooped in to rescue the hostages on that July day.

Beforehand, one of the hostages had been taken to the hospital, to receive medical care. She was Dora Bloch, a 75-year-old Israeli. When the other hostages were rescued, Amin was furious, of course. His agents dragged the old lady out of her hospital bed and murdered her, stuffing the corpse into the trunk of a car. The body was discovered after Amin's fall from power.

And it was the view of Faisal Wangita's mother, Sarah, that the Cohen in the Home Office was retaliating against the Amin family for the murder of Dora Bloch.

Khadija Amin was also living in London, and she commented on her brother and his troubles. Faisal "has no respect for law," she said, "and is most likely to lose his life if he is let out again on the streets of London." Even back in Saudi Arabia, she said, he had been out of control. On one occasion, he broke into the car of agents charged with guarding the family. Then he drove off. "Dad was very angry," said Khadija, "but Faisal always knew that, because of Dad's status in the country, even when he was locked up, he would be released the very next day." Saudi authorities shed no tears when Faisal left the country for good. They "were so happy to see the back of his head," said Khadija. She expressed the opinion that deportation to Uganda might be the best thing for Faisal.

The British deported him a second time, and the Ugandans accepted him. I asked Jaffar how Faisal was doing. (Jaffar has been in Uganda since 1990.) He said that his younger brother's prison stint and subsequent deportation were "a blessing in disguise." He added, "I would request the rest of them to come home, please."

One brother, Haji, ran for mayor of a town called Njeru in 2002, a year before his father died. "I feel proud of my father," said the candidate, "and people here like me for that. As the English say, 'Like father, like son.' My father was a ruler, and I am following in his footsteps." He defended his father staunchly, even the expulsion of Asians in 1972. It helped modernize the country, Haji claimed. He lost the mayoral election narrowly. But he may try again for office sometime soon.

Another brother, Hussein, plans to run for parliament. His full name is Hussein Juruga Lumumba Amin. "Hussein" is his Muslim name. "Juruga" is his African, or indigenous, name. "Lumumba" is a kind of pet name that his father gave him—in honor of Patrice Lumumba, the Congolese prime minister, slain in 1961. Some people call this son "Hussein," others call him "Lumumba." At one point in his life, he was going without the name Amin, but then took it back.

In the mid-2000s, he was not using "Amin." He was known as Hussein Lumumba. And he applied for a job with a Ugandan radio station, KFM. Those who had interviewed him found him clearly the best candidate. But they were nervous about what the boss would think: His father had been murdered by the candidate's father.

The boss was Conrad Nkutu, son of Shaban Nkutu, a key government minister before Amin came to power. Shaban Nkutu was also the uncle of one of Amin's wives, incidentally. Amin had him killed in 1973. His body had never been found. Conrad Nkutu approved the hiring of Hussein Lumumba right away. In an article he wrote years later, he said that he "gently chastised" those who were nervous about his reaction. He would not visit the sins of the father, namely Amin, on the son, namely Lumumba (as Nkutu and the others called him).

Lumumba did a superb job for KFM, Nkutu wrote. And it was clear that Lumumba had no idea about Nkutu's father. He was completely in the dark. Nkutu had no intention of raising the issue, and he did not want anyone else to, either.

Then, in January 2005, the newspapers ran a story: Retired gravediggers had revealed the site of a mass grave, where Shaban Nkutu's body was buried. In these articles, the story of Nkutu's murder—typically grotesque and horrifying—was told. This had a notable effect on Hussein Lumumba. I will turn to Conrad Nkutu, to relate what happened:

> Soon after the [staff] meeting ended that morning, KFM's controller, Peter Kabba, came to my office and reported with a shaky voice that Hussein Lumumba Amin had read the newspaper story in shock and collapsed in Kabba's office.
>
> Kabba sought guidance on what to do as Lumumba had somewhat recovered but was weeping inconsolably and all the KFM staff were discussing the matter after realising that Lumumba was Amin's son, and that I had knowingly employed the son of my father's killer.
>
> Lumumba had asked Kabba if I was willing to see him in my office to enable him to express regrets for what had happened to my Dad. I consented and he walked into my office trembling and weeping uncontrollably, supported to stand upright by Peter Kabba, and, if I recall well, Joseph Beyanga, the station's Head of Production. Lumumba attempted to say something to me and mumbled a vague "I'm so sorry ..." but had lost his voice and was inaudible as well as pretty incoherent.
>
> I got the sense that while he had obviously grown up surrounded by press reports describing his late father as a killer, he was living in denial and had possibly never been confronted with a detailed murder case involving his father as the orchestrator. He was in a very bad emotional state and we were all very sorry for him. I asked Peter to get a company car to take him home and later asked Martha [the human-resources manager] to assure him that I held no grudge against him and he could take a few days off to recover from the shock then return to work.
>
> Unfortunately, but perhaps understandably, Hussein Lumumba Amin did not return to work at KFM and did not send in a resignation letter. We understood his dilemma and did not pursue him though we remained sorry for how he had found out, and KFM missed his good work.

In recent years, Hussein (as he is now generally known) has been a rather feisty son of Amin, not a meek or contrite one. He stands up for what he regards as his and his family's rights. In 2013, he sent a letter to the Ugandan president, Museveni, saying that the government had reneged on a promise to return Amin properties to Amin hands. When he visited one of these properties, he said, soldiers threatened to shoot him. Jaffar felt the same as his brother. He remarked to the press, "I think this country thinks we are supposed to suffer. Unfortunately, people think we are not Ugandans. Until we overcome this problem politically, we will continue suffering."

A few months later, Hussein wrote an interesting article for a Ugandan magazine, *The Independent*. It was about the tense relations between Ugandans and Asians. He said, "I would like to hereby apologize on behalf of the Amin family for any undue suffering Asians have had to bear during the historic events of 1972 that saw thousands of Asians flee." That was putting it delicately: Amin uprooted these people, expelling them from the country. But at least it was an apology (for a momentous act that the apologizer had no role in). At the same time, Hussein called on Asians to apologize to Ugandans, for various offenses—chiefly a certain uppityness, as far as I can tell.

Several months after *that*—in November 2014—Hussein sent a curious letter to the *Guardian* in Britain, complaining about the paper's obituary of his father—which had of course run in 2003. Why was Hussein writing in to complain eleven years later? He had recently seen the obit on social media. Also, he was preparing to run for office, and perhaps wanted to improve his father's reputation. "Allow me to raise my displeasure," he wrote to the *Guardian*. He said that the obit in question had contained many errors: concerning Amin's service as a soldier, his death toll as a dictator, and so on. Hussein wrote, "I am not sure if you can take this from Idi Amin's son, however factual my criticism is."

After receiving Hussein's letter, the *Guardian* re-researched its Amin obituary and left it as it was: There was no need to amend it. The paper's "readers' editor," Chris Elliott, wrote, "While we are used to a wide range of complaints and complainants it was a surprise to receive an email from Idi Amin's son Hussein."

Earlier in the year, Hussein had announced his intention to run for parliament in 2016. He did so in a letter to "friends and well-wishers."

Jaffar Amin

"This has been a very important decision for me," he wrote, "and indeed it isn't a light one, particularly with my late father's legacy in mind." He said that being Amin's son had been "complex"—an excellent word in his case, and in the cases of many of the sons and daughters we are studying. Hussein made a statement about his fundamental political stance: "I embraced democracy a long time ago in the 80's as a student in France," and "now it is time for me to become a guarantor of democracy amongst others." He said he did not yet know what district he would run in. "But what is as sure as steel is what I stand for: Human Rights, Rule of Law, Freedom, A Better Democracy, Good Governance and Economic Prosperity."

Now we turn to Jaffar—whose full name is Jaffar Remo Amin. He has a pet name from his father, like Hussein's "Lumumba": It is "Tshombe." Moïse Tshombe was a separatist leader in Congo, and a foe of Lumumba. As for "Remo," it is Jaffar's indigenous name, from the Kakwa tribe. He told me that the name can mean "to spear" in Kakwa, "and I like to think I am spearheading peace activists in Africa."

He was born in 1967. When he was 30, he married "Lady Issa," as he calls his wife, and they have six children. Jaffar is a big man: 6 foot 1, and broad and muscular. He says he is one of the smaller men in his family, though. Most of his brothers tower over him. His father was taller than he, too. In his book, Jaffar writes, "I am considered an XL in my society, but well below Dad's 6'4" and XXXL."

That is a fairly charming line, you may agree—and Jaffar has charm, in abundance. He has a ready wit, an easy laugh, and a sense of fun. He also has a flair for the dramatic. He is a bit of a performer, actually. He has a deep, rich, and musical speaking voice. Indeed, he makes a living, in part, by doing voiceovers for radio and television.

His book came out in 2010. It is called "Idi Amin: Hero or Villain?" Obviously, he has a great love and admiration for his father. Amin is no villain, in his book. In our interview—an extensive exchange over e-mail—I asked, "Are you 100 percent on the 'hero' side?" He quickly acknowledged "filial biases." Then he said, "The jury is still out," where Amin is concerned. Jaffar wants a truth and reconciliation commission in Uganda, like the ones established in South Africa and Sierra Leone. Such a commission would conduct a thorough investigation, come to conclusions, and leave some sort of harmony.

Many in his family were not pleased when Jaffar wrote his book. They preferred silence. Even now, he told me, his siblings "grit their teeth" when he publicly discusses or debates their father. One of his aims is to show "the human face" of the dictator. I asked him, "Do you feel the need to defend everything your father did? Or are you disposed to concede some points and then move on?" He said, again, that he wanted a truth and reconciliation commission.

But he also said that he was determined to puncture certain myths. For example, there has long been the tale that Amin killed his son Moses and then went on to eat him. One version of the tale goes, "He sacrificed his favorite son, Moses, then ate his liver." As Jaffar pointed out, Moses is alive and well and living in Paris. Moses could put the myth to rest once and for all, said Jaffar, "but, like Greta Garbo, he wants to be left alone."

Jaffar was twelve when his father was overthrown. Coming of age in Saudi Arabia, he read articles and books about his father. He knew what the charges were. And he was of course rattled by them. In his own book, he writes that he had many "tough questions" for his father. He asked them from the time he was 13 until he was 18. And he says that Amin gave him candid answers. I asked Jaffar, "Was he patient with you? Irked? Some of each?" Jaffar described him as "irritable." He said that his father had the habit of answering today's question tomorrow. On the day you asked your question, he would brush it aside, or seem to do so. The next day, he would be ready with the answer.

He told his son, "Look: People fought me, and I fought them back. But I never killed innocent people. God will be the one to judge me." I asked Jaffar whether he accepted his father's line: that he never killed innocent people. Once more, he expressed a preference for a truth and reconciliation commission. But he has a view of the Amin death toll. He does not accept 300,000 or higher. The soundest research, he says, puts the toll at about 10,800. Some obviously consider this scandalously, insultingly, and outrageously low. It probably is. But it is still a lot of deaths, isn't it?

In 1989, Jaffar was admitted to Schiller International University, an American institution with campuses in several countries. Jaffar wanted to study in London. But the Saudis would not let him go, he writes in his book—because the university had a "Jewish-sounding" name. (As you might guess, the university was named after Friedrich Schiller, one of Germany's hero-poets, and not exactly Jewish.) Idi Amin was a ferocious anti-Semite, in addition to other things. He spoke approvingly of the Holocaust. Reading Jaffar's book, I got the impression that he himself was not anti-Jewish. (He is a Muslim, by the way, like his father.) I raised the issue with him. He gave me one sentence: "The secret to peace on earth is resolving the Isaac-and-Ishmael problem."

Jaffar went back to live in Uganda in 1990, when he was in his early twenties. Was he nervous? Nervous about what people would think and say, and how he would be treated? Yes, very. "The fear of the unknown was intense," he told me, "and I kept looking over my shoulder." From most Ugandans, he received a warm welcome.

He went to work for DHL Express, the air courier. He rose in management. He encountered no obstacles for being Amin's son. He also did his voiceover work, and emceeing—that is, he would serve as master of ceremonies for events all over Kampala, the Ugandan capital. But his heart lies in reconciliation work. He has a foundation, the Al-Amin Foundation. He has participated in many "regional reconciliation convocations," whereby Ugandans talk out their problems and grievances, and often achieve healing.

In recent years, he has been featured in at least two documentaries. One is called "Sons of Africa," made by James Becket. An ad says, "Out of a brutal past, two sons climb towards peace." The sons are of different nationalities: Jaffar Amin and Madaraka Nyerere. The latter, of course, is a son of the late president of Tanzania, a country with which Idi Amin warred. In the documentary, Jaffar and Madaraka climb Mount Kilimanjaro, in Tanzania. It is the continent's highest peak, known as "The Roof of Africa." The two sons also talk about the past, and its burden—not neglecting the present and future.

In this film, as elsewhere, Jaffar notes two views of his father: the villain and the hero, in short. He makes clear his own view. "When it comes to Africans, by God, he is a hero. I think he took a stand and said, 'You guys, colonialism was wrong, slavery was wrong, racism was wrong.'" In his book, Jaffar writes that Amin stood against "Perennial Caucasian Supremacy." To me, he described his father as a "revolutionary" whose role on the world stage was to break "the colonial yoke." (For a defender and champion of the black African, Amin certainly killed a lot of them.)

Madaraka Nyerere, speaking in *Sons of Africa*, says of Jaffar, "The first time I met him, I thought he was trying too much to protect his father's past. ... I tried to tell him just to stay away from the past and try and focus on the present and the future, and I think he is managing to do that." Jaffar, for his part, is warmed by Madaraka's acceptance of him. He says it is a "miracle" that he and Nyerere's son are friends, and in fact "brothers." For him, a development such as this means "I can live my life out of the shadow of my father."

Another film comes in the *On the Spot* series of Eszter Cseke and András S. Takács, a Hungarian team. The film features two Ugandans: Jaffar, of course, and Godfrey Ofumbi. He is a son of Charles Oboth Ofumbi, who was a friend of Idi Amin's and a cabinet minister under him. Amin had him murdered in 1977. Jaffar and Godfrey are friends, laughing and joking and reminiscing. But the discussion naturally turns serious.

Jaffar refers to the murder delicately—as "the tragedy" or "the incident." He finds it hard to believe that the murder of Ofumbi had Idi Amin's "blessing." He believes that there has been some terrible misunderstanding, separating the Amin and Ofumbi families, who ought to be friends. It is not, to him, a clear-cut case of murder. But his confidence is visibly shaken when Godfrey Ofumbi speaks about the murder—in painful detail. "My throat is dry," says Jaffar. "I can't even say sorry ..."

Godfrey says, "I see the burden of the cross you're carrying, and let me tell you one thing, frankly: I feel sorry for you. Because you are really a genuine, decent, and honest person, and a true friend of mine. But what you're going through—I wouldn't want it in a thousand years. We can't change the past. We can only learn from it and move forward."

The two sons travel to the Ofumbi home, where the widow is still living. Jaffar speaks at her husband's grave. He kisses her hands. There is a reconciliation. Jaffar is embraced in the Ofumbi family.

There is talk that he will run for office in Uganda one day. I asked him about this, and he said no: He would concentrate on running reconciliation projects for the rest of his life. (He has to make a living, though, and he works various jobs to keep bread on the table.) I said, "What are your politics? Are you a democrat?" He said, "Social democrat on the Norwegian model." That is a very far cry from Idi Amin's Uganda. I said, "Can outsiders really understand what it's like to be in your shoes?" "Never," said Jaffar—but the reconciliation projects "I believe will bring healing and hopefully understanding."

At times, Jaffar Amin is a rank apologist for his father: a whitewasher, a denier. That can be hard to take. Other times, he seems to stare reality in the face, boldly. In any event, he is willing to engage with issues, and take on all comers (including me). He is open and "stand-up." Furthermore, he is unique among the sons and daughters of dictators, as far as I can tell. He has done valuable work. He has played the "hand" he was dealt in an interesting way. I admire him.

19

MENGISTU

Mengistu has three children. He had them with his wife, Wubanchi Bishaw. She is described as a gentle, good, pious woman. Mengistu is very different. He is described as "the Stalin of Africa"—a designation he earned. He was the Communist dictator of Ethiopia, presiding over a Red Terror, mass famine, and atrocity after atrocity.

About Mengistu's birth date, there is some mystery, but he was probably born in 1937. His full name is Mengistu Haile Mariam. He became an army officer, whose big moment arrived in 1974: He was part of the military group that overthrew the emperor, Haile Selassie. The emperor had been on the throne since 1930. Quickly, Mengistu clawed and killed his way to Number 1. He would rule for the next 17 years. Communist though he was, he enjoyed an imperial trapping or two. He liked to ride around in Haile Selassie's 1959 Cadillac limo (emerald green).

Mengistu created the Marxist-Leninist Workers Party and decreed a new name for the country: "the People's Democratic Republic of Ethiopia." He nationalized everything, nationalized the country, in short: land, banks, retail businesses, etc. This was a nation of farmers, but millions starved. And the stories of Mengistu's atrocities rival those of any dictator's, anywhere.

With personal information, Mengistu and his regime were very stingy. No official biography of the dictator was permitted until the mid-1980s—when a brief one was published. If little was known about the dictator himself, even less was known about his family. We know he has three children, however: a daughter, Tigist, and two sons, Andenet and Tilahun. Their names are quite nice. "Tigist" means "patience." "Andenet" means "unity." And "Tilahun"? It relates to providing shade, an umbrella against the hot sun. The children attended French and English schools in Addis Ababa, the Ethiopian capital.

The Soviet Union was Mengistu's great patron and sponsor. When it weakened, he weakened. Mengistu's dictatorship was an embarrassment to the Kremlin of Mikhail Gorbachev. The Kremlin cut off aid to Mengistu. In 1991, an armed rebellion in Ethiopia gathered strength and overthrew the dictator in May. He bitterly blamed Gorbachev: both for the Soviet Union's demise and for his own.

If Gorbachev was no friend, Robert Mugabe, the dictator in Zimbabwe, was. He took Mengistu in. The new Ethiopian government wanted Mengistu tried for crimes against humanity, but Mugabe refused to turn him over. "Yes, he has committed crimes," Mugabe said, "but he is now a political refugee and is entitled to rights as such."

Before he himself fled, Mengistu had sent his children to Harare, the Zimbabwean capital. They stayed with their uncle, Asrat Wolde, who was Mengistu's ambassador to Zimbabwe.

Mugabe set up Mengistu and his family nicely. They have villas or mansions in the best neighborhoods of Harare: Gun Hill and Emerald Hill. They may have a farm or two as well. In 1992, a curious event occurred: Four of the five Ethiopian bodyguards protecting Mengistu fled from his villa (or one of them) and asked for political asylum in Canada. To quote a Reuters report, "The bodyguards apparently scaled the 3-meter (10-foot) wall around the villa and escaped Monday with their AK-47 assault rifles and pistols." In 1995, two Ethiopians tried to assassinate Mengistu, probably at that same villa, and failed.

The ex-dictator has long been kept under tight restrictions by the Mugabe regime: He is to keep a very low profile. He is not to talk to the press or to diplomats or to anyone in the public realm. As a Zimbabwean official said in 1995, guests such as Mengistu are expected to live "silently." Very rarely is Mengistu seen in public. When he is, there is a frisson

The dictator and his children

of excitement. Mengistu might be out for a walk, or playing tennis at an army base.

In Ethiopia, he was put on trial—in absentia, of course. He was found guilty of genocide and sentenced to death. Mugabe said he would be kept safe and sound in Zimbabwe. In December 1994, Mengistu made a stray remark about his rule, sort of interesting: "Things went wrong."

About the three children, we know next to nothing—and we know the most about Tigist, the daughter. She is a doctor. She went to Girls High School in Harare. She then went to the University of Zimbabwe, in the same city. And she studied medicine in Uganda: Makerere University. In 2001, a Zimbabwean newspaper, the *Standard*, discovered that she was working at a local hospital. She was then 27 years old. Contacted by the paper, she confirmed her identity but said, "I decline to talk about my stay in the country with the press. Can you please leave me and my family alone? I would appreciate it if you would let me continue with my life and work under normal conditions."

Her brother Andenet, too, went to the University of Zimbabwe. He is also said to have studied abroad. He is further said to look after whatever Mengistu-family business interests there are in Zimbabwe. About the other brother, Tilahun, there is nary a scrap. Those who know, or may know, about the family are tight-lipped (certainly with me).

In 2001, Mugabe's government conferred on Mengistu and his family the status of permanent residents. They have Zimbabwean passports and travel on them. The ex-dictator had rather a scare in 2000. He had gone to Johannesburg, South Africa, for medical treatment (stomach ulcers). When the Ethiopian government found out about this, they sent an urgent request to the South African government: Extradite him. Mengistu speedily left the hospital and hightailed it back to Zimbabwe.

About ten years later, he wrote a memoir, titled "Tiglachin," or "Our Struggle." (The title "My Struggle"—which in German is "Mein Kampf"—had already been used.) Today, Robert Mugabe is 91 years old, whereas Mengistu is a spring chicken of 78 or so. What if Mugabe dies before Mengistu, and his successor is less friendly to the Ethiopian? Does Mengistu face extradition? According to reports, he has contingency arrangements with both China and North Korea. Most likely, the Mengistu children could stay in Zimbabwe, unmolested. They are blameless in their father's crimes. Of course, they are affected.

20

POL POT

Over the third weekend of March in 2014, a happy and beautiful wedding took place. It was a two-day ceremony. The location was a village called Kbal Spean in the Malai district of Banteay Meanchey Province, in northwestern Cambodia. The bride was in her late twenties and beautiful. She wore a tiara and a glittering pink dress. Beaming alongside her were her mother and father.

Actually, the man was her stepfather: Tep Khunnal, who had been Pol Pot's secretary, his closest aide. The bride's father was Pol Pot himself.

Pol Pot was the leader of the Khmer Rouge, "Brother Number 1." The Khmer Rouge seized power in Cambodia on April 17, 1975; they stayed in power until January 7, 1979. Their rule was one of the most savage episodes in human history. They killed about 2 million people, or between a fifth and a quarter of the population. After their overthrow, Pol Pot and his gang took to the hills, or the jungles, fighting a guerrilla war to regain power.

Years before, on Bastille Day 1956, Pol Pot married a woman named Khieu Ponnary. Their wedding date was significant: They were both French-trained Communists. At some point in the 1970s, Khieu Ponnary developed schizophrenia. After the overthrow of his regime, Pol Pot divorced her. They had had no children.

In the mid-1980s, Pol Pot was about 60, and Khmer Rouge officials decided that he needed a wife. As the journalist Nate Thayer writes, "they handpicked a small group of young women, chosen for their revolutionary commitment and the purity of their class background." Pol Pot could choose from this lineup. He chose Mea Son, who had been an ammunition porter.

They soon had a daughter, named Mea Sitha. Not just Pol Pot but other Khmer Rouge leaders bounced her on their knee: There is a somewhat creepy photo of the tot with Nuon Chea, Brother Number 2. The family lived a primitive life in the jungles. They were often on the run. After all, Pol Pot, being one of the greatest genocidal killers in history, was a wanted man.

In October 1997, Nate Thayer pulled off an extraordinary coup: an interview with Pol Pot. Among other subjects, they discussed Mea Sitha. Thayer writes, "When Pol Pot spoke of his 12-year-old daughter, he became animated and whimsical, exuding a gentle fatherly love that was clearly sincere and typical for the father of a young girl." Pol Pot told him, "She is a good girl. She is kind and plays well with others. She studies hard and she helps her mother."

Thayer asked him an excellent and pointed question: "When your daughter grows up and people know she is the daughter of Pol Pot, will she be proud of you?" Pol Pot was taken aback by the question, disturbed. Then he answered softly, "I don't know about that. History will have to judge."

Pol Pot died in April of the next year. His parting words were about his only child. His widow told the child about them—and the child recounted them in an interview with the *Cambodia Daily* in 2004: "My father told my mother to make sure when I grow up, I study hard to be a good person."

After Pol Pot's death, his widow told Nate Thayer what she wanted the world to know: "that he was a good man, a patriot, a good father." She also had a comment for the *Phnom Penh Post*: "He was a good husband to me. We met in 1985. I am very sad that he has died, and I do not know what the future may bring."

One thing it brought was marriage to Tep Khunnal, her husband's secretary. He had promised Pol Pot, as the boss lay dying, that he would take care of his wife and daughter. He was as good as his word. He quickly married Mea Son and brought up Mea Sitha as his own.

At about the time Tep Khunnal and Mea Son were marrying, they came in from the cold, so to speak: They left the Khmer Rouge movement—which was as dead as Pol Pot anyway—and reconciled with the government. Mea Sitha lived under a variety of pseudonyms until she started high school in the town of Sisophon. From then on, she would be known as Sar Patchata. Her stepfather chose this change of identity for her. It was time, he thought, for the girl to be openly and proudly associated with her father. "Pol Pot" was just a nom de guerre; the old revolutionary was born Saloth Sar.

In 2004, as I mentioned, Sar Patchata gave an interview to the *Cambodia Daily*. She was 19, and still a student in Sisophon. This was an extraordinary interview—just about the only time we have heard Pol Pot's girl speak:

> "I want to study to be an accountant so I can keep money for my family," the shy, soft-spoken teenager said as she shifted awkwardly in a classroom seat. Accounting may seem like an odd career choice for a young woman whose father oversaw the elimination of all currency in the country in his attempts to turn Cambodia into an agrarian utopia. But, Sar Patchata said, "It's a popular subject.... It's easy to find a job."

The *Daily*'s reporters also talked to a teacher, Chhun Huy. He said that the school did not teach the Khmer Rouge as a subject. This was doubly true when Sar Patchata was around.

> Any discussion of that era of Cambodia's history "can attack her feelings," Chhun Huy said, adding that in contrast with her father's public image, Sar Patchata is a polite, sensitive and gentle student.
>
> Sar Patchata's peers are also protective of her, always careful not to mention the brutality and destruction associated with her father, the teacher said. "She has a lot of friends. Everybody likes her here," he said.

The teacher was a survivor of the Khmer Rouge period, and of the forced labor he was subjected to. Several of his family were not so lucky.

> But, he said, he has no problem separating his past hardships from his fondness for Sar Patchata. "This is her father," Chhun Huy said, extending one palm. "This is her," he added, extending the other. "We cannot think about her father."

Sar Patchata had a chaperone, a minder, during the interview (understandably). He was the school's headmaster, a friend of Tep Khunnal's. He admonished the reporters not to ask Sar Patchata about politics or the past. Still, they did a little gentle probing.

> Asked what she recalls of Pol Pot, Sar Patchata, whose physical resemblance to her father is apparent in her heavy chin and thick eyebrows, smiled bashfully, and said she has fond memories. "I remember when I was a baby, I used to sit on his lap," she said, brushing the hair away from her face. "I would just play with him and hug and kiss him."

She said that she thought about her father often. "I used to dream that my father would visit me." She also said that she prayed for him often. It is of some interest, I think, that the daughter of one of history's hardest and purest Communists prays. "I go to the pagoda every Pchum Ben," she said. Pchum Ben is a Buddhist festival during which people pray for their ancestors. "I want to meet my father and spend time with him in the next life, if the next life exists."

The stepfather, Tep Khunnal, did very well after he came in from the cold. He became a wealthy businessman. He also became governor of the Malai district, in Banteay Meanchey Province. Malai is typically described as a "former rebel stronghold"—a onetime Khmer Rouge redoubt. Former Khmers Rouges still rule the roost in this remote pocket of Cambodia.

Sar Patchata went from living a primitive, fugitive life to living a modern, fairly normal one, complete with smartphone, Facebook, and Twitter. She kept in touch with children of other Khmer Rouge leaders. Like young women around the world, she admired David Beckham, the handsome British soccer player, and Beyoncé, the American pop star (one of Mutassim Qaddafi's guests or hirees, you may recall).

The bride, Sar Patchata, with her groom

When it came time for graduate school, Sar Patchata went to Malaysia, to earn a master's degree in English literature. While in Malaysia, she met her future husband: a Cambodian named Sy Vicheka.

It was, to say it again, a happy, colorful, festive, beautiful wedding. There were pink-and-white tents, with glass chandeliers. Tep Khunnal, though a public figure, said little to the press. He did say, "It's only a small wedding ceremony with our friends and relatives."

Among these guests were Khmer Rouge veterans. Indeed, the wedding had the aspect of a Khmer Rouge reunion. May Titthara covered the event for the *Phnom Penh Post*. A former soldier told him, "It's a good opportunity. We can meet with the seniors after we have lived apart for years. You don't know how delighted we are." A former official of the regime said, "It's not a meeting of politics. It is a show of friendship." Pol Pot's daughter was not involved in politics, he said. Rather, the Khmers Rouges form a community, and a network of support. "We love and respect each other as one and help one another."

One lady in attendance was So Socheat, whose husband could not make it: He was Khieu Samphan, Brother Number 4. He was in Phnom Penh before an international tribunal, on trial for crimes against humanity.

After the wedding, the bride would stay in the area to run a rice mill belonging to her uncle and aunt. That is what a guest said. Another guest had known Sar Patchata in years past. She did not know her very well any longer. But one thing she did know: Sar Patchata "is very different from her father."

AFTERWORD

To study the children of dictators is to spend a lot of time with unpleasantness. Dropping the understatement, I will put it another way: To write a book such as mine, you have to spend a lot of time with evil—the evil of dictators and their regimes. Sometimes, the children become part of it all. They join the machinery of oppression. You are perhaps ready to be done with dictators and their families. So am I.

I had to laugh a little in December 2014, when I was listening to Christmas carols and looking into the ghastly crimes of Idi Amin. On Christmas Day itself, I was checking some facts about Mengistu Haile Mariam's "Red Terror." And how did *you* spend that Christmas?

A few days after, I was texting Tep Khunnal in Cambodia. It was a strange feeling, I can tell you: to be sending a polite text to Pol Pot's former secretary, and the husband of his widow, and the stepfather of his daughter.

Paul Johnson, the great English historian, once planned to write a book called "Monsters." It was to be part of a series of books he had written, or would write—including *Creators* and *Heroes*. *Monsters* was to be about the worst of men. But Johnson decided not to write it because, he told me, he did not want to spend so much time in the company of such people. I understand.

Though, I might add, Johnson *did* decide to write a biography of Stalin—a short one.

Here is something that may amuse you: For months on end, I borrowed books about dictators—psychopaths, mass murderers—from the library. I was worried that the librarians would have concerns about such a borrower.

243

As I said in my foreword, this book is a psychological study, in part. I see it as a book about individuals, mainly. But it is also a book about individuals with a common fate, or a common situation. They would have a lot to talk about, if they ever got together.

Edda Mussolini could talk to Saddam Hussein's daughters Raghdad and Rana. Their fathers had their husbands killed. Marie-Denise Duvalier might make an interesting contribution to the conversation as well: Her husband was spared, but it was a close call. (He later lived with her sister in a common-law marriage, remember.)

Marie-Denise has something in common with Kim Jong-il's daughter Sol-song, and with Bushra Assad: Each of those women could have succeeded her father, if she had been a man, not a woman.

Few of the children have had a serene life. They have experienced war, prison, exile, and other upheaval. Some have been victims, some have been victimizers. Some—many—have been a mixture of the two.

We could easily draw up some categories. There are the monster sons, the unspeakable brutes, the worst chips off the old blocks: Vasily Stalin, Nicu Ceauşescu, several of the Qaddafi boys, two of the Assad boys, Saddam Hussein's sons—maybe Kongulu Mobutu.

There are the lieutenants, the close political and personal aides. The Khomeini sons, at different periods, are probably the best examples in this category. Then there are the successors: Jean-Claude Duvalier, Kim Jong-il, Bashar Assad, and Kim Jong-un.

What about the sons who *would* have succeeded, if their father had been able to hang on (to power, that is)? Nicu might have made it, crazy and drunk as he was. One of the Qaddafis would have succeeded Moammar, probably. Mobutu was grooming Niwa, who predeceased him. Apparently, Mobutu did not line another son up. Bokassa the First tapped a *prince héritier*, who was but five when his dad was toppled—there would be no Bokassa the Second.

There is also a category of what we might call normal people, or comparatively normal people: Carmen Franco, Romano Mussolini, the Tojo children as a group, Valentin Ceauşescu, Nzanga Mobutu, Pol Pot's girl Sar Patchata. While normal—normal-ish—they revere their dictator father, or most of them do.

A few *almost* broke from the dictatorial orbit, knowing it was dark and wrong, but could not quite make it: I of course think of Saif al-Islam

Qaddafi, and of yet another Ceaușescu child, Zoia. At one time, she said that her last name had become a "dirty word" to her. Mao's eldest, Anying, had some doubts and disgust, too. I wonder what his life would have been like, if he hadn't been struck down in the Korean War, age 28. Kim Jong-il's son Jong-nam, the exile, has made criticisms of his family's dynasty. But he may be bitter, having been passed over for succession in favor of a much younger half-brother. And if he ever engaged in full-blown dissent, that would sign his death warrant.

Two of the "children" succeeded in breaking out altogether: the defectors Svetlana Stalin and Alina Fernández (Castro's daughter). They defected not just literally—physically—but mentally and spiritually. This mental or spiritual defection preceded the literal one.

Jaffar Amin, I would say, is in a category of his own. He is both a loyalist—a defender of his father, a champion of his father—and a reacher-out to his father's victims. He is a paradox and, on balance, a mensch. That may seem strange or offensive to say, but I believe it is true.

I will repeat what I said in my chapter on the Ceaușescus: Valentin and Nicu were born to the same parents, and were raised in the same environment. They had the same opportunities. Nicu chose—if "chose" is the word—to be a monster. Valentin has lived quietly and more or less blamelessly, as far as I can tell. I don't think he has ever harmed a hair on anyone's head. Why the disparity between the two brothers?

Here, you get into ancient debates, concerning "nature," "nurture," and much else. Those claiming to have the answers should be viewed with skepticism, I think.

Loyalty, in the normal scheme of things, is to be admired. I will give you a memory from American politics: In the 1988 presidential race, Reagan's vice president, George Bush, was accused of being slavishly and comically loyal to the president. He said, repeatedly, "In my family, loyalty is not a character flaw." Twelve years later, when his son George W. Bush was running for president, the candidate was invited by the press to take issue with his father's 1990 budget deal—a deal that harmed the first Bush's presidency. It was pretty obvious that George W. regarded the 1990 deal as a big mistake. But he said, in effect, "If you think I'm going to criticize my dad, you're barking up the wrong tree."

And we may allow even the sons and daughters of dictators their loyalty. Do you recall what Ilir Hoxha's prison mates said? "Everyone has the right to stand up for his father." I agree with this. But what if your father is Enver Hoxha? This complicates things, for he enslaved and immiserated and entombed a great many.

In the first paragraphs of my foreword, I explained the genesis of this book. Visiting Albania, I wondered, "What must it be like to be a son or daughter of Hoxha? To live in this country and bear that freighted name?" As I was to discover, the Hoxha kids are just fine with it. From all available evidence, they are proud of their father, their name, and themselves.

Denialism is common to the children of dictators. Maybe it is necessary, as a "coping mechanism," to use a modern term. Many of them, most of them, have lived by lies. While I was writing my book, I noticed a poster on the streets of New York. It was for a Broadway show, *Jersey Boys*, which is about old-time rock-'n'-roll. The poster said, "Everybody remembers it how they need to." Sons and daughters of dictators, like other people, have often remembered it the way they needed to: the "it" being their father and his regime.

They have help, too. What I mean is, there is always a remnant, a core of supporters, collaborators, and well-wishers from the past. Also, there are younger people who have gotten it into their heads that the defunct dictatorship was a golden age. When she first ran for office, people gave Alessandra Mussolini the Fascist salute. And General Mao Xinyu finds great enthusiasm for his genocidal grandfather in China.

I now pose the question, "How much slack should we cut these characters?" I'm referring to the dictators' sons and daughters. While I was writing the Stalin chapter of my book, I happened to talk to my friend Ignat Solzhenitsyn, a son of Alexander Solzhenitsyn, the writer and hero. We were talking about Vasily in particular. I said, "Remember, he was the son, through no fault of his own, of the worst man in Soviet history. You are the son of the *best* man in Soviet history. Come to think of it, you are Vasily's counterpart!"

This does not relieve Vasily Stalin of moral responsibility. He was a vicious, despicable thug. He also, you could concede, had a lot to overcome. It might have been hard for him to turn out non-vicious. He was raised by Stalin's personal security agents.

I never thought I would be quoting, in a moral discussion, a man who believes himself to be the grandson of Hitler, but here I go: Philippe

Loret said (if you remember), "I don't think evil passes on. Of course, qualities from your parents pass on to you, but you build your own life, and you make it what it is."

Before we finish, we might play a kind of parlor game—beginning with the question, "Who was the best father, among these dictators?" The truth is, almost none of them was big on fatherhood. They barely knew their children. Of course, this is true of countless salesmen, restaurateurs, and other working people (and non-working people—fathers who are simply absent). It may be truer, though, of dictators, consumed in their colossal egos, and busy smothering a country.

That said, I think probably the best father was Franco, though that may be cheating: He is a relative lamb amid our monsters. He was a picture of normality by comparison to the others. And he greatly loved his only child, Carmen. His relationship with her was evidently the most prized in his life. Also, Tojo seems to have been a good and (dare I say?) conscientious father. Idi Amin was a fun-loving "Big Daddy" to his dozens, especially in exile.

Who was the worst father? The competition is tough here. We have one great tie—though Mao somehow stands out in his utter lack of human feeling.

Who was the best of the children? I think it should be said that the Tojo children, as a class, have conducted themselves with exemplary dignity. They have not disowned their father; they have praised the old war criminal, in their few public statements. But they have never told a lie about Tojo and the war, so far as I'm aware.

The children I admire most, as you can tell, are the defectors: the women who had uprisings of conscience and saw reality for what it was. Svetlana's task was greater than Alina's, probably. For one thing, she lived with her father, at least through her girlhood. Alina barely knew Castro, who acknowledged her but ignored her. Svetlana said, "My father would have shot me for what I have done." Yes, he would have. I will say again, she was brave. Flawed and sometimes confused, but brave, and also, as I have argued, touched with greatness.

The worst of the children? It's hard to say anyone but Uday Hussein. But then I remember that the field also includes the successor sons—particularly Kim Jong-il, Bashar Assad, and Kim Jong-un. Can we say that Uday was worse than they?

In my foreword, I quoted the reaction of my friend Tom Griesa when I told him what I was writing about: "People are interesting." Yes, and they are strange, too. The adoration of dictators is strange. They are adored by their children (fine). They are also adored by ordinary people—masses. Often, they are adored by their victims.

I will quote another friend, David Pryce-Jones—who in his book *The Strange Death of the Soviet Empire* writes about a German Communist named Werner Eberlein. Eberlein's parents were founders of the German Communist Party. After the rise of the Nazis, the family went to the Soviet Union. When Werner was 17, his father and two of his uncles—loyal Communists and Stalinists all—were shot by Stalin. Werner himself was sent to Siberia, where he worked in a sawmill for twelve hours a day for seven years.

He of course remained a loyal Communist and Party worker. Pryce-Jones writes, "When I asked him, indeed pressed him, to explain how in spite of these horrors he could have devoted his life sincerely to the Party, his reply was that he had been too busy surviving to dwell on grievances. [What a word here, *grievances*.] And besides, Stalin had been a god on high, supernatural, someone whom it had been inconceivable to criticize."

This is a mentality that you and I don't have, probably. If a man, a party, and a system had murdered our father and uncles, and sentenced us to slave labor in Siberia, we would probably have been a little cross. But such a mentality does exist, in many. That, we know.

We are not sons and daughters of dictators, you and I. But many—hundreds—have been. And we might muse for a second on how we would handle it. For us, thankfully, the matter is purely theoretical.

A NOTE ON SOURCES

Way back in the foreword, I mentioned the difficulties of writing about dictators' families—or of writing about closed societies in general. And in my chapter on the Kims, I used the word "driblets." We have "driblets from defectors and other informed parties," I said. About other families, we have generous helpings of information.

I have used everything I can, everything possible: every scrap or remark or hint. Tiny items in yellowed newspapers served me well. For example, it was noted in 1959 that a Japanese general had received the Legion of Merit from the U.S. Armed Forces. He was married to the late Tojo's eldest daughter—which is all I cared about, of course.

When people have spoken of dictators, over the years, they have occasionally mentioned the dictators' children, just in passing. Dictators are big players on the world stage; children are bit players, at best (usually). The passing remarks made my eyes widen. They were like trumpet calls, for this book.

I was in a position of scavenger, or excavator—even garbageman. When information is scarce, you seize on anything that may help build a picture.

Back to faded and buried publications for a moment. In 1981, Chinese state media reported that a banquet had been held for Mobutu Sese Seko's envoy, his son Niwa. That was dull and routine for anyone who happened to be reading that scrap at the time, and what normal person would be interested in it today? For me, though, it was a find.

Luckily, there are yearbooks from the Martha Cook residence hall at the University of Michigan. Kimie Tojo arrived there in 1959. My mother happened to live in Martha Cook, too. Unluckily, for me, she left in 1958.

The Central African Empire was not a fount of information (although it was a fount of fascination—ghastly fascination). A U.S. ambassador, Goodwin Cooke, told me that, in his two years there, the newspaper, *Terre africaine*, came out three times. And it was full of mistakes and lies. Also, you just about never saw a foreign reporter in that part of the world. Or a local reporter. One foreign reporter, Michael Goldsmith of the Associated Press, was almost beaten to death by Bokassa.

And I will quote, for the third time, a subhead in the *Miami Herald*: "Fidel's private life with his wife and sons is so secret that even the CIA is left to wonder."

I have used, as you have seen, a great many biographies and memoirs. I have also used other books, including histories. Often, the accounts given in these books conflict. Someone in my position has to resolve the conflicts, or if that is impossible, simply report that the conflicts exist. Usually, everyone in a drama deserves his say (if he has given his say).

Some of these "children of monsters" have written books—although not many have, really. Others have given interviews. It seems that Pol Pot's daughter has given just one interview in her life—when she was 19, to the *Cambodia Daily*. That interview is a treasure chest, for our purposes. It is almost a unicorn sighting.

I could not reach that unicorn, Sar Patchata. As a rule, dictators' children want to be left alone. They certainly want to be left alone by someone like me, writing a book about the sons and daughters of dictators. They are liable to take offense at the very notion that their dad was a dictator. To Ilir Hoxha, for example, Enver Hoxha was "a true democrat."

Also, friends and associates of dictators and their children tend to fall silent when someone like me makes an inquiry—no matter how gentle or benign that inquiry is. I was led to people who are in touch with Mengistu. They remained silent. There is a certain *omertà* in this world of dictators, or fallen dictators. But fortunately, there are also people who will share what they know, or some of what they know (almost never on the record).

When it came to children themselves, Jaffar Amin was quite open, as you have seen. I had some exchanges with his brother Hussein—useful exchanges—although he declined to be interviewed. At Davos one year, I had an encounter with Saif al-Islam Qaddafi. Since 2011, though, he has been in a Libyan prison, not giving interviews as he once did.

Many of the "children" we are dealing with are dead, of course (or otherwise indisposed, as Saif is). A few others seemed possible to reach. I made several approaches to Valentin Ceaușescu, through various avenues. No biting. Same with Kiki Bokassa: no biting. Kimie Tojo Gilbertson sent me a polite no-thank-you, as I mentioned.

Alina Fernández, one of Castro's daughters in Miami, agreed to be interviewed. Or maybe I should say she *appeared* to agree, through a mutual friend. Then she changed her mind. Why? I don't know, but I can tell you this: In the very month we are speaking of, she returned to Cuba, I believe for the first time since her defection more than 20 years before. She went to see her ailing mother. Perhaps she did not want to do anything that might irritate the Cuban regime. I don't know. In any case, she wrote a memoir that is blazing, and rare, in its honesty.

Around dictators and their children, rumors swirl, of course. In some cases I reported rumors; in other cases not. In my job as scavenger, I often asked, "What smells right?" Your nose is an important organ in composing a book such as this.

I have not given footnotes in this book, but I have attributed—probably overattributed—all through. I consulted everything I could get my hands on. (The New York Public Library had a fragile, off-site copy of Mussolini's little book about his son, *Parlo con Bruno*.) I also consulted scores or hundreds of people, directly. I will address this in my next and final note, the acknowledgements.

ACKNOWLEDGEMENTS

Barely a page went by that did not require, or benefit from, consultation with someone—or two or three someones. Expertise was constantly called on; insider knowledge was gold. Some people talked to me way off the record, precluding their acknowledgement. But there are plenty to acknowledge.

What follows is a list, and lists are generally boring for people to read—but they mean a lot to authors like me, who are grateful for the assistance.

For Hitler and Germany: Sir Ian Kershaw. For Mussolini and Italy: Andrea Mancia, Krilla Missiroli, Mariuccia Zerilli-Marimò. For Franco and Spain: Stanley G. Payne. For Stalin and the Soviet Union: Robert Conquest, Richard Pipes, Ignat Solzhenitsyn. For Tojo and Japan: Frederick R. Dickinson, Christopher W. A. Szpilman.

For Mao and China: Jung Chang, Steven I. Levine, Perry Link, Roderick MacFarquhar, Andrew Nathan, Alexander V. Pantsov, Ross Terrill, Arthur Waldron, Jianli Yang. For Kim and North Korea: Michael Breen, Aidan Foster-Carter, Bradley K. Martin.

For Hoxha and Albania: Ruben Avxhiu, Cvetin Chilimanov, Saimir Lolja, Dritan Nesho, Stephen Suleyman Schwartz. For Ceaușescu and Romania: Jessica Douglas-Home, Ion Mihai Pacepa, Juliana Geran Pilon.

For Duvalier and Haiti: Elizabeth Abbott. For Castro and Cuba: Mauricio Claver-Carone, Luis Domínguez, Otto Reich, Félix Rodríguez, Armando Valladares.

For Assad and Syria: Farid Ghadry, Robert Ford. For Saddam Hussein and Iraq: Joseph Sassoon. For Khomeini and Iran: Ali Alfoneh, Manuchehr Honarmand, Michael Ledeen, Neil MacFarquhar, Gary Sick, Steven Stalinsky, Elliot Zweig.

For Mobutu and Zaire: Brandon Grove, Daniel Simpson, Michela Wrong. For Bokassa and the Central African Republic (or Empire): Goodwin Cooke, Anthony Quainton. For Amin and Uganda: Hussein Juruga Amin, Jaffar Remo Amin, James Becket. For Mengistu and Ethiopia: Berhane Arefaine, Meron Estefanos, Donald N. Levine.

And for Pol Pot and Cambodia: Chea Bunseang, Sophal Ear, Nate Thayer, May Titthara.

The following friends supplied what might come under the category of General Help: Buntzie Churchill, Javier El-Hage, Denisa Feddersen, Fred Fransen, Jamie Hancock, Paul Johnson, and Elijah Stevens.

Speaking of friends who help, I wish to thank my *National Review* colleague Chris McEvoy plus a slew of other NR colleagues: Jack Fowler, Rich Lowry, Luba Kolomytseva, and Mike Potemra.

Further thanks go to the team at Encounter Books, whose president is my wise, energetic, and admirable friend Roger Kimball. My editor, as before, was the brilliant Carol Staswick. I have invented an adjective: *Staswickian*, meaning learned, thoughtful, and precise.

My heart overruns in gratitude to my friend and ally Martha Apgar (a daughter of Florida, America, and God).

It was because of Ellen Toomey that I got to Albania in the first place—and this was the experience that started the book. And it was because of JoDell Shields that I knew Ellen.

David Pryce-Jones, to return to the beginning of this book, is my dedicatee. I don't think this is done in Acknowledgements, or ought to be—but I'm going to repeat what I said in the dedication: "an exemplary thinker, writer, and friend." No kidding.

PHOTO CREDITS

HITLER: German Federal Archive via Wikimedia Commons, Creative Commons: Bundesarchiv, Bild 183-S33882/ CC-BY-SA

JEAN-MARIE LORET: *Paris Match*

MUSSOLINI: Wikimedia Commons

EDDA CIANO: © Massimo & Sonia Cirulli Archive, New York

FRANCO: Government of Spain via Wikimedia Commons

CARMEN FRANCO: José Demaría Vázquez in *La Vanguardia* via CampuaFotografo.es

STALIN: Wikimedia Commons

YAKOV DZHUGASHVILI: Wikimedia Commons

VASILY & SVETLANA WITH STALIN: Wikimedia Commons

SVETLANA & FATHER: Wikimedia Commons

TOJO: *Rekidai Shusho tou Shashin* via Wikimedia Commons

KIMIE TOJO & MOTHER: © Bettmann / Corbis

MAO: Zhang Zhenshi via Wikimedia Commons

LI NA & LI MIN WITH MAO: Wikimedia Commons

KIM: Gilad Rom via Wikimedia Commons, Creative Commons

KIM JONG-IL: Presidential Press and Information Office via Wikimedia Commons, Creative Commons

KIM JONG-UN: Peter Stevens via Flickr, Creative Commons

HOXHA: Forrásjelölés Hasonló via Wikimedia Commons, Creative Commons

ILIR HOXHA: *Bota Sot*

CEAUŞESCU: © Gianni Ferrari / Contributor / Getty Images

NICU CEAUŞESCU: Communism in Romania Photo Collection via Wikimedia Commons

VALENTIN CEAUŞESCU: Cristian Otopeanu via Wikimedia Commons, Creative Commons

DUVALIER: © Hulton Archive / Stringer / Getty Images

PAPA DOC & BABY DOC DUVALIER: BlackPast. org

CASTRO: Antonio Milena via Wikimedia Commons, Creative Commons

ANTONIO CASTRO: © Adalberto Roque / Staff / Getty Images

ALINA FERNÁNDEZ: Wikimedia Commons

QADDAFI: U.S. Navy photo by Mass Communication Specialist 2nd Class Jesse B. Awalt via Wikimedia Commons

SAIF AL-ISLAM QADDAFI: © John Schults / Reuters / Corbis

ASSAD: Government Photographer via Wikimedia Commons

BASSEL ASSAD: Wikimedia Commons

BASHAR ASSAD: Fabio Rodrigues Pozzebom via Wikimedia Commons, Creative Commons

SADDAM HUSSEIN: Wikimedia Commons

UDAY & QUSAY WITH SADDAM: © Associated Press

KHOMEINI: Wikimedia Commons

AHMAD KHOMEINI: Wikimedia Commons

MOBUTU: Frank Hall via Wikimedia Commons

NZANGA MOBUTU: Radio Okapi via Wikimedia Commons

BOKASSA: Romanian Communism Online Photo Collection via Wikimedia Commons, Creative Commons

JEAN-BÉDEL BOKASSA JR.: © Keystone / Stinger / Getty Images

AMIN: BlackPast.org

JAFFAR AMIN: Courtesy of Jaffar Amin

MENGISTU: Wikimedia Commons, Creative Commons: אדעולם at Hebrew Wikipedia

MENGISTU WITH CHILDREN: *Durame*

POL POT: Lazer Horse

SAR PATCHATA: Heng Chivoan via *Phnom Penh Post*

INDEX

Praise for *Children of Monsters*

"A magnetic page-turner that nonetheless is complex and deep. The fascinating and horrific details Nordlinger unearths flow together to pose important and disturbing questions about love, loyalty, history, and human nature."

—Mark Helprin, author of *Winter's Tale* and *A Soldier of the Great War*

"This extraordinary book makes us all ask of ourselves: What would we do if we realized that our beloved father was also a blood-stained tyrant?...Jay Nordlinger's exceptional investigation into the children of 20 modern dictators grips and convinces."

—Andrew Roberts, author of *The Storm of War* and *Napoleon: A Life*

"a riveting and informative read"

—Juliana Geran Pilon, in the *Washington Free Beacon*

"sobering, albeit relentlessly fascinating and entertaining"

—Mark Tapson, in *FrontPage Magazine*

"gripping...At the risk of cliché, I will say, *Children of Monsters* is impossible to put down."

—Mona Charen, in her syndicated column

"peerless...Like a good tragedian, Nordlinger infuses *Children of Monsters* with catharsis. Nearly each of his 20 chapters culminates in a release of tension....Without humanizing the dictators, Nordlinger's study of their children reveals their fathers' humanity."

—Michael T. Hamilton, in *Dissident*

"oddly compelling...As surprising as the book's subject is at first glance, as one begins reading it one wonders why such a book was not written a long time ago."

—John Daniel Davidson, in *The Federalist*

Previous Praise for the Author

"Jay Nordlinger is one of America's most versatile and pungent writers."
—Paul Johnson, author of *Modern Times*

"Few writers are well qualified to write about the world's cultures, and none more so than Jay Nordlinger."
—Robert Conquest, author of *The Great Terror*

"Nordlinger offers a unique combination of depth and accuracy of knowledge with clarity and elegance of style. It is a pleasure to read sophistication without affectation."
—Bernard Lewis, author of *What Went Wrong?*
The Clash between Islam and Modernity in the Middle East